WAR'S LONG SHADOW

Many survivors of the Second World War have lived beneath its long shadow for the last sixty years. This book brings together the experiences of men, women and children from all walks of life as the war progresses over sixty-nine months. These highly personal accounts give an extraordinary depth of insight into the realities of war. Harrowing, inspiring, touching, surprising, they shed a new and richer light on the meaning of war.

Edited by
CHARLOTTE POPESCU

◆

WAR'S
LONG SHADOW

69 MONTHS OF
THE
SECOND WORLD WAR

Complete and Unabridged

ULVERSCROFT
Leicester

First published in Great Britain in 2002 by
Cavalier Paperbacks
Wiltshire

First Large Print Edition
published 2003
by arrangement with
Cavalier Books
Upavon
Wiltshire

British Library CIP Data

War's long shadow: 69 months of the Second World War.
  —Large print ed.—
  Ulverscroft large print series: non-fiction
  1. World War, *1939 – 1945*—Personal narratives, British
  2. Large type books
  I. Popescu, Charlotte
  940.5'48141

  ISBN 0–7089–4955–X

Published by
F. A. Thorpe (Publishing)
Anstey, Leicestershire

Set by Words & Graphics Ltd.
Anstey, Leicestershire
Printed and bound in Great Britain by
T. J. International Ltd., Padstow, Cornwall

This book is printed on acid-free paper

CONTENTS

FOREWORD

by Earl Kitchener of Khartoum

All too soon there will be no one left to pass on first-hand accounts of the 1939–1945 War. The Editor has done future generations an important service by collecting together these previously unpublished eye-witness records. They bring vividly to life the very personal and frequently moving experiences of soldiers, sailors, airmen and civilians in most theatres and campaigns of that titanic struggle. From the first days of the Phoney War, through the many grim reverses during the early 1940s, to the Normandy Landings and the final exhausted relief of VE Day, this unique collection of diary entries demonstrates above all the fortitude, courage and resolve of ordinary people caught up in extraordinary events.

I commend it to you — 'lest we forget'.

Earl Kitchener retires in 2002 as President of the 8th Army Veterans Association.

INTRODUCTION

As the wife of a serving army officer and the mother of three boys I've sometimes found myself wondering how I would cope with the stress and anxiety of war or disaster. Perhaps this is why I was so intrigued when I unexpectedly received by post three short diary extracts, sent to me by children's writer Jessica Frank. Jessica had recently read my book *The Tears of War*, a poignant wartime love story that ends in tragedy, and she had been moved by it to ask me to consider publishing her extracts in some form of anthology, for posterity's sake. Thus was *War's Long Shadow* conceived. Being an orderly individual, I could think of no better framework than a neat month-by-month chronicle of the Second World War, covering the sixty-nine months from September 1939 to VE Day in May 1945. Now all I needed to find from somewhere was another 66 suitably interesting — and previously unpublished — diary entries.

Uncertain of the likely response, I wrote a letter to the editors of all the regional newspapers in the UK, explaining the project and appealing for personal wartime memories from their readers. I also asked friends, relatives and neighbours for diary extracts and I turned to the Internet in search of wartime accounts from those who had moved abroad after the war. To my relief and delight submissions began to flood in. At once it was clear that I had struck a chord with many veterans, who fully realising that their cherished memories would not be of sufficient interest in their entirety, nonetheless knew that they could offer many fascinating individual entries that might well be suitable for inclusion.

Now began some hard editing as I sought to fill each month's slot from the amazing mass of material that for months littered every flat surface in my study. Very quickly I decided to retain a primarily British focus to the book (although I admit I just couldn't resist several outstanding accounts from US servicemen towards the end of the war). I aimed for as varied a selection of anecdotes as possible, juxtaposing, for example, a visit to a brothel by the Marquess of Aberdeen with the horror of a soldier being wounded and then captured by the Germans. There are heartbreaking stories of mothers evacuating their children and living through the Blitz; there are stirring accounts by sailors who survived the sinking of their ships; there are harrowing memories of life as a POW, which range from the boredom of captivity to the thrill of escape, followed by life on the run in North Africa or occupied Europe. There is a fascinating account of operations by Lord Henniker, who worked with Fitzroy MacLean and the Partisans in Yugoslavia, and three stories by Colonel Walker Brown including a daring mission with the SAS behind the lines in France. Above all I have sought to achieve a balance between the three services and the home front and to cover most theatres of operations.

Contributions from over 50 individual diarists lend this anthology, I trust and believe, a rich and unique diversity. Of added interest, I hope, is the fact that a number of contributors appear more than once in the book, allowing the reader to follow their progress through the war. For clarity of context I have tried to set the scene at the beginning of each month with a short description of what is happening in the larger panorama of war. Any perceived inadequacies in these are of course my own.

Inevitably much excellent material could not be found a home between the covers of this book, often because I already had several ideal entries for a particular month. But so impressed was I by the eye-witness accounts of so many of my unused diarists that I am planning a second volume. If any reader would like to submit previously unpublished personal wartime memories for consideration I would be delighted to receive a copy (preferably in typescript or on disk) at: Cavalier Paperbacks, Burnham House, Jarvis Street, Upavon, Wilts SN9 6DU.

Finally, I would like to thank my husband — Alistair Fyfe, friend — David Eccles, my mother — Christine Pullein-Thompson, and literary agent, Robin Wade for their help and guidance during the compilation of this book.

SEPTEMBER 1939

On the 1ˢᵗ Germany invades Poland and Britain declares war on the 3ʳᵈ September. The British Expeditionary Force (BEF) consisting of four Divisions crosses the English Channel to take up position alongside the French army. At the end of the month Hitler and Stalin sign an agreement, the Soviet German Boundary and Friendship Treaty, dividing Poland between Germany and the Soviet Union — neither the boundary nor the friendship will survive the next two years.

ON A FARM IN POLAND
AS WAR BREAKS OUT
Michael Bereznicki

Michael Joseph Bereznicki was born in Eastern Poland in 1922. He moved to Stanislaw in 1938.

I lived on a farm near the town of Kaluch, which was not far away from the provincial

1

capital of Stanislaw in Eastern Poland. Although this farming district was officially located in Poland, there were lots of Ukrainians and even a few Russians living there as well. I remember the early part of September 1939. I was 17 years old at the time, and my father sent me into town to buy provisions. When I arrived there, I noticed lots of people milling about in the town square; so many, in fact, that I couldn't get through to the store because of the size of the crowd. I got off my horse and cart and pushed my way through, but still couldn't hear what was going on. I asked an older man standing next to me.

'Didn't you hear? War has been declared.'

'Really! That's amazing. But, why the big crowd?' I asked.

'The military district is announcing a general mobilisation. They're calling out the names of people who'll have to report for military service.'

I couldn't believe it! Everybody in Poland heard rumours about an impending conflict, but nobody ever thought that it would actually happen. Being only 17, I was still considered too young for military duty. I pushed my way through the crowd and made it to the store eventually. I bought the provisions and hurried home. I ran up to my

2

father and said, 'Have you heard?'

'Heard what?' he replied.

'There's going to be a war.'

'Nah,' he nodded disagreeably, 'They'll never really attack. Hitler is just scare-mongering.'

'No, I'm afraid it's true. The military district in town is mobilising the reservists.'

My father looked dismayed. He said nothing. Instead, he gestured for me to help him unload the wagon and completely refused to talk about this any further.

About three days later, I was out working in the fields when I heard a loud 'whooshing' sound. I looked up into the bright blue sky and saw about four or five black aeroplanes flying together in a 'V' formation. I looked carefully, but couldn't tell whose they were. It was a very sunny and bright September day and the sun glared into my eyes. As these planes streaked by, I realised that they were German. I dropped my spade and ran quickly to the nearest tree. The planes did not shoot at me, instead they kept right on flying. I think they were heading for Stanislaw. I knew then for sure that this was no joke. This was serious. The Germans were actually invading Poland.

Bereznicki's story continues in February 1940 on page 41.

3

18 YEARS OLD
AND TOO YOUNG FOR FRANCE
Alec Barthorpe

Alec James Barthorpe was born in 1921. Here he remembers the declaration of war.

War was officially declared at 11 a.m. on 3rd September and on that day, and at that time Teddy and Peter Hicks and I were sitting with Mr Hicks, their father, in their house indulging in our favourite pastime — drinking beer! Peter, Teddy and I had a weekend pass from the Drill Hall, so Mr Hicks had invited us around to have a beer and listen to the Prime Minister's important announcement. Within a few minutes of the end of the announcement, the air raid siren sounded, but we all decided that it was just as safe staying where we were as going outside, so we carried on drinking beer.

We were three of the five who had signed up in the Territorial Army to be together if hostilities broke out. On our return to the Drill Hall, we were informed that the Regiment was being formed and our Battery was being integrated with the Surrey Yeomanry, so that we would become the Surrey and Sussex Yeomanry. Then the

Regiment was off to France with the BEF, and would be equipped with all the available guns, limbers and transport we possessed at the Drill Hall and further equipment would be issued to us in due course. We would also be moving into the Hove County Cricket Ground immediately, where all this equipment would be assembled. All ranks were billeted in private houses in the vicinity of the ground and days full of activity passed quickly assembling all the equipment and transport for the newly formed Regiment.

Then out of the blue, came the bombshell for me. No soldier under 19 years of age would be allowed to go to France with the BEF, but would remain behind to form our second battery. I did everything I could think of to get back to the unit, I even volunteered as a batman — but all to no avail, so when the Battery moved off I stayed behind and helped to form and train men for the 389th Battery, of the 144th Field Regiment, Royal Artillery (Surrey and Sussex Yeomanry). By the end of September our First Line Battery had moved out to an assembly camp and was on its way to France. The handful of us who stayed behind cleaned up the County Ground and prepared it for our reinforcements to arrive for training.

Barthorpe continues his story in January 1941 on page 116.

LIFE ON HMS HOOD AS
WAR IS DECLARED
Leonard Williams

Leonard Charles Williams was born in 1911 into a naval family in Portsmouth. He went to Greenwich Royal Naval School when he was 13 and joined the Navy at 15. In 1936 he joined HMS Hood as a Seaman Torpedo-man.

After hearing the declaration of war, we sat for a while around the portable radio. We

6

were sitting on ventilators, boat crutches, on anything else available, for we were up on the boat deck. It was a fine morning, with the ship lazily lifting her bows to the long Atlantic swell. Over on the port beam steamed one of our escort. I watched the thin spiral of smoke languidly rising from the destroyer's galley funnel, while the brilliance of this September morning warmed my bones. I saw her crew going about their duties on the upper deck, and the forecastle gun's crew huddled behind their gun shield. Every now and then she would dip her bows to the swell, and, occasionally, the sea would break on board, to sweep aft in a shower of spray which sparkled in the sunlight like cascading diamonds. It was a day to be at sea. Only one thought marred the peaceful scene and beauty of the morning. Somewhere beneath this heaving ocean enemy submarines were at their war stations and we were a prize target. As a single man with no responsibilities, I received the news with a certain amount of indifference. I was annoyed, of course, because the tenor of my life was now about to be disturbed, which was I suppose, a selfish way of looking at it. There was the other side to be considered too. For years, we had trained for just such a possibility as this. Now it was up to us to see that the taxpayer got a return for his money. I tried to assess my ability to face up to the new situation. I knew my limits under normal conditions, but how would I react under war conditions, possible action, with all it could mean? I tried to detach myself like a shadow, and study myself from a position outside. Will you be afraid, I asked myself, or will you be the stuff of which heroes are made? I am afraid we all asked ourselves similar questions, and, like myself, received the same answer: 'Wait and see!' . . .

Whilst the Phoney War was going on in France, and the RAF were plastering the Germans with leaflets, the war at sea began immediately and, before the first day was over the liner *Athenia* had been torpedoed and sunk in the Atlantic.

Our new Captain, Irvine Glennie, broadcast the news to us over the ship's loudspeaker system, with a few choice comments of his own. *Athenia's* loss served to bring us all down to earth. We now knew that we were dealing with the same old Hun that our fathers had known. These people were inhuman monsters. There was no possible excuse for sinking *Athenia*. She was carrying passengers, of whom a large percentage were women and children. We were very bitter about this outrage, and it left us resolved, more than ever, to settle

Germany's hash once and for all.

After about two more days, we returned to Scapa Flow to re-fuel. I think the only reason we had gone to sea was to keep clear of Scapa when war was declared, in case of a concentrated air attack on the anchorage. Whilst at Scapa we had several air raid alerts, but apart from one of our own aircraft which was fired on by the shore batteries, for approaching the Flow from the wrong direction, we had little interference at this time.

Towards the end of September, one of our submarines, *HMS Spearfish*, was heavily depth charged whilst on patrol in the Heligoland Bight. The damage sustained was such that she was unable to dive and could only proceed on the surface at a reduced speed. The Commander-in-Chief, Admiral Sir Charles Forbes, decided to take the entire fleet to Heligoland on a rescue operation, presumably also, in the hope of catching any German vessels who may be tempted to interfere with *Spearfish*. It was a big decision to take, for the area concerned was right on Germany's doorstep. However, we in the Navy have a reputation for looking after our own, and we soon found ourselves headed on a south easterly direction towards *Spearfish*. When the fleet first arrived in the Bight,

Spearfish was slowly struggling homewards, but was constantly in danger of air attack. Whereas a solitary submarine could possibly have avoided detection, a fleet spread over several miles of ocean, certainly could not. It was not long, therefore, before we were spotted by a German patrol aircraft and our position duly reported to its base. We could now expect severe air attacks. We were not disappointed!

Within a short space of time the fleet was attacked by bombers coming down out of the sun, for it was a beautiful day, with a smooth sea. *Hood* being positioned well out on the screen, was not immediately involved. The carrier *Ark Royal* was severely bombed, and at times, was completely obliterated by smoke and spray. The pilot of the aircraft concerned, claimed *Ark Royal* as sunk, and we later learned that he was awarded an Iron Cross for his 'brilliant feat' and made a national hero. The truth was, *Ark Royal* was not even hit, and suffered no damage whatsoever. For months afterwards, the enemy maintained that she had been sunk and repeatedly asked over their propaganda radio, 'Where is your *Ark Royal*?'

Our AA gunners in *Hood* had a grand-stand view, since we were some five miles away from the main attack. Then, quite suddenly, and without any noise or other warning, a Dornier bomber approached *Hood* from astern and out of the sun. As it passed over our mainmast, it dropped a fair sized bomb. Not satisfied with this, the pilot waved his hand as he sped by. Fortunately, the missile bounced off the ship and struck the water about 15 feet off our port beam. It blew a hole in our torpedo protection bulge; but apart from scattering the tiles in the stoker's bathroom and covering everything with debris and dust, it did little damage and no casualties were incurred.

So sudden had been the attack, we had not even been able to fire a shot. Captain Glennie immediately broadcast orders that the gun's crews were in future to open fire without waiting for orders. The attacks on the fleet eased off on the approach of darkness, and finally ceased altogether, and we made our way homewards, escorting the badly damaged *Spearfish*. We had been very lucky this day, for we were all intact. It had been our first brush with the Luftwaffe, and, whilst we now knew their fibre, we had also found the chinks in our own armour.

Leonard Williams continues his story in April 1940 on page 50.

OCTOBER 1939

The battleship, *The Royal Oak*, is sunk in a daring raid by a German U-boat on the Royal Navy base at Scapa Flow.

RAW RECRUIT
Vic S Senior

Vic Senior was an articled accountant before war started. In October 1939 he joined the Royal Tank Regiment as a trooper.

We had arrived at Wool station in Dorset about nine o'clock; it was raining; we had been pushed into the back of a lorry and brought to this hut in Bovington Camp. I say 'we' because there were six of us altogether; we had travelled separately from London and had met on the platform at Bournemouth, where we had to change trains. We all seemed to possess the same vague lost look and instinctively were drawn together, to find as I suspected, that we were all heading for Bovvy — raw recruits.

Lance-Corporal Blash, for that was how he introduced himself (not his real name), had shown us into this hut in which there were 32 iron bedsteads. On each were three hard, brown rectangular objects — which we discovered together formed a mattress and which, later I was to learn, were called 'biscuits' — three bristly blankets, two straw pillows, two stiff calico sheets and two pillowcases. In the middle of this ill-lit hut were two coke slow combustion stoves, alight but smoking vaguely, two scrubbed wooden tables, and four equally well-scrubbed forms. Beside each bed was a green wooden chest and a bedside locker. Blash had shown us the wash house and latrines, some 40 yards away and had taken us to the dining hall where laid out on more of those same white, scrubbed tables, were rows of thick china plates, on each of which were slabs of bread and cheese, a dollop of plum jam and a cube of margarine.

'There's your supper,' he said, 'You can help yourself to a mug of cocoa from that tea-pail over there.' We were too tired to notice the incongruity of his remark.

He left us, but before doing so, advised us peremptorily, 'I shall be round to wake you up at six o'clock in the morning . . . I'm the non-commissioned officer responsible for you lot. We've got plenty to do tomorrow so I don't want no malingering. No idle bastards in my squad. Good night all, no snoring and don't piss the beds.'

We were later to learn that Blash was a regular soldier, not too bright, with a sadistic streak who had been given an acting-unpaid-lance stripe to look after our batch of recruits. He was anxious to succeed in the hope that this modest promotion would be made permanent. He knew only the pre-war Regular Army way of dealing with recruits and this involved being tough during the initial period of training. Discipline was strict and orders were to be obeyed unequivocally, automatically, and without question. NCOs were expected to be hard, to make a lot of noise, but underneath as we were soon to find, they were always considerate and almost paternally interested in the welfare of those in their charge. They were proud when their squaddies did well and purred when any compliment was received from a superior officer, for example on the excellence of the turn out and drill of their squad at a passing-out parade. Blash was no exception and we hated the sight of him until later when we came to know him better.

We leapt from our beds and in pitch darkness made our way to the ablutions, cursing and swearing. 'Bloody hell' was the lucid comment of one of our number when he realised there was no hot water. Inept perhaps, but it summed up our feelings admirably. We returned to the fetid atmosphere of the hut where someone was trying to light one of the stoves which had gone out overnight. He was surrounded by a mound of clinkers, half-burnt coke, charred wood and paper as he tried unsuccessfully to coax the cast-iron brute to life. In the end, he gave up.

We took stock of each other. All of the beds had been slept in and there were about 30 of us altogether, as motley a collection — of all ages — as you ever did see. There was a Cockney hairdresser, two labourers from South Wales, one bank cashier, a professional footballer, an Irish navvy, two waiters from Cornwall, an undergraduate, a nattily dressed grocer from Lincoln, an old soldier of the cavalry who had rejoined, a merchant seaman who spoke with a Canadian accent, someone who called himself Tex because, he said, he had been a cowhand in the States whilst the rest of us were mostly nondescript individuals from the suburbs of big cities or from small country towns. We went to breakfast as the first dim streaks of dawn were showing in the stormy eastern sky, a mist drifted in from the sea, the cookhouse windows, inadequately

15

blacked-out, winked at us in the gloom. Within the dining-hall, orderlies dolloped out to each of us liberal helpings of half-liquid porridge, tea and a greasy meat rissole, swimming in tinned tomatoes. We ate with relish for it seemed that we had been up for hours.

We learnt that we were not to remain at Bovington for our recruit training. We were informed that we were to be posted to under-strength Territorial Army regiments in the locations to which they had proceeded on mobilisation but that we would have to wait a week or two for our individual posting orders. We were issued with battledress, cavalry greatcoats and cheese-cutter caps.

As we were soon to discover, most of the time was to be spent on something called fatigues; washing up mounds of pans, thick with congealed fat in the cookhouse, peeling potatoes, cleaning up the dining hall after meals, sweeping leaves outside the officers' mess or humping barrels and crates for the sergeants. Under the somewhat bovine tuition of Lance Corporal Blash, we learnt to prepare the hut for daily inspection; to make up our beds and lockers; to scrub and clean the corners, how to use the bumper to polish the floors, to knock down cobwebs and to buff up items which in civilian life few of us would ever have considered needed cleaning at all.

Basher Blash introduced us to the spurious delights of the Kit Inspection. Every Saturday morning, we would lay out and exhibit all those items with which we had been issued, to be checked and inspected by an officer from the headquarters of the Depot. If anything was lost, it had to be paid for, and we were detailed to go to the squadron-quarter-master-sergeant to sign a chit admitting our deficiency, authorising him to recover the amount due from our meagre pay.

'Knife, fork, spoon, razor, comb and lather-brush.' That was the ludicrous ditty which Blash taught us to sing to ensure that we remembered the correct order in which to lay these items on top of the canvas hold-all on the bed.

In spite of the frustration, discomfort and almost continuous harassment most of us enjoyed our time at Bovington. Every evening we would gather in the NAAFI canteen. We played darts, dominoes and pontoon. I found someone to play chess and we had egg and chips for supper. One night the RTR band gave a marvellous concert in the Garrison Hall.

In 1941 Senior was posted to the Middle East and was commissioned in 1942. Having fought with the 8th Army in the Western Desert, he took part in the invasion of Sicily in July 1943 and was in Italy in 1944. By December of that year he was fighting in the streets of Athens during the Communist uprising and was awarded the Military Cross and Bar. He remained with his regiment in Greece teaching the Greek Army how to use tanks. He married while in Greece and was by now a Colonel. In 1953 he went with the 1st Royal Tank Regiment to Korea for the final stages of war and finally retired from the Army in 1971 after nearly 32 years of service. Colonel Senior has one son and one daughter and four grandchildren. He now lives in Limerick, Ireland.

BALANCE OF PAYMENTS
Peter A L Vaux

Peter Vaux was commissioned into the Royal Tank Corps in July 1937. At the start of the war he was a troop leader and recce officer with the 4th RTC and was stationed in France from September 1939 to June 1940.

In early October soon after our arrival at Martinvast, Major Conrad Lee, commanding Headquarter Squadron, instructed me — as the Squadron 2nd Lieutenant and dogsbody — to collect from all ranks their English money and take it to the Field Cashier in Cherbourg for exchange into francs. I undertook this task with the seriousness it deserved. Armed with a large exercise book and a stout canvas bag I visited all 200 souls, from the highest to the lowest, requiring each to empty his pockets into my bag and to initial the entry in the book. When added up there was a considerable sum, while the bag weighed a ton as I staggered with it into the Field Cashier's office.

The Base Cash Office was established in an upstairs room near the docks. There a number of officers and attendant NCOs were busy behind a makeshift counter of six foot tables. The awkward newness of their uniforms revealed how recently they had replaced the banker's pinstripes. I had never before seen so much money lying about. The Cashier, who at last condescended to notice me, was a thin-faced captain with hair the colour of his unpolished Sam Browne. His expression of chronic irritation and barely-concealed fury betrayed his conviction of being beset by fools. After a glance at the total in my book, he made a brief calculation on the back of an envelope and instructed an underling to give me some immense sum in francs. He then hurled my bag into a corner of the office.

'Aren't you going to count it?' I asked, but he looked at me with contempt and turned away. As I attempted myself to count the piles of unfamiliar notes which had been placed upon the counter he addressed me for the first time: 'Will you kindly stop playing the fool and get out of this office.'

Returning to the chateau I called on the Squadron Pay Clerk to help in the tedious task of converting each individual's sterling contribution into francs. The rate, as I recall, was Fr124 to £1 so that we were soon juggling with astronomical figures. When all was done the books would not balance — we had at least 8,000 too many francs. We went through the whole thing again and yet again, always with the same result. Finally, I reported to my Squadron Commander who sternly ordered me to return the surplus to the Field Cashier as soon as I had paid the officers and men their due.

None having disagreed with my figures, I took the bundle of notes back to Cherbourg. There the same Cashier eyed me with dislike, half listened to what I had to say and then angrily told me to get out and stop being a nuisance. In confusion I withdrew to the Austin Seven and returned to Major Lee. He looked at me even more sternly, exclaiming that I simply could not have explained the matter properly. I was to go back to the Cashier at once.

This time my particular Cashier was busy and another tried to help — but I was insistent that no one else would do. A silence fell, and all eyes were upon me, as my man looked up in recognition, gradually turned puce and, half rising from his chair, hissed, 'If you don't get out of my office at once and stay out I will have you arrested. Now GO.' I made one more attempted protest and then fled. I thought I would rather be arrested by my Squadron Commander than by that man. But, to my delight, Major Lee was in expansive mood, for by now it was nearly 9 p.m. 'Well, well,' he said, 'You had better put the money in a sealed envelope in the (locked) squadron stationery box.' (I have never before dared to tell how it was that all ranks of Regimental Headquarters and Headquarters Squadron, 4 RTR fed so sumptuously upon roast pork that Christmas 1939 and for some days afterwards at the village of Fienvillers in Picardy.)

After being captured and escaping while stationed in France, Vaux was in action in the Western Desert with the 4th Royal Tank

21

Regiment and subsequently with the 7th Armoured Division, fighting at Tobruk, Alam Halfa and El Alamein until December 1942. He was Brigade Major of the 7th Armoured Brigade in Italy from January until September 1944 when he was wounded and out of action in hospital in the UK until April 1945. He remained in the army after the war becoming a Brigadier in the Sixties. Having retired from the army in 1981, Vaux lives with his wife in Hampshire.

NOVEMBER 1939

British ships are sunk by the new German magnetic mines in the North Sea. At the end of the month Russia attacks Finland. Germans continue to kill Poles and Polish Jews in their hundreds.

GETTING USED TO THE FRENCH
Robert Clemishaw

Robert Charles Clemishaw was born in Nottingham in 1920 and moved to Formby, Lancashire when he was eight. Before the war he was an apprentice glove cutter in the leather industry. In May 1939 he joined the Territorial Army and became a driver in the RASC (Royal Army Service Corps).

We arrived in the French port of Cherbourg on 1st November 1939, having sailed from Southampton by night convoy. Three days were spent in Cherbourg while the vehicles were off-loaded. We were billeted in French

cavalry horse stables and on 3rd November we moved out. Driving on the right hand side of the road was quite a novelty. Eventually we arrived in Rouen and bedded down in our trucks. Nights were now getting colder. Next stop was at a French artillery barracks in Amiens for a midday meal laid on by the French who knew we were coming, and made us so welcome. The meal was first class! We said our farewells and were on our way once more. We arrived at our forward location about 4.30 p.m. A mining village by the name of Fouquires, East of Lens, West of Lille, close to the Belgian border was to be our base for the next six months. Arnold James and I were billeted with a Monsieur and Madame

Deverelle. They turned out to be a fantastic couple. Having no children of their own we were treated as sons. I shall always remember them with great affection. Two remarkable people who had so little yet gave their all to complete strangers from another land. They owned a small estaminet, and generally the whole area seemed dark, dismal, grey and very poor. The house was a terraced two up and two down type. We were shown our room which was dark with just a skylight in the roof of about 18 inches square. We had a double bed with a feather mattress and rather dodgy springs! Better than the back of a truck! An oil lamp lit the room up. The only other furniture was a small table and a threadbare carpet covered the floor. There was a kind of outhouse next to the lavatory and water pump containing a long, low bench with a white enamel wash basin — all the comforts of home!

Monsieur was about 5ft 4in, short, fat, round-faced and swarthy. He always seemed to be in need of a shave but was quite bald. Monsieur had fought at Verdun in the First War, and was serving as a Gendarme in the Second War (armed with pistol).

Madame was somewhat larger in every way, quite grey and arms like a prize fighter. Arnold's ability to speak French was a great asset. The Deverelles were about 54 years of age but looked about 70. Not surprising as they must have had a very hard life. Before we left for company parade in the morning large, strong coffees were produced well and truly laced with cognac brandy! Many a time in the early days we were three sheets to the wind.

Clemishaw was at Dunkirk and fought in North Africa. In 1944 he married Corra McDowell and they had two daughters. After the war he returned to work for a manufacturer of leather gloves and became Managing Director of a Liverpool firm. Clemishaw died of lung cancer in 1994.

DECEMBER 1939

The German pocket battleship, *Graf Spee*, is scuttled as described in the following account.

HMS EXETER AT THE RIVER PLATE
Norman Schofield

Norman Schofield was born in 1920 in Cheshire and joined the Royal Navy as a boy entrant in 1936, specialising in radio. His early years were spent on HMS Exeter and at the time of the River Plate action he was a telegraphist.

We steamed northward towards Montevideo; this was to be our oiling place for several days. Eventually we received a message from the Commodore to rendezvous with *Ajax* and *Achilles* in a position off Montevideo. He had received information that led him to calculate the course of a Pocket Battleship (PB), which was en-route for the Plate area, presumably to fuel, and her probable position at 6 a.m.

27

on the 13th. We treated the report quite calmly as it was about the ninth one we had received with no after results. The PB had already accounted for eight ships but she always managed to disappear before we closed our claws. However, this would most probably be our last rendezvous so this took a little of the coldness from the atmosphere.

On the morning of the 13th I awoke with the sound of action mingled with the clattering of heavy footsteps audible on the ironclad deck above me, and there was much excitement in the passageway outside the office. Chief arrived and we asked him what the commotion was. The answer came not from him but from the loudspeakers, 'Captain speaking! Captain speaking! Every man to his action station at the double! *Admiral Graf Spee* in sight!' This call was repeated and was followed almost simultaneously by the thunder of the eight-inch guns. At last we had met with the wolf of the high seas and as I dashed upwards to my station above the bridge (the Director Control Tower) I thought this then was the day for which I have waited so long — I, like many more of the ship's company, was about to experience my first taste of a naval action!

I ran onto the upper deck, bumping into men going down below, then to the flag locker, upwards past the signal deck — where I caught a glimpse of my chums in the Remote Control W/T [Wireless Telegraphy] Office (RCO) — and emerged on the bridge. The sun was shining and the sea was calm except for the bursts of enemy shrapnel in the water. I peered out over the sea and saw for the first time an enemy warship in action. The *Graf Spee's* guns were blazing away with as much gusto as our own — as each salvo left her turrets, massive smoke rings oozed upwards and sped skywards in ever increasing circles. With this vision in sight and amidst the roar of gunfire and shell burst, I crawled into the Director Control Tower and settled myself near the Gunnery Officer who seemed to be having the time of his life adjusting his instruments and shouting orders down the different voice pipes.

It must have been about five minutes later, when there was a blinding flash which seemed to envelope me. Then I heard shouts from the bridge — surely we had been hit? The Gunnery Officer supplied the necessary answer by clearing the tower — apparently his lines of communication had been cut. He crawled out and the crew followed — they were bound for the after control. We had an operator up there, so my job was finished for a while, anyway. I hopped down onto the bridge and had a quick look around — the aerials had been blown away and the after mast was severed with the rigging hanging free. The Telegraphist Air Gunner was freeing the planes from the loose wires and stays — he made short work of both planes later — both were riddled with shrapnel so they were useless and were just pushed over the side. On the bridge itself, many were dead and much blood streamed about the deck. The Captain was clothed in tennis rig (probably what he had slept in). He was dashing about from one voicepipe to another with complete mastery of the situation. He really proved himself that day in many ways — the chief one being that we dodged two torpedoes by about three feet! Then the Signal Officer arrived, dressed ready for a take off in the plane. He was rigged in his observer's flying kit and limped badly (a wound in the leg most probably). He reported the planes overboard then limped off again leaving the Captain as busy as he found him.

Whoosh! Another flash! That was close. I looked round; a group of men who had been behind the Director Control Tower had disappeared and a great hole was all that remained to show the passage of the deadly missile. I made my way down to the signal deck where again a mass of debris confronted me. A shell had hit the wheel-house diagonally and in line with the deck, had ploughed its way through the passage and RCO to leave the bridge seconds before explosion! Dashing through that passageway I glanced again at the once orderly office. What a sight; it couldn't be true! But yes; there were all my chums — there was Arthur and Sam, my watch mates for three years past. They were punched into a hole (which the shell had left), Arthur's face now only half a pale mask, no legs. Pary was there, stretched mutilated, with his head dangling through the rent in the deck. Micky was quite dead, and Buck, who had stood my watches in Port Stanley, had no legs but was trying to rise feebly. He gave one convulsive cry and bowled over.

All this, I saw in a second and obviously was of no help in the RCO so I ran down to the flag locker. The action was continuing, not so fiercely but nevertheless, although the fo'c'sle [forecastle] turrets were silent, the after turret — Lazy Y we called her because of her obstinacy to complete her firings in the many exercises we had completed — was still going to our great surprise. She certainly redeemed herself that day! In this locker more disaster met me. The Petty Officer

Telegraphist was there huddled in a corner away from the other dead. He was very badly knocked about but still had enough spirit to sing out, 'That's the idea boys — give em hell!' I went down another deck to the sick-bay.

This had been hit so that most of the injured were lying around on lockers and in the various stores. There was about a foot of water washing around the deck and it was thick with smoke — obviously we were on fire below, somewhere. The doctor was in desperation, moving around with a hypo-syringe, dealing out morphine and bandages; he was very busy. Hatchways to both wastes had gone and smoke poured from them. My only hope to reach the main office was across the upper deck, so off I went, passing the gun's crew who were sweating heavily — some had bandages round their heads but were unperturbed as they carried on heaving shell after shell into the gun. Our office was a hive of industry and the main transmitter was pumping out signals continuously. Two or three hands, who had been away to rig jury aerials, came back with the news, which I already knew — half the staff were gone — in the RCO all my watch was killed.

The signals received showed that *Exeter* had taken the brunt of the action. We had gone in close to the enemy to avoid her shells exploding on us, and also to bring her in range of our secondary armament. *Ajax* and *Achilles* had put themselves on the other side of the *Spee*, so as to draw some of her gunfire away from us; The *Spee* was on fire amidships and was hit in quite a number of places with only one gun remaining. Just so, she had put us out of action — our Y turret was the only one firing after an hour. However, all that remained was for *Ajax* and *Achilles* to carry on the pounding. The last signal was 'Proceed to Falkland Islands with all speed'. This turned out to be ten knots. The ship was like a red hot tin box full of holes. One hole amidships had to be counteracted and this was done with application of a collision mat and by listing the ship at an angle. It was really a blessing that we didn't hit one of the many storms prevalent down there — even a little torpedo boat could have made us tremble!

Clearing up operations began and our dead were checked as 64 — five died afterwards on shore. The wounded were many and the wardroom was converted into a sick-bay. The cable locker was damaged, a shell had cleared the Chief's flat of almost everything, on explosion. All the dead were draped in blankets, canvas and weights with chains.

They were laid on the fo'c'sle and quarter-deck and the burial at sea took place. Chums of three years' friendship were reverently committed to the deep in three minutes. I think many of us who were watching had to quell the sickly lump, which rose in our throats as their remains hit the water and sank. Everyone was given a tot of rum; an old naval custom. It was new to me and my brother received half of my ration. I shan't forget him — he was dressed in overalls, now black with all his hair badly singed; he'd barely escaped with a mate of his in the Chief's flat explosion, they had been the fire party down there.

I was made a first operator right away and was very busy till we arrived in Port Stanley. More signals reached us of the battle. On seeing the other two cruisers appear, the *Spee* had made a run for it: she was heavily damaged and was seeking refuge in Montevideo harbour. That day and night I don't think anyone slept and only a few of the really old sailors ate anything. On the radio, next day we heard of the battle. It was a victory for us and most of the commentators gave much praise to *Exeter* — the little cruiser which had struck blow after blow at Germany's pride and joy.

The day following, in which the ship was

cleared up as much as possible, we heard that *Graf Spee's* time in the neutral port of Montevideo was ended — 48 hours was the maximum given. Reports of a big force waiting outside to engage her convinced us all of her final downfall. However, *Graf Spee* did not come out. She made for the deepest spot in the channel and after most of the crew had disembarked, she scuttled herself and sank in the centre of the bay. The water there is not very deep and her masts still remained above the surface. Her Captain — Langsdorff — afterwards shot himself in one of the hotels ashore in Montevideo — he was found lying on the ensign of the old Germany — the Eagle.

Meanwhile, we were proceeding towards dear old Port Stanley again, of course the ship was in no condition for another action and when the men started rumours of another PB coming across from South Africa, we were all somewhat perturbed. The atmosphere was very tense as we neared Port Stanley. 'We simply must make it!' was the thought ringing through our heads and in view of the fact that one of the executive officers had taken over the navigation duty (the latter had been killed) I imagine his feelings were much the same as ours. We eventually steamed into the harbour and gave a sigh of relief. Many of the wounded cheered with joy as the familiar cry of the seagulls swooping down to the refuse shoot and the clanging of the anchor cable leaving the locker heralded the ship's anchoring. The people ashore must have been warned of our coming, as hundreds stood cheering and waving on the hilltops.

Our wounded were the first ashore, serious cases to the little hospital and the others into people's houses. Some even gave up their own bedrooms for patients. Then leave was granted to nearly everyone and we all proceeded ashore.

HMS Exeter now returned to Britain for repair. Schofield rejoined her as she was deployed for convoy duties in the Far East. Sadly HMS Exeter was sunk in the Battle of the Java Sea at the beginning of March 1942 and Schofield spent the remainder of his war on the Japanese Island of Honshu as a prisoner. He married Marian in 1945 and stayed in the Navy until the late Fifties. Then returning to Cheshire with his family (he had a son and daughter) Schofield worked in various fields until he retired in 1980. He died in 1999.

JANUARY 1940

The Finns are still resisting Soviet efforts to break through their defences and the Germans continue their persecution of Polish Jews unabated.

THE PHONEY WAR AND HOME LIFE
May Wedderburn Cannan

May Wedderburn Cannan was born in 1893. She was a war poet and had three volumes of her poetry published during and just after the First World War. She became engaged to Bevil Quiller-Couch at the end of the war but he died in February 1919. She married Percival James Slater in 1924 and had one son, James Slater. In January 1940 May was living on a smallholding while Percival went on a Senior Officer's course.

It was the time that became known as the Phoney War. We had gone to war over Poland, but because we had left it till too late, there was nothing we could do for Poland, and the

37

Germans did nothing except what they did there. The French garrisoned the Maginot Line and the BBC had done a broadcast from it at Christmas and you could hear men walking and talking in the fortifications waiting for no one quite knew what. The British did a bit of defence work along the unfortified Belgian Frontier and Hore-Belisha said it wasn't enough and Chamberlain dismissed him. 'There'll always be an England' became a smash hit and someone wrote 'Hang out the washing on the Siegfried Line', and 'Run Rabbit Run', — brash and boastful, written, I am thankful to say, by a professional song writer which made those of us who knew war and knew what would be coming to us, feel physically sick whenever we heard them.

Meanwhile what I suppose I had always known would happen happened and we were told to reduce our poultry stock to a figure that would make my egg production and poultry farming completely uneconomic. Fruit was unsaleable since sugar rationing had begun and taking the sheep down to the lower pasture in the village, Mr Brazier told me he would no longer be able to keep them. The bottom he said is out of that market — ploughing up everything, that's the plan. No place for small mixed holdings — he would take a job at one of the big farms — and he would be only too welcome . . . So I wrote to PJ [Percival] and a day or two later got the answer. Always cheerful even in the face of a bitter blow, he wrote: 'There is no use making a misery of this war. It is a shame that all our efforts to produce a food unit that might be useful in war have come to nothing; stock reduced and everything unwanted, but at least you have improved the fields if they are to be ploughed and I have been thinking that you should become a rolling stone and follow my fortunes . . . Do you think you could sell up or let our house — there will be people soon wanting to get out of the bombing who might like it — wind everything up and join me? You would be able to get the odd job, paid, or unpaid near wherever I am and we should see each other sometimes.'

May Cannan moved to Streatley, Berkshire to be near PJ's battery and then to Chilmark in Wiltshire. Their son was at Eton at this time. Cannan's accounts of life during the war continue in August 1940 on page 80 and September 1941 on page 172.

FEBRUARY 1940

The Soviets break through the Finnish defences. In Josing Fiord in Norway *HMS Cossack* under the command of Captain Philip Vian intercepts the *Altmark*, the German vessel that was the auxiliary of the *Spee* and which was a floating prison for the crews of sunk merchant ships. With no help from the Norwegians, Captain Vian's men board the *Altmark* and release 300 British seamen.

DEPORTATION
Michael Bereznicki

Michael Bereznicki, whose account of life in Poland in September 1939 is told on page 1, continues his story. Poland had been divided into two, with Germany possessing the western half and Russia the eastern half. Stalin decided to deport the Poles from their homes, partly as revenge for Poland's victory over the Red Army in 1920, partly to eliminate capitalists and other bourgeoisie from their sphere of influence and partly to appease Ukrainian nationalists who claimed the land as theirs.

We were still living on our farm during the winter of 1939-40. Papa thought that we might be able to peacefully coexist with our Russian overlords. But this forlorn hope ended on the 10th February 1940, when I heard a loud knocking on our door at 4 a.m. My father opened the door and saw a squad of Cossacks and NKVD officers [Soviet Secret Police] standing on our doorstep. One of them asked (in Russian), 'How many in your family?'

'About six of us,' my father replied.

'It is not safe for your family to stay here. Your neighbours are complaining. Therefore, we must help you to leave at once,' the official said.

'But where will we go?' my father pleaded.

'Don't worry about that. Everything has been arranged. Gather your belongings and come with us immediately.'

So, we grabbed whatever we could carry and then stumbled out into the frosty twilight. We were ordered to climb into a horse cart, which the six of us did. The entire family — my mother and father, my two brothers, my sister, and myself — squeezed together into the back of this wagon. Our group arrived at the town of Kaluch a few hours later. When we got there, all six of us climbed out of the cart and walked out onto the train platform. The train had small slits for windows with coils of barbed-wire running through the frame. We were transferred from a horse cart to a carriage for cattle. Next, our family was herded like animals onto the train, and the door was bolted shut from the outside.

Our group travelled for a long, long time. Some people got sick, some began to push each other, others began to argue, and so on. Our family must have travelled for 24 hours without food. I don't ever remember being as hungry as I was back then. We didn't eat anything for the entire trip. Everybody felt starved.

After many hours of travel, the train arrived at our destination — Lvov. We stopped there because that was the point where the Polish and Russian train systems met. Polish rails were slightly narrower than Russian rails. Everybody had to leave the railway carriage and file onto another, which was built to travel along the Russian rail system. The transfer point was about half a kilometre away and so the passengers and their armed escorts had to walk. I don't remember how, but I managed to slip away from the crowd and hide behind a building. When the crowd left, I realised that I was free. Maybe I should have run away, made a plan, or perhaps returned to the farm. But our farm was probably nationalised by now and all our possessions were probably redistributed amongst our neighbours. Where would I go? I didn't know anybody in Lvov. I had no tools, possessions, food, job or money. I would probably be labelled a fugitive, and I would have to run constantly from the NKVD. A cloud of pessimism intruded itself upon my previously bright and sunny plans. Looking down the snow-covered streets, I realised right there and then that I had no choice but to return to the train and my family. I ran toward the Russian side of Lvov.

When I arrived at the loading zone, I was stopped by a tall lanky Russian army officer wearing a fur hat and holding a large clip board.

'Where do you think you're going?' he asked rather gruffly.

'I have to be on that train,' I replied.

'No, everybody on that train has been specially selected. You obviously don't belong there.'

'But I do belong there. I slipped away

44

during the walk between the two train stations.'

'No, I'm afraid I'm going to have to ask you to leave,' he said. And he began to push me away.

'Look at your list,' I implored. He stopped pushing and said, 'Okay. I'll check. What's your name?'

I told him and he looked at the list for a long time. I could hear the locomotive starting up. I stood there nervously shifting my weight from foot to foot. 'Please hurry, I think the train is about to leave,' I said.

'Oh yes. Right here. You're supposed to be on railway carriage number 507. I'll tell them to stop immediately.'

The two of us ran frantically towards the carriages and shouted at some soldiers to halt the locomotive. It stopped and I got on. The door slammed shut behind me, and I pushed my way through until I rejoined my family.

MARCH 1940

Finland capitulates, ending the Soviet-Finnish War and signs a peace-treaty with Russia. On March 18th Hitler meets Mussolini at the Brenner Pass.

THE PHONEY WAR
Arthur Heartfield

Arthur Heartfield was born in London in 1919 and was employed as a motor vehicle mechanic when he left school in 1935. When war broke out he enlisted in the Territorial Army in the 1/7th Battalion, Middlesex Regiment and joined the BEF in France in January 1940. He was a Lance Corporal Driver Mechanic in charge of the Battalion Medical Officer's three 15cwt Morris trucks.

The 1/7th Battalion, Middlesex Regiment were enduring a very cold winter and the vicissitudes of the Phoney War in the Houplin-Seclin-Lille area of North France during the early months of 1940. We passed the time in training and practising 'tactical withdrawals' from simulated lines of defence on rivers and canals in the countryside around Lille. The overall plan, as we found out later, was for us to advance into Belgium moving easterly to counter the German attack which would come from the east. As Belgium was neutral we could not practise on Belgian soil, and had to rely on the Belgians establishing defence lines on their eastern frontier so that we could move up to reinforce them when attacked. This meant that we knew nothing of these Belgian defences until they were under attack.

The area around Lille had been in German hands for four years during WW1. Many of the locals had German fathers and were rabid German sympathisers, which made for strained relations with the British troops, although they were happy enough to take our money in the cafes and estaminets! We were only allowed to draw roughly the same amount of pay as that of a French Army private (poilu) — 50 centimes per day to avoid further conflict because of our much higher rate of pay (2/- per day less deductions plus rank and trade pay). The remainder of our pay was banked for us in Britain.

The French countryside and people were extremely poor, and many signs of the ravages of WW1 fighting were still to be seen — fences made of barbed wire from No Man's Land, houses built of petrol cans and papered inside with newspapers were not unusual. It was common to see German signs such as 'Trinkwasser' still painted on the walls of the French houses. As the Medical Officer's driver I saw a lot of this desolation because all civilian doctors in the area had been drafted into the French Army, so our doctor did what he could to service emergency cases in the surrounding villages, making home calls on these people who often did not even have a horse and cart. The other British doctors in the area did the same, but often got little thanks for their services. The roads were mostly cobblestone and until almost the end of our time there were overlaid with a thick layer of ice. Since our vehicles were fitted with very wide tyres intended for desert use, driving on ice was very difficult, and sometimes impossible. Our food supply sometimes ceased for some days because the trucks could not get through, and we had to rely on what was left in unit stores and what we could scrounge.

Our Battalion Quartermaster Captain had been the Signals Sergeant with the same unit in the British trenches in the same area during WW1. On Sundays during this time he would get parties of us young soldiers together and take us to places in the old trench lines that he knew where famous battles had taken place. In that way I got to see Vimy Ridge and several other well-known sites, and some of the cemeteries. Near to us was a blown-up fort of the 1917–18 Hindenburg Line, part of the German defences thrown up when the Allies at last started to advance and overrun their trenches.

Arthur Heartfield was evacuated at Dunkirk. Having transferred to the REME (Royal Electrical and Mechanical Engineers) he was eventually posted to Iraq and was involved in the reconditioning of tanks and other vehicles which were then sent out to the Russian front. He was demobilised in 1946 and ran a garage business until emigrating to Canada in the Fifties with his wife and two children, where he still lives today.

APRIL 1940

On the 8th April British ships steam towards Norway in order to lay mines and try to prevent the Germans shipping iron ore from Narvik. Meanwhile the Germans, having already overrun Denmark, begin their invasion of Norway. British and French troops are sent to help in the battle for Norway but by the end of the month the Germans are practically in control, the Norwegian King has been evacuated to England and British troops are withdrawing.

LIFE CONTINUES ON HMS HOOD
Leonard Williams

Leonard Williams whose account of life on HMS Hood in September 1939 is recounted on page 6 continues his story.

About the beginning of April, we again went to Devonport Dockyard to have our obsolete 5.5 inch guns removed, and twin mounted dual purpose 4 inch guns installed in their place. We also gave our ship's company 14 days' leave. I, for my second week, went to Wembley and met a girl, spent a wonderful time, and became engaged before returning on board. During this refit period at Devonport, life for those left on board was most uncomfortable. The dockyard men were working day and night, getting the old guns out, and putting the new twin mountings in. The clattering of the rivetting hammers kept us from getting any sleep, and it was a frequent occurrence to have a shower of red hot fragments and sparks descend on one's midday meal, when the white hot giant rivets holding down the new mountings came through the deck head.

As soon as our refit came to an end, *Hood* (complete with 14 new 4 inch guns in seven twin mountings) sailed for the Mersey, and went into the Gladstone dock at Liverpool for a bottom scrape and the supposed fitting of an armour bomb proof deck. In actual fact, we only managed the bottom scrape and then we were hurriedly re-floated and sent post haste to Gibraltar, where we formed and became, the first flagship of the famous Force H, with Admiral Sir James Somerville as our Flag Officer.

A further account by Leonard Williams appears in July 1940 on page 76.

MAY 1940

On 10th May Germany invades the Low Countries. With 136 divisions the Germans advance through Holland and Belgium. British, French, Belgian and Dutch troops combined are only half the size of the German force.

BRIEF ACTION AND SPEEDY RETREAT TO DUNKIRK
Basil Rabbits

Basil Rabbits was born in 1920. He started working for the Local Authority, Twickenham Borough Council in 1937 and also joined the Territorial Army in that year. As a territorial soldier he was one of the first to be called up and served in the Royal Artillery.

Early in May it came — everything had been quiet; but suddenly Germany invaded Holland and Belgium. Then we got orders to move from our base near Amiens. Sandbag walls were pulled down, ammunition loaded, kits packed and billets cleared. It was a very swift operation and we assembled in the village main street that same day. The whole village turned out to see us off. Leyland trucks towed our semi-mobile guns and three tonners carried the other things. On the cab of one of the three tonners reposed our three-seater loo. The loo is always one of the first considerations of an army on the move and we were not leaving it behind. The locals considered it a huge joke.

We travelled towards Belgium. Our destination was Merville on the French border. There was a small grass airfield occupied by the RAF just outside and it was our job to help defend it. Jerry seemed to give us time to build our walls and then he came, a small speck in the sky at 30,000 feet. We could not touch him because our effective ceiling was only 16,000 feet. He was just on reconnaissance, but we did get off a couple of shots to indicate his position to the RAF. They did not catch him though.

One day the cook wagon was up with a meal when the spotter cried out — 'plane!' Sure enough there it was coming low over a railway embankment about half a mile away. Away went our food on the wagon and we jumped to our jobs. I was spare man that day which meant I was one of half a dozen who had the only six rifles and the Bren gun, ostensibly for defence against infantry attacks. On came the plane, but he was not alone. There was a whole squadron of Dornier 215 medium bombers, with a machine gunner in the belly of the plane facing backwards. Our number one gun got off only two shots before they were on us, but the planes had not seen us either. Number two gun swung round ready as they passed over us and they let go with their shrapnel as the Dorniers were passing and going away. When the Jerries saw us their belly gunners opened and bullets flew all around us. It was all over pretty quick and nobody was hurt. An exciting action, but one nervous NCO had called out, 'Take cover.' Some of us did automatically move to do so and the officer did threaten to shoot us if we did it again. We had learnt our lesson and we were strengthened by it. We had had our baptism of fire. The gun commanders standing up in the middle of it all with their heads and shoulders exposed were an example.

We did not know the full position, but it was clear that the Germans had, on entering Belgium, swung round the end of the French Maginot Line and into France. Their use of fast moving armoured columns was something new. They did not bother to move the whole front forward, but while keeping us all occupied, the flying columns moved into France and swung round behind us towards the channel. Germany therefore had us all trapped so that we had to inevitably retreat towards the coast. Our supply lines via Boulogne and Cherbourg were cut.

Meanwhile our Captain had to make up his own mind about what arrangements to make. We could hardly stay. We kept in touch with the other two guns by runner and checked the airfield which was deserted. We commandeered a Crossley wireless van left by the RAF and a tractor used for towing aircraft and ammunition and bombs to the plane.

The guns were mobiles so were on their own wheels. We hooked two guns behind the Crossley van and two behind the tractor. That evening we moved to the other side of the town, bivouacking in some woods.

The Captain went off to reconnoitre. He came back with little hopeful news and before dawn we moved off again, a strange little convoy. We went through some of the 1914–18 towns again — Ypres, Armentieres, Ballieul, Poperinghe, sometimes stopping for a quick action, sometimes when taken by surprise by dive bombers, taking cover in a ditch or under the guns. On that journey we brought down one definite and possibly two German planes.

We came into the outskirts of Dunkirk and somehow made contact with Battery HQ who had also arrived in the area. We set up our two guns 200 yards from a French battery of 75mm guns. They were in constant action and firing away like machine guns at any German aircraft that appeared. The Major decided to send some of us home as we had only two guns but a full complement of men. That first night outside Dunkirk we lay in the open on our ground sheets with our gas capes over us. We stayed fully clothed except for our boots. Putting one boot inside the other and inverting them we kept them dry, for, of course, it rained. I slept with my tin hat for a pillow.

The following morning about half of us were marched off leaving two gun crew, the officers and a few men with the rifles. They did not call for volunteers to stay but we would have all volunteered. Our party arrived in the docks area later that day. We were kept hanging about a long time avoiding air raids. Then we were shepherded onto the quayside. There was one ship there and already plenty on board her, but we were also packed onto her and packed below decks. It was a cross channel ferry and some time later, when we could take no more on board, we moved off. As we moved away the Jerries came over again. They hit the quay and I doubt if many more boats went alongside after that. There were not many casualties, but few boats of any size used it again. Then began the saga of the little boats.

After Dunkirk Rabbits remained with the Heavy Anti-Aircraft branch of the Artillery and served in the air defence of Great Britain until early in 1944. His battery was then attached to the Canadian Army and went across to Normandy landing a few days after D-Day. His battery were then used as field artillery in a ground role at Nijmegen and Arnhem. As the war ended his battery spent some time rounding up German prisoners and mine clearing on the islands of Zeeland. He was demobbed in 1946 and returned to his job working for the Council. He now lives in Devizes, Wiltshire.

DUNKIRK
James W Fyfe

James Wilson Fyfe was born in Glasgow in 1920. He joined the Officer Training Corps while at Glasgow High School. He left school in 1937 and was employed as a junior by a firm of coal exporters. In February 1939 he joined the 52nd Lowland Division Signals Regiment as a Signalman and trained as an Operator on Wireless and Line. He travelled with the BEF to France as part of 51 Heavy Regiment RA Signal Section on 19th September 1939 but saw no action during the winter of 1939/40.

We knew something was going to happen when we were told to pack up and the next day we started to move. Our convoy was long — each 9.2 inch Howitzer had three Scammells plus several three ton admin vehicles so from the leading vehicle to the end it covered about three miles. We had a clear run to the west until almost lunchtime when the convoy was forced to slow down. The roads were fairly well blocked with all the traffic trying to crawl through the refugees and vehicles already abandoned with stores and kit scattered all over the place. We were ordered to abandon our vehicles taking our personal weapons and haversack rations.

Everything was done in an orderly fashion with no panic whatsoever. We all walked in the direction indicated by our officers. We never saw any sign of the enemy and probably wouldn't have recognised one if he had popped up. At one point the RHQ had halted and as always a Bren gun was mounted on a tripod and positioned just inside the office area. I was walking through RHQ when I heard a light spotter plane very close by and could see the pilot coming overhead. I looked at the Bren and wanted to aim it, as there was no one else about but I could not move as I knew nothing about a Bren and felt very angry with myself for this inefficiency. The plane, I discovered later, had been brought down by one of the batteries.

We arrived at the sand-dunes North of Dunkirk in the late afternoon and settled down for a rest. We saw the sea far out on low tide with queues of soldiers, some in the water waiting to be picked up and we knew then that we were to be evacuated to UK. I scooped out a trench in the sand with a piece of wood and settling down, fell asleep. I have no idea how long I slept nor the time I eventually awoke but emerging from my cold sand pit I found the others had all gone. I got a tremendous fright and with dusk coming on and an empty beach in front of me I walked up towards the road where I joined other strays walking in the direction of Dunkirk. After a short time I saw a 15cwt truck that contained the Adjutant. He had already picked up some members of the unit and I was relieved to climb aboard. We picked up other stragglers as we made our way towards Dunkirk.

It was a good feeling to rejoin the others in the Signal Section. We rested that night against buildings on the main road outside the town and on the following morning turned up a side street that had been badly bombed. It was here that we had our first taste of enemy action. Stukas were dive bombing the roads wherever they could see our troops. The planes dived down low over the rooftops and we all scrambled for cover amongst the rubble from previous raids. Fortunately no one in our area was injured. Thankfully it did not rain but we had no rations or facilities for cooking and after almost 48 hours without food we were all hungry, anxious and worried about what was going to happen next and how we were going to get away. We saw very few locals on the edge of the town and I imagine they had all left for the countryside to the south and west.

Eventually we were directed towards a destroyer, which was tied up alongside in the harbour. It was very low in the water and we had great difficulty climbing down ladders from the quayside onto the deck. We were fortunate to get on board as the ship was very overloaded and the crew cast off as soon as we had boarded. Relieved at getting away, I was very glad of the mug of tea provided by the Navy soon after we had cleared the harbour mouth but there was no question of feeding us. As we left the harbour all the sailors were at action stations manning the guns the whole time we were in sight of Dunkirk. We were packed so tightly, standing room only throughout most of the ship that the crew had to force their way along the deck. I squeezed myself into the stern area so did not see any casualties other than walking wounded on board. Heading out to sea we passed many small boats moving towards the shore and others, fully loaded, sailing for home. In the distance we could see several larger boats picking the troops up from the water.

On arrival in Dover or Folkestone we walked off the destroyer and were directed straight onto waiting trains that moved off the second it was full. Before each train left, ladies ran along the outside of the carriages handing in postcards to anyone at the window. I wrote my name and address on the postcard that would tell my parents that I had got back from Dunkirk. As all signs and names of stations had been removed for security reasons we had no idea where we were going. When we did get off the train it was near an army camp. Here we were herded into the NAAFI, fed at last, and given a bed.

After Dunkirk Fyfe's regiment was re-formed and became responsible for coastal defence around Devon. In August 1942 he joined the 11 Corps Signal Regiment and in December having been promoted to Sergeant, embarked for the Middle East as part of an Army Corps reserve. However, as the battle in the desert had ended the ship was diverted via Cape Town to Bombay. After serving in India he was commissioned in August 1945 and after a motor-cycle accident in 1946 he returned to Glasgow via hospital ship. Fyfe retired from the army in 1975 as a Major and now lives in Worcestershire.

JUNE 1940

On June 14 German troops entered Paris and Germany took control of the Channel coast and Northern France. On June 17 (the day the *Lancastria* sank at St Nazaire and at least 3,000 drowned) France capitulated. Hitler agreed to the Central and Southern part of France being governed by Petain as unoccupied France with Vichy as its capital. Italy under Mussolini declared war on France and Britain and Italian bombers started bombing Malta and Aden. On the Desert border between Libya and Egypt, Britain faced a new war zone.

THE LANCASTRIA GOES DOWN
Edwin Quittenton

Edwin Richard George Quittenton was born in 1901. As a young man of 17 he was trapped in a loveless marriage by a 21-year-old woman who convinced him she was pregnant. After 21 years of marriage and no children, he met his second wife, Lily. By now a musician and 38 he and Lily set up home in London. Quittenton joined the Territorial Army in April 1940 and, attached to the RASC, was sent immediately to Northern France.

Evacuation seemed to be the general order. Scattered remnants of English troops were being marshalled and taken away. Our orders had come through and I reported back at Rennes to do an evacuation run to St Nazaire and then back to Rennes. The air battle was on in real earnest, but my job had to be done. The railway station and goods yards were blown to bits and a direct hit on the ammunition dumps sealed the fate of those barracks. There was panic everywhere. I was glad to get away with my last officers, and we settled down at St Nazaire. Those 18 hours at St Nazaire on this last Sunday were as a nightmare. Thousands of troops were hiding in fields from air gunners. Still, we had to take a chance and I don't think many casualties occurred during this whole period.

Boats of all descriptions were being used to transport troops to England. The time seemed long for us awaiting our turn. Again and again our hopes rose, but still we had to wait. I was asleep in the car with a major and two captains when a shout was heard across the flats. It was for our Major; at last we were on the move. It was 3.30 a.m. AA guns were shelling German planes, but none of our boys were dismayed; we were going home! We moved off at 4 a.m. and had a three mile walk to the docks. Arriving at 5.15 a.m. we halted for a snack and drink of water; later tea was made. It was a long business ferrying the troops out to the waiting ships. I, with four more pals, had been detailed in advance with records and officers kit. We were in advance of the company and reached the *SS Lancastria* first. On getting aboard, it was obvious that the ship was full and there was room for only a few more. I, with my four chums, was detailed with the other troops to the bottom hold of the ship, aft of the engine room. It was stuffy and warm, and before long everyone was drowsy or sleeping. We five had a sleep of about two hours, then we had a feed of tinned rations. Again we all settled down to sleep; an air raid had been reported, but that did not bother anyone.

At 4 p.m. I asked one of my pals (who was awake) if he would come up for a drink as it was so hot and stuffy. He said he would come up for a wash, so we left the other three boys asleep and climbed up two decks. Hundreds of boys were sleeping at this time, down below in what would have been holds in peacetime. My pal left me at the top of the stairs, I went about 13 paces along the corridor to the wet canteen; I looked round to see where he was and saw him talking to someone he knew. Just then there was a double thud outside which shook the boat. Nobody took any notice of it and we all moved up a pace. I looked round again to see where my pal was and had just caught a glimpse of him when there was a crash and he was flung into the air. The boat took a list. Lights went out and I felt a hot draught and a bang on the head. It was hell let loose. I couldn't turn back as it was a raging furnace. I felt sick with fumes, groping about in the dark. I went forward and stumbled over bodies. There were moans and shouts everywhere. I mumbled to myself, 'This is my lot. No dammit there must be way out!' I groped along in the dark, feeling along the wall, when suddenly a flap gave way letting through a streak of light. A sudden ray of hope and a way to freedom entered my mind. I pushed hard and the flap opened, showing light coming through an open porthole, revealing what looked like the dry canteen. I dived through, followed by other fellows, and made for the porthole; I got jammed half way through. Something had to be done. A horrible feeling passed over me of being trapped in the jaws of a trap. I saw water immediately beneath me and heard the shouts of the men behind me, 'For Christ's sake man get through!' They pushed me, but I did not move, only got rammed tighter in the porthole. 'I can't move!' I shouted, 'Pull me back inside.' At last I was pulled back inside, whilst slimmer fellows swarmed through the porthole as fast as they entered the room, and I saw another porthole to help more of them escape. I opened it to enable more light to enter. As I looked round the place I saw another chance in a wooden door. What lay behind the door I did not know only the fact that I had still got to find a way out. The door was locked, but, being made of matchwood did not offer much resistance to my boots. It took several hefty kicks and it burst open, revealing the iron doors mid ships. With even mind I tackled the screw bolts and the doors gave, but owing to the 45 degree angle of the ship, it was impossible to open the four sections of door. Voices were shouting behind me in all kinds of babble, but I took no notice; instead, I shouted, 'Come on boys, if you want to get out help me to open these doors!' It was not long before we had the doors fast open, giving all who could reach it the way to freedom. A quick glance and I made up my mind, saying 'Well, old boy, you cannot swim, but you must take a chance.' I saw a rope dangling about nine feet out in the water, and without hesitation I jumped, measuring my distance and catching the rope in my two hands. I went under the water, and after taking a little more than I could hold I came to the surface, and seeing a lifeboat a few feet from me, made for it by kicking out in the water.

Fate was with me and I succeeded in reaching the boat and getting into it. The next thing was to get the boat nearer the ship, and, with the help of a few men already in the boat, and not thinking of our safety (the ship had got a very bad list and was towering above us) we succeeded in pulling in near enough to fill the boat far beyond capacity. We had to shout 'Enough men! No more, or we shall capsize'. There was a frenzy, but we had to get away from the ship, so we got oars out and began pushing away from the side. Still more men, came along, clinging to the ropes either side. Eventually, with careful avoidance using the oars, we moved off.

The fear on the faces of everyone as we moved slowly away was terrible. It seemed that we were getting no further from the ship. I heard myself shouting, almost frenziedly, to the men (including myself) at the oars, to pull with every ounce away from the ship. It was babble and panic again. I shouted, 'Will someone take command and tell the men on the left to keep their oars out of the water! We must turn round and move away from the ship, otherwise, if she turns turtle, we shall go under with the suction!' We all pulled like demons, and, inch by inch, we began to pull away. Struggling bodies, trying to grab the oars, making it more difficult for us to move. 'In — out, in — out, in — out,' we started yelling, making believe we were having a race against the other lifeboat in front. 'Come on boys!' I shouted, 'in — out, in — out. We're catching them up.'

Suddenly, out of the sky like hawks, streaked German planes, diving on us. Flattening out, they started machine-gunning us. Rat-tat-tat-tat-tat. Yells went up from the boat, from the water, all round. Cries of, 'For Christ's sake help!' Bodies floated by, and we struck a big patch of oil. Suddenly the raiders began dropping flares on the oil, but our luck held out a little longer, and eventually, with a little more persuasion, we managed to reach the side of a French trawler. Rat-tat-tat-tat went the machine guns, and the French gunner replied with a sharp burst which drove the raiders off.

We managed to scramble aboard, many

injured amongst us, and, after seeing to them and their comfort, we formed ourselves into small parties, throwing ropes overboard and helping to save many more lives. Three of us, including myself applied Sohaeffers method of artificial respiration and were successful in many cases in bringing men to life. I myself failed only once.

In the engine room, bunks, cabins, bridge, in fact everywhere one looked were bodies, and what a terrible picture! Men covered from head to foot in oil; naked men; mutilated bodies; men badly burned, and amongst us, one woman and a child. Out on the sea were hundreds of bodies, many past recognition, shot to pieces, machine-gunned or blown to pieces. At last came the order from the French Captain that he could not take on any more men. They had worked hard, as had we boys. Shivering, we stood watching a battle between the RAF and the raiders, who were eventually driven off after an attack on a British destroyer.

As we moved off towards the *Oronsay*, three German mines were exploded, causing more anxiety to us all, but finally we were taken aboard and made a lot more comfortable.

Never shall I forget the last minute of the *Lancastria*, as she lay with that terrible list, hundreds of men clinging to the top of her, screaming, rolling off her as she finally turned over and the water swallowed her. Graceful was the *Lancastria*, and quietly and gracefully she went under, and the waters stilled over her. We hovered around on the *Oronsay* until 8 p.m. when orders were given that she was to proceed and take a chance. Slowly she moved away, zigzagging slowly in the dark. The journey seemed endless. Dawn broke at last but how far were we from land? How long before we landed? Had we any escorts? Questions were being asked, but nobody could give a true answer.

At about 10.30 a.m. all survivors of the *Lancastria* were marshalled together in the well deck saloon for a roll call. There were 500 aboard. The order was given for all to form their own detachments, each company of men under an NCO to keep their places until arrival at Plymouth. There, as each regiment was called, they would be taken off. As a final instruction all were warned not to move about the ship, or she would turn turtle. We were to land at 8.30 p.m. At about 4 p.m. volunteer semaphore signallers were asked for, to send a message ashore. Again the question was asked, what was wrong with the wireless in the *Oronsay*? At 6 p.m. the order came for us to get ready to land and we finally set foot on the jetty at 8.30 p.m. as predicted, where we were fed and given tea and cigarettes. We then moved off to our billet and examination by the medical officer.

It was then that we were told the story of the *Oronsay*, and we paid tribute to a gallant Captain. The *Oronsay* had received a direct hit on the bridge (before the attack on the *Lancastria*). The bomb took away the bridge, chart rooms, steering and wireless room, and broke the Captain's leg. The *Oronsay* was holed and taking in three feet of water, but the auxiliary pumps were just capable of taking out as much water from the ship. After the Captain had been told he could land the men back in St Nazaire, he chanced a dash for England, alone. The die was cast, and by the aid of the auxiliary steering gear, sextant and memory, the Captain brought his badly crippled ship safely into port. Only his skill and daring brought us back to safety, for within half an hour of the landing of the last soldier the pumps failed, but the Captain had done his job.

After Dunkirk Quittenton developed emphysema and chronic asthma and was no longer fit for service. After the war he ran a private car hire business and he and his wife had six children. He died in 1967.

CLEARING UP AFTER DUNKIRK
Silvester Macdonald

Silvester Macdonald was born in SE London in 1919, one of four sons. He was working on various docks in the port of London with his father and older brother when war broke out. Macdonald joined up and trained as a medical assistant in the Naval Brigade.

Higgins and I had reported as usual to the Chief Petty Officer, but instead of his usual welcome, he told us that he had been waiting to give us a special assignment. Higgins and myself were each given four seamen as stretcher-bearers and were provided with a truck and driver. We were told to go over to the Navy Dockyard and remove all the bodies from a ship that had come in during the preceding evening. The ship was *HMS Ivanhoe*, a British destroyer used during the last day of the evacuation from Dunkirk. Every available foot of space aboard this ship had been used to evacuate as many soldiers as the ship could possibly carry. They had fought their way down to the beaches, and the Navy knew that this would be the last trip that the ship could make. They crammed themselves into all available space below decks, and then filled the open decks.

73

However, after the ship had left Dunkirk, she was attacked from the air by the Luftwaffe and although she fought back, suffered severe damage. Her guns were practically put out of action which enabled the enemy aircraft to continue the rain of bombs and devastatingly strafe the ship with gunfire. I later learned that there was a medic aboard who worked like a demon to apply tourniquets and to try to ease the suffering of the injured and dying. There was so much carnage that he could not even let the dead rest in peace, for he had to pile the bodies in a heap so that space could be made available for the ship to be operated and defended. I never did learn this person's name but I bow my head to this young unknown who did his best with little more than a morphine syringe to help ease the lot of others. He performed in such a heroic manner that there are no medals or awards that could even come close to recognition of his performance, even though he was exposed to personal danger on the open decks for most of the attacks. The *Ivanhoe* just about made the crossing without sinking and was immediately placed in a dry dock so that she would not sink overnight. The soldiers and ship's crew who had survived were disembarked and the wounded were removed and taken to hospital. Such were the conditions when our little party arrived at dockside. It was a beautiful summer morning, but there was an unnatural quietness hanging all around. Even the view from dockside brought a hushed feeling to all who looked. It was a macabre scene that the devil himself could not have imagined to see bodies hanging over the bridge rails, lying around gun turrets, sprawled on the decks both fore and aft and the bodies in navy blue and in khaki that were entangled in death in a grotesque heap on the after deck. It took little imagination to hear the ghostly echoes of far off bugles calling for their spirits to assemble again and be counted. We just went back to the barracks and did not even discuss it before we tried to sleep. I believe that it was a very rude awakening for me. The fun and games were definitely finished.

A further account by Silvester Macdonald occurs in August 1941 on page 162.

JULY 1940

The British neutralise the French fleet at Oran as the following account describes. Petain and his Vichy government in France break all ties with Britain.

TRAGEDY AT ORAN
Leonard Williams

Leonard Williams continues his story of Life on HMS Hood which was recounted in September 1939 on page 6 and April 1940 on page 50.

At 5 p.m. on the 2nd July, Force H led by *HMS Hood*, left Gibraltar and steamed towards Oran. We knew that the French had a considerable naval force in Mers-el-Kebir harbour, and as we slid through the quiet, starlit night, we hoped that our old comrades-in-arms would join us in the common effort against Germany and Italy. We arrived off Oran at approximately 7 a.m. the next morning. It was a brilliant day, with a calm sea and blue skies. We could see the French Fleet ranged alongside the break-water, and behind them, the white buildings drowsing in the early morning sunlight.

Force H began cruising up and down outside the breakwater. Captain Holland, who spoke fluent French and who had recently been the British Naval Attache in Paris, was sent ashore to negotiate the terms with the Admiral-in-Charge, Vice Admiral Gensoul. The forenoon passed uneventfully and, apart from the defence watch, the hands went to dinner. After dinner Force H went to Action Stations as a precautionary measure; meanwhile the talks ashore seemed to be meeting difficulties, since no result had been forthcoming.

As the hot afternoon wore on, we hoped that the French Admiral and his staff would see reason, and that it would not be our miserable lot to have to fire on our old Allies. At 4.30 p.m. the French asked for an extension of the 5.30 p.m. time limit. This was readily granted and for another hour the haggling went on. It was noticed however, that the French ships had been raising steam and furling their awnings; a sure sign of preparation for sea. We did not know whether this meant that they were contemplating coming out to join us, or whether they were preparing to fight us. We were therefore on the horns of a dilemma! A further signal was sent to us asking for more time, but on instructions from London, and taking into consideration the approaching darkness, a final time limit of 5.55 p.m. was given. Beyond this, we would take such action as was necessary to render their fleet inoperable. Besides this, we had received reports that further French reinforcements from Algiers were at sea and we did not want further complications.

Captain Holland had managed to get back to *HMS Foxhound* and at 5.55 p.m. sharp, Force H opened fire on the vessels in Mers-el-Kebir harbour. For the next 20 minutes the bombardment continued, without respite, causing severe damage to the French fleet. We, in our turn, received the attention of forts behind Mers-el-Kebir and the combined guns of the vessels in the harbour.

Our ships were fortunate, since none were hit. We, in *Hood*, received only superficial damage from shell splinters. Our casualties amounted to two men wounded. It had been hot while it had lasted, and as darkness fell, we left the burning shambles, and made our way back to Gibraltar. We returned, not as exultant victors, but as extremely sad Allies, forced by circumstances beyond our control, to bring death and destruction to those we had called our friends. Never had the uselessness of war been brought home to us so starkly. It was a sorry squadron that finally berthed under the shadow of the Rock. It had been our first involvement in a fleet action. It was not a pleasant experience to be fired on, particularly when it is known that the projectiles coming your way weighed almost a ton. We were all very thankful when the gunfire ceased and we were told that the action was over. Our highly strung nerves relaxed and we began to live again. It was some time before the memory of Oran faded from our minds.

Leonard Williams married in January 1941. In February he left HMS Hood on promotion to Petty Officer, in order to take the Leading Torpedo-man's course. On 24th May 1941 HMS Hood sank with the loss of 1500 men; there were three survivors. It was a long time before Williams got over the shock of the loss of Hood. He went on to serve on HMS Ledbury and Resource during the war and remained in the Navy until 1953. He was then employed by the Post Office until retirement and died in 1990. He and his wife Kay had one son.

AUGUST 1940

The German air offensive against Britain is launched on 9th August. Approximately 300 German aircraft fly over the Channel to attack radar stations. In the next few days there are more attacks on radar targets and aircraft factories. British fighters retaliate; this period of fighting in the air became known as The Battle of Britain.

BOMBS AND LIFE IN THE COUNTRY
May Wedderburn Cannan

May Cannan's previous account of the Phoney War appears in January 1940. Now she moves to a cottage in Wiltshire to be near her husband who is in command of the new 76th Searchlight Regiment.

We had got the cottage, it seemed, because it was near an RAF bomb dump — a great underground place where the bombs were brought by trains at night. There was a village

80

shop where one was not very welcome because everything, including the rations, was in short supply and they were only delivered once a fortnight and went bad in the hot weather.

There didn't seem much that one could do in the way of war work: the village was small and isolated and I had so little petrol, so I persuaded the man in the next cottage who was working in the dump to let me lift his potatoes which he had no time to do and dig his patch, and when he found that I knew what I was about, we became friends and I got to know the villagers, and when I did go into Salisbury with the car, would shop for them. However there was no coal for the winter ahead and the ration for oil for cooking, heating and the lamps was two gallons a week and did not always come.

We were a new regiment with nothing in hand in the way of comforts. I wrote to the Daily Sketch and got a crate full of pullovers, balaclavas and mitts, collected some money, begged knitting needles, which were impossible to get, from my friends and bought wool. Our young wives who had begun to come down from Scotland (we had two batteries of Scots), organised knitting sessions with tea and biscuits and a couple of WIs volunteered to knit for us too. And then we had an influx of evacuees from London belonging to our two London batteries — people from the East End who had never walked in a field, and were terrified of cows.

We got them billeted in the little town, five miles from headquarters and the older women with children were thankful to be out of it but the young ones, especially all the real East Enders used to the excitements and Life-in-the-Street, were bored and some went back. They missed the fun in the shelters, they said.

One was brought to my attention because when she did go out she never went farther than the churchyard and sat there huddled on a tombstone. I had tried to get them over, two or three at a time, to tea with me, but they couldn't face the four mile walk and I hadn't enough petrol for transport so that hadn't been a success. This one wore a little black frock and a string of pearls the size of pigeons' eggs when she came to knit, and looked disparagingly at my shabby tweeds and small row of pearls, and told me, whatever her husband said, she was going back. She wasn't staying 'ere with nothing but mud and cows. She preferred the bombs.

I used to take pregnant wives to hospital with the petrol that I had and find accommodation for wives who came down.

On one such day I set out just as the siren at the dump went off. Up on top of the Downs, a great German bomber, hedge-hopping, swooped suddenly out of the murk and let fly at me with his machine guns. The pilot was flying so low that I could see his face — inhuman, a robot, something in a film. If I had had a revolver I could have shot him, and would have for they had killed 20 old ladies the week before waiting on the platform for a train. Thinking that he went faster than me and would get out of range I slowed up but he only circled and came over and did it again, and then, in the field on my right he dropped a bomb. I suppose he wanted to be rid of it before he went home.

I stood on the accelerator and tore down the road to the farm where Margaret (a friend) was staying; I ran in and asked, 'Where's the babe?' 'Oh,' she said, 'I heard something so I brought the pram in and put it by the window.' 'Not the window,' I said, 'Glass,' and seizing the pram, dragged them both into the passage. Another bomb fell and presently I went to see and the German bomber was streaking away with two Spits on his tail. I heard afterwards that they had got him.

A further account by May Cannan appears in September 1941 on page 172.

SEPTEMBER 1940

On 7th September the Germans launched their first raid on London with 300 bombers and 600 fighters. In the first week of the London Blitz 1,286 people were killed. The Germans also bombed the docks in Liverpool, Cardiff and Swansea and during September other provincial cities were also attacked including Bristol and Manchester. Between 7th September and 3rd November the Luftwaffe were to attack London every night.

AIR RAIDS

There follows an anonymous letter contributed by Judy Cederholm which was found amongst some old papers belonging to her mother. Both the sender and the recipient are a mystery but the original letter has been donated to the library at Battersea.

4, Ascalon House, Savona Estate, Battersea, London, SW11

Dearest Pal:

I suppose you've heard all the news by now. Isn't it terrible? Well I must start from where I left off before.

I was in Hunwick when I wrote last but I have been back nearly two weeks now. Russ had an accident last Friday fortnight on a motorcycle. He was taking a dispatch to Scotland and a car ran into him and he went into the telephone pole. I was pleased I was up there. Johnny (that's Russ's pal) came and told me and the padre got an army lorry and took me into the hospital to see Russ. He had concussion, cuts on the right side of his face and shock. He looked a mess. The padre took me in on the Sunday and told me Russ would be out on Monday as they were moving Wednesday. Russ came out and on the Wednesday I came home and spent the night in the air raid shelter, seven hours we had of it, but not much action.

The next day I got a telegram from Russ saying he'd be home on the afternoon train. I met several trains but no Russ. I went home feeling fed up and miserable. Russ arrived home Friday afternoon. He had come to a different station and also the trains had all been late. He was home for eight days' sick leave and we thoroughly enjoyed it. I slept through the air raids and we had a lovely time. He went back to Yorkshire last Friday and then Hitler started. Saturday afternoon at about five the siren went. We raced out of the shelter and gosh you should have seen the German planes overhead. There were about 200 of them. They started a fire at some docks not very far from here and talk about blaze. The sky was full of smoke and red glare. Then the all-clear went.

We had tea and talked and Amy got ready to go home when the siren went again. We decided not to go to the shelter, but gosh did we change our minds quick. We heard the weirdest sound like a whistling whine growing louder and louder and suddenly a terrific thud and explosion. Hell Peg, my stomach turned right over. We grabbed our gas masks, knitting, books, coat and whatnot, and before we could get to the shelter two more screaming bombs fell, followed by an explosion, each one louder than the last. I fell down the steps in my rush to get to the shelter and broke both heels off Rose's sandals. Meanwhile the guns were booming nearby and we suddenly realised that there was a war on. Gosh it was awful. Bombs fell all around, the sky was as light as day with the fire and guns and planes. It was frightful. One of the bombs fell very, very close and the walls of the shelter shook. The woman I was sitting next to fainted in my arms and I felt as sick as a dog.

Mum took me to the sink so I could be sick and then the damned lights went out very, very slowly. What an experience. The lights came on after about half an hour.

Anyway, bombs fell all around and the raid lasted until a quarter to five and we were sure glad to get back to bed. It all seemed like a horrible nightmare.

At half past seven I went with Amy to the station and we were told there were no trains running as four of the railway lines had been blown up near Battersea.

There's hardly a district in London that the Jerries missed. We are scared to move out of the house now. Mum and I went to my cousin Doll's for dinner and she asked me to go to a road about five minutes' walk from where she lives. There were four houses blown to bits and several others in a lovely mess. All the windows were out and a warden told us that there were three women buried in the debris. I felt really ill when we went back to Doll's.

There was an air raid warning at one o'clock Saturday afternoon, but nothing much happened, just a plane or two around.

We, Mum and I, came home and then at eight o'clock the siren went as a bomb dropped and we rushed to the shelter. A couple of bombs fell on the railway near here. The marshal of our shelter told us to lie on our faces as we heard a whistling bomb. I pushed my fingers in my ears and the marshal held us down. Gosh it was an awful feeling, Peg, waiting for a bomb to blow you to bits. I was tired as I had only one hour's sleep in 48 hours, so I lay down and about quarter to three fell asleep with bombs and the huge guns firing. At 6 o'clock a lady woke me up and said, 'There's the all-clear'. Mum said I had missed a lot by going to sleep, thank goodness. Mum and I went to bed and at 8 o'clock we were practically blown out of bed by a bomb explosion. The siren hadn't gone but we rushed to the shelter. It was a time bomb and had fallen two streets away, demolishing two houses. There were two women buried in the debris again.

There were five time bombs that went off and we came indoors again, when somebody came and told us there was another bomb in the school about 100 yards from here, so we went back to the shelter, but our air raid warden told us there wasn't much danger as it was far in the earth.

And that's my adventure so far. God we

prayed that they'd stay away but we know it's silly as Hitler said he'd blow London to bits. I'm a darned coward now, but I am hoping if a bomb does fall that we will be blown to bits and not get buried alive in the debris. Wouldn't it be terrible?

I haven't heard from Russ today and I feel awfully worried as they are in tents and in an industrial area near Sheffield and tents aren't much protection against shrapnel.

Well Peg, here I am again. The siren went as I was writing and we had to rush to the shelter. There were a lot of Jerries overhead and a few Spitfires. When the all-clear went, we came in and there was a letter from Russ. He's moving again and maybe it's to Egypt. Gosh, with the air raids and worry over Russ I'll be grey.

We got our beds ready in the shelter and now all we're doing is waiting for the siren to go. Gosh, Peg I can't describe the feeling it gives you. You feel sick at the stomach and every time a bomb falls, your stomach turns over and your heart goes into your mouth.

Considering everything, I think everyone is remarkably calm. The kids go to sleep and most of them sleep through it all. Poor little things. Isn't it awful? When poor, innocent, little babies have to go through this? We have two darling little babies in our shelter and they help to take your mind off other things.

It's getting near eight o'clock and I am really dreading tonight as one of the men saw one of the German planes dive on Battersea Power Station, apparently photographing it. It's about 200 yards from here, and it's awful high. It could do a lot of damage but I wish it had been blown up as it is a great worry to us. It's a military objective, I suppose.

I wish I could be with Russ. I shouldn't be frightened then. It's not a bad feeling when you know you would at least be going together, but if anything did happen to me, I don't know what Russ would do, and I don't like the idea of leaving him. Gosh, aren't I morbid? In a year or two I'll be out there telling you of all these horrors and may perhaps be able to forget all the terror that grips us when the bombs are falling, and then this war will be a thing of the past.

Well I think I had better close and get ready to fly to the shelter. I'll write a better letter when the raids are over and I can think of other things besides air raids. I only wanted you to know we are still alive and kicking. I hope you are all keeping well. Lots of love to your Mum and Dad.

Love from all of us

Anne

OCTOBER 1940

Mussolini orders Italian troops based in Albania to invade Greece and the British send a small force to help the Greeks. America agrees to equip and maintain ten British Divisions, manufacturing the weapons in the US.

EVACUATION
Mrs Evans

Mrs Evans gave this account to Jessica Frank, when they met in hospital in the mid Seventies. Nothing more is known about Mrs Evans. Jessica Frank's account: Waiting for the Return of the Bomber Squadron is recounted on page 121.

The siren went off at 11.30 p.m. and the all-clear didn't sound till gone 3 a.m. with only 20 minutes respite in between. At one point there was this deafening crash followed by the rumbling sound of falling masonry. It sounded just as if someone was tipping a load

91

of rubble in through the entrance of our shelter.

And then our oil lamp went out. In the darkness I could hear all three children screaming — even our Derek who is 12 and not easily frightened. I tried to put my arms round all three of them.

Then there was a pause — as there often is — between one stick of bomb falling and the next lot. Apart from the children's sobs there was complete silence. I think we were all too shocked to speak. My husband, Jim asked if anyone was hurt but no one answered then he found a torch and relit our oil lamp. The floor was covered by all the debris which had blown in and on top of that a thin layer of black dust. Our faces too, were covered in the same black dust, we looked like a gang of miners just up from the pit face!

But the strange thing was, that there — right on the top of all the stones and rubble — was a lady's shoe, just one and underneath the dust you could see that it was almost new.

I really don't know why, but for some reason Derek thought that he could see the foot that had been inside that shoe half hidden! 'There's the foot,' he said. Well, when she heard that, Cathie went almost hysterical. She was already terrified, poor little mite and

Derek, saying that about the foot, was the finishing touch.

Then Jim let fly at Derek — told him not to talk so daft. Why did he have to frighten the life out of his little sister? I could see Derek's eyes fill with tears and his lip begin to tremble (he thinks the world of his Dad). I know he never meant to scare Cathie so then I had a right go at Jim for being hard on him. He got an earful from me! This isn't the way we normally go on, it's not like us. It's just that with fear and lack of sleep everyone's nerves are in tatters.

When the siren went off last night the children were fast asleep so of course it woke them up. As soon as he heard it Bobby started screaming, 'Make it stop, make it stop.' He knows now what will follow but because he is only three he seems to believe that grown ups can do anything if they try — even stop an air raid!

Jim carried him down to the shelter still screaming at the top of his voice. Once we got there it was a little better; he buried his head and most of his upper body underneath my cardigan like a little rabbit going down a hole and fell fast asleep. He was so tired that he slept through the first part of the bombing and only woke when the worst of it began.

Well one thing is certain, after last night

our minds are made up, the kids have got to be evacuated and just as soon as it can be arranged. I have been very foolish not to have done it before.

It was only the day before yesterday that the lady from the WVS [Women's Voluntary Service] called — her name is Mrs Woodward — This was the second time she has been to see us. The first time she came the air raids hadn't started — not so as you'd notice — and Jim and I didn't want to send our kids off to live with complete strangers.

This last time we were in two minds about it. I think we would have agreed but we had just had three days without even an air raid warning and (stupidly as it has turned out) we thought the raids might be coming to an end.

But Mrs Woodward didn't think so. She made it clear that she thought we were plain crazy to keep them here, she made out that ours were about the last children left in London and that we were risking their lives. Well that upset me no end. I couldn't help myself, I just broke down in tears. I think she felt that she had overdone it, she was really kind and put her arm round my shoulder and said, 'Believe me, I do understand how you feel. I know what a difficult decision it is, but honestly these air raids are going to continue

— probably even get more frequent — and, if they leave now, Derek and Catherine can live with the same family and we can arrange for Bobby to be in the same village.'

How right she was about the air raids. Jim is going to phone her from the depot this morning to say that we would like them to leave as soon as she can fix it.

Jim had to be at work at seven this morning so he can't have had more than three hours' sleep. I only woke up when I heard him close the front door. It is now 8 a.m. and all three kids are sleeping soundly — Grandma too — judging from the snores coming from her bedroom.

Last night she was on again about how she 'wasn't going to the shelter, she'd prefer to die in her own bed, thank you very much.' The annoying part is that she doesn't really mean it, all the time she is saying this, she is collecting her belongings to take with her. Last night she was even slower than usual, because she couldn't find her teeth.

Jim has tried his hardest to persuade me to be evacuated with the kids — officially I am entitled to go with them because Bobby is under age, but how could I leave Grandma? Come to that — how could I leave Jim when he is in such a dangerous job? They report casualties in the armed services but they never seem to mention the firemen nor the ARP who have suffered as much as any.

I have just been to the corner shop to buy a loaf of bread. There was a long queue for cracked and broken eggs outside the shop but I didn't want to wait that long. When I looked round the corner at the street that's directly behind ours, I went weak at the knees. Oh my God, how blooming lucky we were last night! Three houses are flattened — just rubble — and another looks like a child's doll's house does when you open up the front and can see every room at a glance. There is nothing but a big crater where the little newsagents used to be. I know that family lived above the shop, I just hope they got out in time. Sometimes I wonder if we would be wiser to go to Whitechapel tube station which would give better protection than our little shelter, but it's farther away and I doubt whether Grandma would make the distance. Another good reason for staying where we are is that we've made such friends with Evie and her husband Andy who share our shelter. At present he's on leave from the Merchant Navy. Last night he was wonderful with our kids; whenever there was a pause in the bombing he told them jokes and riddles. Evie has been such a help — she keeps an eye on my three while I go to my house cleaning job every Monday and Friday.

I can hear the children are awake — Cathie and Derek are having an argument by the sound of it. Oh Lord I hear Bobby making that sort of whimpering noise — I know what that means — it means he has wet himself and is too ashamed to tell me. It's really not his fault, with all these terrible air raids, he gets so overtired that when he finally falls asleep he is dead to the world. But suppose he does it when he gets to his new home. They may be angry with him — even smack him for it and if he is very unhappy how will I ever know when he's too young to write and tell me. If only all three could be together, but as Mrs Woodward says, not many people are prepared to look after a three year old and not many have the room for three children.

11th October

It has all been arranged; the children leave for Wiltshire the day after tomorrow. I wanted to take them to their new homes myself and see them settled in, but Mrs Woodward said it would be better if I just bring them as far as Paddington where they will meet up with the other evacuees. She thinks it would be best to visit them in a month's time; that she says, will give them something to look forward to. But I want to see where they are going and I want to meet these strangers who will be in charge of my kids so tomorrow I am taking the train to Salisbury and then a bus to Copthorn. First I have fixed up to meet Mrs Hammond who lives at the Manor House — just fancy our Derek and Cathie living at the Manor. Then I'm going to see Mrs Harvey at Orchard Cottage, where Bobby will be. Mrs Woodward says that anyone who has room available must accept evacuees, so I do hope that these two ladies don't mind too much. I told Derek and Cathie that they were leaving us and going to live in the country. Derek wanted me to go in his place. He said, 'I've got used to being bombed, it doesn't bother me,' but of course he is scared stiff, same as everyone else. What a brave lad he is. I don't think Bobby quite understood, he kept on asking, 'Will there be elephants?' He has kept on about elephants ever since we took him to London Zoo.

12th October
The first train from Paddington to Salisbury leaves at 10 a.m. I decided to wear my best coat and hat; I want to look my best so that they will know that our children come from a respectable family. I arrived at Salisbury with time on my hands — enough to look at the shops and visit the cathedral. The bus to

Copthorn went at a snail's pace, it seems that in the country anyone can stop a bus anywhere they like! I had no difficulty in finding the Manor House, it's at the end of a tree-lined drive so you can't see it from the road but there was a sign pointing to it. There is a gravel sweep up to the front door and on either side of the door two high stone pillars. It looked huge!

I rang the bell and Mrs Hammond opened the door. She is tall and very slim and looks no more than 45 although her hair is almost as white as Grandma's.

'You must be Mrs Evans? Do come in — I'll get Nanna to bring some tea in a minute.' I followed her into a big square hall. I reckon the stairs were as wide as the average small car. They don't go up in a straight line like most stairs but in three big loops. The sitting room was even larger than the hall. The fire surround was made of marble and that too was bigger than any I have ever seen. Nanna is not, as I had at first thought, Mrs Hammond's children's grandmother, but she was their nurse and stayed on with their family after they grew up as a sort of housekeeper and help. She came in and put a silver tea tray down on a small table. There were lots of questions I had meant to ask Mrs Hammond but sitting there and trying to balance a small china cup on my knee made everything go out of my head.

Mrs Hammond asked me the children's names and she asked what Jim did. She told me she had two children — a boy of 23 who was a soldier and a girl of 18 who had just joined the WRENS. After this, conversation seemed to flag and I felt as if she was a little bored. I was just about to leave when she asked me if I'd like to see the children's bedrooms. I followed her up a wide corridor and she showed me two single rooms quite a way apart, all beautifully decorated. Try as I might I couldn't quite imagine Derek and Cathie sleeping in such rooms as these. At home they share a double bed, sleeping head to toe and Bobby sleeps in our bedroom.

When we reached the front door I turned to Mrs Hammond and said, 'You'll find they are good kids really. If they do anything wrong they only need telling.'

'I'm sure they are,' Mrs Hammond said.

It wasn't far to walk to Orchard Cottage which was as different as could be to the Manor. It was like a fairy tale cottage painted white with a thatched roof. Mrs Harvey came out to meet me. She was a little older than I had imagined, I guess mid fifties, a small dumpy woman with dark hair. What a nice lady! She showed me round the cottage which didn't take long as there are only three bedrooms. Bobby will sleep in a little room next to her. I told her about Bobby's bed wetting problem. 'Poor little chap,' she said, 'No wonder after all he's been through. It's just a question of rubber sheets, that's all.' There is a little boy the same age as Bobby living next door, so he will have someone to play with. Going back on the train I thought how strange it was that I had been more worried about where Bobby was going — not nearly so much about the other two — now it turns out to be just the reverse.

13th October
This afternoon I took the children to Paddington. They had to have a label sewn onto their sleeve with their name and address. They must be labelled and have their gas masks firmly attached and one small suitcase each. It was dreadful seeing them off. I kept reminding Derek that he must write and tell me how they are getting on. Although Cathie is nearly seven she is not much of a hand at letter writing. Bobby was still on about the elephants until he was actually in the train. When it started to move and he saw that I was still on the platform he suddenly realised that I was not coming with them. He tried to struggle out of Derek's hold to get to me. The

last I saw of him was his little nose squashed against the window crying as if his heart would break.

19th October
The air raids have been pretty well continuous. We've hardly had one night without. We are now so certain that the siren will go as soon as darkness falls that we have given up attempting to sleep in the house. We just go straight to the shelter and sleep in our clothes. We have taken our mattresses down there and at least with the children gone and Jim working, there is more room to stretch out.

20th October
I was cheered up no end because a letter arrived from Derek this morning. He wrote: 'Dear Mam and Dad, I hope you are not too bothered with the bombs. The day before yesterday the weather was fine all day but yesterday it rained in the morning then it cleared. Today has started off wet but the sun is a bit out now so I think it will stay fine. Love Derek.' I had hoped to hear how they were getting on. I didn't want a blooming weather report! I have had a card from Rose Harvey. She says Bobby has settled down a treat. The last card she sent me had a picture

of two people drinking a toast with the word, 'congratulations'. Underneath Rose had written — Dry two nights running!

I have got a cleaning job at the hospital at Bethnal Green. Jim and I put every single penny extra we earn into a Post Office savings account. It's the fund for the bath we aim to have one day. By rights I ought to be putting the extra money I've been earning at the hospital into the bathroom fund — instead I've bought presents for the children. There is one toy in particular that Cathie has always wanted — it's a koala bear. She once saw a little girl on a bus who was carrying one and Cathie went green with envy. I saw one of these koalas in a toy shop window and decided to ask the price. It cost an arm and a leg! Much more than I expected but I could see that it is as life-like as the real thing. Well, I put down a deposit on it and I can just about manage to pay the remainder next week. Of course I have to buy Derek a present of equal value and I know just what to get — he has always wanted football boots, so I have left a deposit on a pair of them as well. Bobby will just have to manage with a toy from the charity shop. I am planning to tell Cathie that I have washed and mended her old school sweater, 'It's in this parcel,' I'll say and underneath I'll hide the bear. I can just imagine her expression when she sees it. I know she'll be over the moon!

31st October

I've arrived in Copthorn to see the kids. Cathie and Derek were waiting in the bus shelter by the village green. As soon as my bus came in sight they ran out waving their arms, all excited. Right away I could see how much better they looked, just as if they had been on a long holiday in the sun. They both started talking at once. Derek said, 'We reckoned you'd be on this bus, but we met the one before just in case. All the time he was talking, Cathie was tugging at my arm to get my attention. 'Mam, Mam, she kept saying, I've got something to show you — it's in the shelter out of the rain.' She ran off to fetch it and what did she come back with but a koala bear. Identical in every way to the one I had brought with me.

Well that really knocked me back. I think I said, 'That's nice, who gave it to you?'

'Mrs Hammond gave it to her,' Derek said, 'When we were shopping in Salisbury and she asked me what I would like so I told her football boots. She bought me the most expensive ones in the shop. I hope it was OK to use some of my clothing coupons?'

'Well what a coincidence,' I said, 'I have

gone and bought you both exactly the same. I don't suppose you'll need two pairs of football boots and two koala bears. I'll have to see if I can change them.' I could see Derek looking thoughtful and a bit worried. 'You'd like two bears, wouldn't you Cathie?' I could see him give his sister an almighty dig with his elbow. Cathie always does what Derek tells her. 'Yes,' she said but I knew she wasn't too bothered either way.

Rose had suggested we had a picnic in her cottage so we went there right away. She came out to meet us holding Bobby by the hand. For a moment I thought he wasn't going to recognize me but he soon remembered and sat on my knee for the rest of the afternoon.

Derek and Cathie had so much to tell me they hardly drew breath. They liked this school better than the one in Stepney. Derek goes fishing with a friend at weekends and Cathie and a friend seem to spend most of their free time with a pony. Well there was no need to ask if they were happy. Mrs Hammond is giving them the time of their life. I misjudged her, it goes to show that you can't tell by first appearances.

My bus to Copthorn didn't leave for Salisbury till 3.30 p.m. but come 3 p.m. I could see that Cathie had her eyes on the clock. 'There's plenty of time yet,' I told her but it wasn't the bus she was thinking of but her riding lesson. I gave her a kiss and told her to run along I'd see her next time I came. Derek came to see me off at the bus stop and Rose brought Bobby. This time he didn't cry at all he just waved and blew kisses and then turned and went off happily with Rose.

On the way back home I saw 20 or 30 bombers, dark outlines against the evening sky, heading away from the Thames and towards the continent. I only know that many of those young men will not be coming home tonight. And I thought of little children probably the ages of Derek, Cathie and Bobby in some far off German city, terrified out of their lives, maybe even killed before this night is over.

NOVEMBER 1940

In November The Germans bomb Coventry as well as Birmingham, Bristol, Liverpool and Southampton.

EVACUATION MEMORIES
Bob Harris

Bob Harris was born in Brighton in 1930.

It is November 1940, two months since I arrived in Rossington, South Yorkshire from my Sussex home. I am already homesick. Christmas looms ahead as a confirmation of separation. Just ten years old, I am billeted with a miner's family, together with my brother John, who is two years older than me, and I look to him for moral support.

I am embarrassed because I don't know what to call this strange lady, who hasn't suggested Auntie or otherwise . . . so I have to rearrange my words to initiate a conversation. Also she is very deaf and can't always interpret my private needs. Our guardian is tall and spare and flits around like a busy bee.

The husband is short and thickset, habitually silent as though harbouring a grievance. When he is stripped to the waist at the sink, I am fascinated by the black weals beneath the skin. On a rare occasion, he told us of a scary experience down the pit. They both seem to enjoy 'the last hour' at what they call The New Boozer.

I offered a tough red-headed boy some sweets today; in exchange he has promised to introduce me to bird-nesting and other country lore in the spring. I'll have to keep the sweets going.

My mother writes every week, sending a postal order and cartoon strips — my favourites — from the Daily Mirror. I wish I could write longer letters to her, but I am so often lost for words without knowing why. I write of swimming in the river at the end of Waddy Lane; of excursions along the Great North Road and the discovery of a pheasant's nest: a jackpot if ever there was one; and cycling along the lane to Finningley aerodrome with the saddle at least six inches too high! And I write of scratching for souvenirs amongst the debris of a downed German aircraft.

Often I am woken by the trudging of miners' feet on their way to a shift down the pit, their gruff voices filling my mind with curiosity as to their eerie journey below ground. War seems remote here. Only *Pathe News* brings the rumblings somewhat closer.

The welfare officer came to the house the other day to look us over. She smiled a lot, asking questions. I'm glad she wasn't told I had wet the bed.

In the village there is a character called Stringy Billy, a retarded youth, who plays with string all day from a wheelchair. The area is named after him. We are a little in awe of him.

School — that notorious stumbling block — becomes an acceptable hurdle with the help of new Yorkshire friends, Archie Pinder and Frank Worsdale. They open up exciting vistas as I am introduced to thrilling country lore in which they revel and excel. I can feel the weals of the cane wielded by the headmaster, Mr Fawcett and Mr Webster, the science teacher (of whom I am terrified) and the gentle approach of dear old Mrs Metthan who is hard-pressed to control the raw exuberance of miners' children — not to mention the Shoreham boys.

The daughter of the house is on leave from the WAAFS. Tall and attractive in her smart uniform she brought us sweets, then took John and me to Doncaster to see The Thief of Baghdad at the posh Gaumont Cinema. We were both enthralled.

So it's church on Sunday, then a trek along the Great North Road before dinner. Gosh, we came back ravenous. We eat whatever's available.

Mother says she'll come up after Christmas. Oh joy!!

After the war Harris worked in the retail book trade and as a supermarket manager. He now lives in Hove and is married with four children and seven grandchildren.

DECEMBER 1940

The British attack the Italians in the Western Desert and capturing Sidi Barrani advance into Ethiopia and Eritrea.

THE NIGHT THE BOMBS FELL
Dennis Farr

Dennis Farr was born in 1929 in Luton, Bedfordshire.

It was winter 1940, and the German nightly raids on London were also beginning to fan out to target industrial towns in the Midlands. I was a ten year old schoolboy when war was declared and was a day boy at Luton Grammar School. We lived in a small terrace house not far from the centre of Luton, a Bedfordshire town once famous for its hat manufacturers, but which by the mid 1930s had become home not only to Vauxhall Motors (where tanks were made in the 1940s) but also to a major ball-bearing company; a truck and van maker; a chemical plant; a precision instrument firm that made bomb sights and naval rangefinders (where my father worked during the war); Electrolux, which then, as now, specialised in electrical goods; and a morale-boosting brewery. So we were a prime target.

Luton lies in a fold in the Lea valley, a modest little river, and two main railway lines from London to the Midlands and the North ran through a convenient gap in the Chiltern hills which surround the town on its southern and western flanks. On these hills were placed rows of the sump oil and cotton waste-filled cylinders which, when lit, gave off smelly black smoke that was meant to provide, in suitable climatic conditions, a thick blanketing haze concealing from enemy air raiders the topography of the town. They were probably quite effective, for Luton, considering its strategic importance, escaped relatively lightly from the bombing.

Nevertheless, I can remember lying awake and listening to the characteristic drone of German bombers as they flew overhead night after night. Although the air raid sirens had sounded none of us took refuge in any shelter. The next door neighbours had one of the mass-produced Anderson shelters in their garden, but my mother, fatalistically perhaps, hated the idea of ruining our neatly kept small back lawn with one of those contraptions. They did not look very strong anyway.

One evening as my mother, my elder sister (by then a young primary school teacher) and I were sitting in our small breakfast room at the back of the house, the sirens sounded the alert; it was probably about eight or nine o'clock and, homework finished, I was about to go to bed. We heard the quick thump of the anti-aircraft guns sited on the hills above the town, and realised we might be in for a lively night. As the drone of enemy aircraft grew more insistent, we became more apprehensive. My partially deaf mother could sense the tension from our strained faces. We were also anxious about my father, who had slipped off to the nearby conservative club for his regular pint.

Then we heard first one distant crump of an exploding bomb, quickly followed by another, nearer to us, and then the hideous screaming whine of a bomb which intensified to the point where I thought it was going to blast us to pieces. It screeched over our house, and by that time we were all huddled under the kitchen table; I screamed in terror as the bomb exploded and shook our house to its foundations. I have never been quite so frightened in all my life since, and even my mother could hear that ear-splitting roaring whoosh. After the explosion, a curious calm followed, and we crawled from under the table. There was that unmistakeable acrid smell of cordite and high explosive. And what had happened to Dad? Was he dead or alive? We waited for him to return, hoping against hope he was unscathed. At last, the all-clear wailed, and we went to see if the house had been much damaged. The front door, with its pretty late Victorian stained glass panels was blown in, other windows were shattered and cold air blew into the hallway.

Then, thank God, our father walked in through the back door, unhurt, but like us, rather shaken. Broken glass was all over the place. The bomb had landed in the middle of the road of a street running parallel to ours, the blast, we later discovered, had permanently skewed the window frames of two smaller rooms, and loosened slates. Quite soon, next day even, workmen arrived to nail roofing felt and laths over our front door and broken windows. Sometime later, crude bubble glass was fitted into the front door and remained there for years after the war, until a better substitute was found. Our blue and red fanlight, amazingly, had survived intact.

After the war Farr became the director of the Birmingham City Museums Art Gallery and later the director of the Courtauld Institute Galleries. He married Diana Pullein-Thompson in 1959. They have two children and three grandchildren and now live in Surrey.

JANUARY 1941

British and Australian troops break into Tripoli taking thousands of Italian prisoners. In Greece the Italians have been driven back across the Albanian border.

THE BATTLE OF KEREN
Alec Barthorpe

Alec Barthorpe, whose previous accounts appear in September 1939 on page 4 and in July 1941 on page 156 had spent most of 1940 in training and helped receive the soldiers evacuated from Dunkirk. In October 1940 he sailed with his regiment (the 144th Field Regiment, Royal Artillery) to Freetown and on down the western coast of Africa to Cape Town. Having rounded the Cape of Good Hope his unit finally arrived in Sudan at the end of 1940.

In January our infantry reported that, as a result of a noticeable lack of enemy movement or activity, patrols had been sent

116

out and revealed that the enemy had vacated Gallabat village and retreated in the direction of Lake Tana, about 60 – 80 miles away. A mobile composite unit was quickly formed, consisting of a company of infantry and a troop of artillery, for which my troop was selected and despatched immediately in pursuit. We eventually caught up with their rearguard after about 15 miles travelling at top speed, which was not that fast in bush country. We wheeled the guns into action, but after firing a few rounds the enemy retreated. We were stood down as it was now getting dark and spent the night in our present positions. The next morning we were advised that the enemy had indeed made good his escape towards Lake Tana, and we were to return to the battery position at Gallabat, and then to proceed at all speed to Keren, where the Italians were making a stand to block our way to the only pass through the mountain range to the high plateau above and the capital Asmara. All our probing attacks, so far, had been repulsed.

It took us a few days to reach Keren as we had to go via Kassala, but on arrival we took up our positions in a sandy valley which was very wide at the mouth, where we came in, but narrowed down as we approached the mountain range ahead and ended at the foot of the pass. What we did not know at the time was that the gun positions we were occupying in the sandy valley were situated in the centre of the area the Italian artillery had used as a firing range before the war! According to information received, the 4th Indian Division had arrived sometime before in their advance from Kassala but had been halted at this spot. Despite patrols being carried out to the north and south of our position, this was the only pass from the low land to the high plateau a few thousand feet above, where Keren, the main Italian supply base, lay. The pass was narrow and winding, both the road and railway line had been hewn out of the rocky face of this narrow gorge, which was overlooked by Fort Dologorodoc, Mount Sanchil, Brigg's Peak and a few other strong points held by the Italians. In order to break through these massive defences the 5th Indian Division was called to assist, and that included us.

We were deployed in a very sandy area which in a way was to our advantage, as despite the frequent shelling we underwent by enemy artillery, the shrapnel was smothered by the sandy soil which saved casualties and on one occasion saved my life. We ate and slept within ten metres of the gun, which was essential in action, and on this occasion we were awakened at first light with a request for defensive fire on a pre-selected target. We started firing at the usual rate of one round per minute. This was very soon increased to two per minute and then almost immediately to the emergency call of gunfire (as fast as you can). This applied to all our four guns in the troop. After about two hours' firing, No 3 gun on our left (we were No 2) ceased firing, and as there had been no order and we had been shelled during this operation, our No 1 enquired the reason. It appeared the recoil system on the gun had leaked oil, rendering the gun unserviceable. As we were running low on ammunition the sergeant on No 2 gun suggested that we send over some men to fetch some of his. I was sent with three others to fetch some. (I must mention here that although I was a driver, when we were in action in a static position I assisted on the guns.) We did several trips to No 2 and back, carrying either a box of four shells or one of eight cartridge cases. As I started back on my last trip carrying a box, the enemy started shelling our position. I was about half way back so to turn back was as dangerous as going on, so I just kept going. I was walking through a particular sandy patch over a low dune when a shell landed literally no more than two metres from my feet but at the foot of the dune. This probably saved my life as I was covered in sand and bits of grass; I swore at the enemy gunners but was unhurt by shrapnel. I was told afterwards that when my friends saw me disappear into a cloud of sand they called to see if I was all right, but once they heard me swearing they knew I was untouched — thanks to the sand!

It was not until March that Italian forces were eventually driven out of Keren.

Barthorpe's story continues in July 1941 on page 156.

FEBRUARY 1941

The Italians are defeated at the Battle of Beda Fomm and thousands of Italians are taken prisoner. Hitler decides to send Rommel with a division of German troops to North Africa. He also orders an increase in the U-boat sinkings of British merchant ships, hoping to cut off Britain's supply line across the Atlantic.

WAITING FOR THE RETURN OF THE BOMBER SQUADRON
Jessica Frank

Jessica Ann Tyrrell was born in Dublin in 1921. In 1941 she married Alan Frank who was in the RAF.

Half asleep I think I hear the sound of distant thunder but it's just another convoy of heavy armoured vehicles making slow progress down the village street. The reverberation is enough to make the windows rattle. I look at Alan sleeping soundly beside me and am amazed that he can sleep through such a racket. Careful not to wake him, I slip out of bed and pull the blackout curtains back a little. It is already daylight. Yesterday's fog has lifted and, although the sky is overcast, I fear that the weather will not be bad enough to prevent them from operating tonight. My heart sinks at the prospect.

Not worth going back to bed, so I wash and dress and start to make breakfast — tea and toast, and porridge — which is a welcome alternative to revolting powdered egg. Alan appears looking for Brasso to clean his buttons. While he does that, we switch on the wireless to hear the news. It is not good but they are adept at making it sound better than it is. At least for the past two nights there have been no air raids on our towns. Last week Liverpool and London got it yet again (we heard that 600 people were killed in that raid). I suppose the bad weather, which prevented our lot from taking off, stopped the Luftwaffe as well. While I am making the toast I keep looking out of the window, silently praying for a lovely, thick pea soup fog to descend. I persuade myself that it is beginning to look a little greyer.

'Good,' I say, 'I really do believe the weather is getting worse.'

'It's not good,' Alan says, 'How the hell can

we win the bloody war if we can't fly?'

I realise I have said the wrong thing. Wives are supposed to sound calm and confident. I feel neither and I'm afraid it shows.

It is strange but the air crews really seem to hate it when operations are cancelled (all their wives have noticed this). You'd think they would be only too glad not to have to fly — but just the reverse, when that happens they come home in a thoroughly grumpy mood, but we dare not risk even the slightest disagreement (perhaps when the war is over we can let rip)!

My two closest friends are also closest in distance. Gay's husband is a captain on one of the Wellingtons in Alan's squadron and Phil's husband, Johnnie, is a tail gunner in another Wellington. Gay has only been married for three months. She says that they met on the train going from Nottingham to London and that by the time they reached London they were engaged. That might be a slight exaggeration but certainly it was a whirlwind affair. Phil and Johnnie have rooms in a house on the outskirts of the village.

Alan and I were so lucky to find this place. It is a big, solid rather ugly Victorian house in the middle of the village. I think we are living in what was once the nursery wing. Mrs Reeves, who owns the house, is very old. Last week we happened to meet on the front door step and she said, 'Now my dear, you must tell Elsie not to use the loud sweeper (the hoover) in the mornings if your husband is trying to sleep after his expeditions,' (expeditions sounds more like a holiday outing) but it was nice of her to think of it. Elsie is Mrs Reeves's cook and my saviour.

Alan leaves for the aerodrome. He will be back for lunch and then I shall know whether or not they will be going tonight. I go and see what is on my larder shelf. Cabbage, parsnips and about half a pound of mince and of course potatoes — one thing we are never short of. I feel a total lack of inspiration but Elsie comes to my rescue and says she will show me how to make shepherd's pie.

Where the villagers are concerned, the RAF can do no wrong — especially the air crews. They spoil them — us — because it must include their wives — in every possible way — from farm eggs to an extra gallon of petrol from the garage. When, well after closing time, the pub is still packed with noisy airmen, their wives and girlfriends, the police just look the other way.

Three Polish squadrons are based on one of the nearby airfields. Despite the language difficulty we have got to know a few quite well. They have beautiful manners. One evening when we were asked to drinks in their mess, a young Polish flying officer introduced himself to me. He bowed very low, clicked his heels together and said, 'My name is Buggar — in English, very funny.'

Until the Poles arrived I don't think any of us fully realised the true horror of the Nazi occupation. The Poles, having had first hand experience of quite ghastly atrocities, loathe and detest Germans. It seems that extreme hatred can override every other emotion so that they have no feelings of fear only an almost fanatical desire to bomb Germany again and again. Alan has heard that once over the target they can hardly contain themselves and are apt to drown conventional radio procedure in their descriptive abuse of all Germans.

As I pass the village green I see that about 20 small children are waiting there. They all have gas masks slung across their shoulders and they have labels with their names and ages on their backs — like so many parcels waiting to be posted or cattle waiting to be auctioned. They are evacuees from Manchester or Liverpool about to be delivered to their new homes. Some of them are clutching bedraggled soft toys, some are crying, and all look bewildered, as well they might.

The weather is improving by the minute.

When I get back with my shopping Elsie shows me how to make shepherd's pie. Alan gets back punctually at 1 p.m. He confirms that tonight is on. He won't know where the target will be until this afternoon. Alan eats a hurried lunch. He gives me a kiss says, 'See you . . . don't worry my love,' and is gone. I watch from the window as he gets into the car and drives off. Many moments are bad but this is always one of the worst. I look round and am appalled to see his lucky mascot on the floor. Ferdinand is a little wooden model of a bull. He has been over Germany 15 times — Alan has never flown without him. Perhaps it is absurd but I've got it into my head that it is desperately important that Ferdinand goes with him. I tear down the drive, hoping against hope that the car will have been held up at the main road, and it has. By great good luck I am in time to hand Ferdinand over.

That evening Phil and Gay come over as usual; both arrive from opposite directions at exactly 7.30 p.m. bringing an odd assortment of food with them and better still Gay has managed to get hold of a third of a bottle of sherry. Churchill is going to speak after the news. When he talks everyone — whatever they are doing — stops to listen. Although he gives no one the illusion that it will be easy, he manages to inspire absolute confidence

126

that, in the end, we will win the war. At the moment it is difficult to imagine how, or when.

At 10.45 p.m. we hear the first aircraft take off and they depart at about three minute intervals. We count 16 in all, that's the whole of one squadron. We still hope that the target will be in France. If it is, we can expect them back in two and a half hour's time. If not it won't be before 3.30 a.m. or even 4 a.m.

Phil is knitting, she often is, but I notice that she knits with tremendous intensity and almost ferocious speed when she is waiting to hear news of Johnnie. Gay and I attempt to do the crossword. Gay says that two pilots' wives in the other squadron have decided to join the Wrens as they can't bear this waiting around any longer. We can well understand how they feel but agree that we want to spend every moment we can with our husbands. From 1 a.m. we strain our ears for the sound of returning aircraft hoping against hope to hear them, but nothing — only two aeroplanes which screech overhead at terrific speed, probably night fighters on the look out for enemy bombers.

We now know that our husbands must have been sent to Germany, so we can't expect them back for a long time. We make sandwiches. At 3.50 a.m. Gay says that she is sure that she can hear an aeroplane. First it's just a faint hum, but soon it's unmistakably coming closer and — yes — the first one is landing. Two arrive in fairly quick succession, a ten minute interval and then another. Then a horribly long gap — perhaps it wasn't really so very long but it seems ages. By 4.30 a.m. 12 have landed, at least we are not too sure if it was 12 or 11. It could be that one had to circle the airfield twice. But at best, four have not returned. There is always a chance that they have landed somewhere else. We keep repeating this, as if saying so will make it more certain.

As soon as they have landed, they will be debriefed so it will be yet another half hour before they can ring home. Phil and Gay have plenty of time to get home before their call comes through. I see them off on the front door step. It is a pitch dark night. A searchlight slowly traces a great arc across the sky methodically moving back and forth and back again as it searches the sky for any sign of enemy aircraft.

I decide to undress and go to bed. I leave the bedroom door wide open so that I can't possibly miss hearing the telephone. We all know that when someone's husband has not returned they always send somebody round to break the news. They would never do this by telephone. So please God let it be the telephone and not the door bell that I hear.

I turn both bars of the electric fire on to get the room warm. Suddenly the telephone rings. I have been on tenterhooks waiting for it and yet the sound makes me jump. At once I feel as if the most enormous weight has been lifted. I thank God he has landed safely and I rush to answer it. Alan says, 'I'll see you in 20 minutes,' but then, 'I am afraid there is bad news — Johnnie is missing.' I am bereft of words, I know that Phil will be totally devastated. I am too shocked, too upset to speak. Alan thinks we have been cut off, 'Are you still there?' he asks. I ask him if there is any hope that he could have crash-landed or parachuted out. Alan says, 'Not much chance,' (I can tell that he thinks there is none at all). 'I know that it is a wretched thing to have to do, but the CO thinks you would be the best person to break the news to Phil.'

At first I say, 'I can't do it,' then, 'Do I have to?' Alan thinks I should. 'You are her closest friend,' he says. 'Would you like to wait till I get back so that I can drive you over?'

It's too much to expect of him. I can tell by the sound of his voice that he is dead beat. 'It's okay,' I say, 'You needn't drive me. I'll get dressed and go now.'

When I get to Phil's house, I just stand in the road looking up at her window. She may be in bed but she won't be asleep, she'll be waiting for that telephone call. I cannot bring myself to knock on the door. I have no idea of the time but there is a thin gold line along the horizon so I suppose the sun is about to rise but still I cannot summon up the courage to ring the door bell.

Then I see the corner of her window blind move just the smallest fraction — an almost furtive movement. Then she is there at the front door in her dressing gown. I don't have to say anything, as soon as she sees me standing there she knows why I have come.

Later in the morning someone will return Johnnie's car to her. As soon as she has packed she is going to drive to York where Johnnie's mother lives. There will be no operations until tomorrow or the day after. As usual we will all meet in the pub tonight — and probably drink rather too much. I am sure that some of the regulars from the village will notice that Johnnie isn't there, they always insist that he plays the piano. But none of us will mention his name nor the names of the others. Perhaps that seems unfeeling. It isn't that, it's just that it happens too often. Talking about it doesn't help anyone. It is best to try to live for the moment and remember that one day this war has got to end.

Gay's husband was killed three weeks later on a comparatively easy raid. Jessica Frank's husband survived and his account of a bombing mission is told on page 263 in March 1943. The Franks had four children after the war and have several grandchildren. Jessica Frank lives in Devizes, Wiltshire.

MARCH 1941

More British troops arrive in Greece and on 28th March the British engage the Italians at the Battle of Cape Matapan, off the coast of Greece, in which the Italians lose five out of their eight cruisers. Meanwhile in North Africa Rommel has succeeded in reversing the Italian defeats and marches eastwards through Cyrenaica driving the British in front of him.

AN INCIDENT IN THE DESERT
Henry J West

Henry John West was born in 1916. He joined the Royal Sussex Regiment in Brighton in 1935. He was posted to the 1st Battalion, Royal Sussex which in 1936 was shipped to Palestine. In 1939 he was stationed in Suez protecting the Shell Company Refinery. Here he met and married a Greek girl and their first child was born in Cairo in November 1940. By March 1941

132

West's Battalion had moved to the Western Desert and joined the 4th Indian Division, 8th Army.

Somewhere between Sollum and Bardia, the truck that I was driving broke down and, as I was the last truck in the convoy, I was soon left behind in the middle of nowhere. I worked on the truck and got it going (the fault was sand in the petrol filter). I hadn't gone very far when I saw an enemy plane coming my way. I didn't take much notice because I had never known them to bomb or machine-gun a single truck on it's own before. Then I noticed that it had circled around me and was coming in an attacking line in front of me.

I started to scramble out of the passenger side when the gear lever got stuck partly up my trouser leg. I had to tear the trouser leg to get free, by then the plane was machine-gunning. I only just managed to throw myself out of the truck, when the petrol tank was hit and my truck exploded. The blast threw me away from it and I landed a few yards away in a sort of hole in the sand, where I skidded face down and just lay there. After a little while I felt myself all over and, as I felt wet and sticky, I thought that I had been hit. I started to move my limbs to see where, and as

I found that I had everything there, I got up and realised that the hole that I had slid into had been used as a loo and I stunk.

Sometime later, when the convoy had stopped, the men realised that I was missing and as I was driving the Officer's Mess truck they sent someone back to look for me. They found me luckily enough by sighting the burning truck. I couldn't understand why they wouldn't let me sit in the front with them, they made me sit in the back so that the wind blew the smell away from them. It took me a long time to live that down.

West was eventually captured in North Africa and sent to a prison camp. The story of his escape appears on page 424.

APRIL 1941

The Germans invade Greece and the British start the evacuation of their troops, withdrawing them to North Africa. In North Africa, Rommel continues his march eastwards and the siege of Tobruk begins — it is the only British garrison left in Cyrenaica and they are determined to hold it.

THE TORPEDOING
OF HMS CAPETOWN
Albert Welch

Albert Welch was born in 1920 in London. He left Dagenham Park School at the age of 14, and worked as a trainee carpenter on local building sites. At the outbreak of war in 1939, he was among the first to volunteer for active service and was selected for the Royal Navy. He was initially sent for basic training at HMS Royal Arthur in Skegness and this was followed by a further period of training at Chatham Barracks where he subsequently became an accomplished cook. *By August of 1940 at the young age of 19, he found himself leaving Liverpool on the converted P&O cruise liner RMS Strathmore. The ship was taking British wives and children to the then comparative safety of the Far East. Although he had crew duties to perform, he was still able to enjoy the novelty of this new experience and the bewildering luxury of an ocean cruise. Leaving the ship at Colombo, Albert then served on a series of ships in the Indian Ocean including HMS Widnes, HMS Centurion and HMS Capetown.*

During the early spring of 1941 *Capetown* was primarily involved in patrolling to the north of Berbera, off the port of Massawa, to ensure that there was no interference from the Italian Red Sea fleet which was based there. There was no evidence of these warships looking for action but over the next few weeks a small number of blockade runners were intercepted. With the continuing land successes, however, it was very apparent that the port of Massawa was likely to fall and consequently there was much concern over what the fleet might do as a last resort. These fears were confirmed when, at the beginning of April, the six remaining destroyers slipped out of Massawa and went north to raid Port Sudan. They were soon spotted, however, and intercepted by a series of air attacks from *Swordfish* of *HMS Eagle*, resulting in four being sunk and two being run aground and scuttled.

With the very high temperatures experienced during the day, many of the crew took to sleeping on deck at night to benefit from the cool breeze. I came off watch at 6.30 p.m. on 7th April and went up on deck for a few hours to chat with a couple of shipmates, including my best mate, Bill Boardman. As this day was in fact the first anniversary of my joining the Navy, much of the conversation was about how much we had seen over the past year and how much our lives had been changed by these events. We then had a light meal and, feeling tired from an early start that morning, we decided to turn in. It was a beautiful moonlit night and Bill and I set up our wire and canvas camp beds on the upper deck. We were on the port side, roughly amidships, with Bill on the inboard side. The cool breeze was a blessing and as we settled down I noticed that we were just off the coast and making about 10 knots. I quickly went off to sleep totally unaware that events were going to change our lives yet again.

What we had not realised was that an Italian Motor Torpedo Boat (MTB) from Massawa had been quietly stalking us in the darkness and had been slowly manoeuvring into a position slightly ahead of us where she had a perfect view of the *Capetown* silhouetted against the moonlight. At 2.30 a.m. the Captain of the MTB fired two torpedoes and promptly turned, accelerating away at high speed. The attack was totally unexpected as *Capetown*, being an old ship, did not have the benefit of the more modern radar and Asdic technologies and was therefore totally dependent on the lookouts. Thankfully the first torpedo narrowly missed us, passing safely across the bow but before we could take evasive action, the second torpedo struck us amidships, adjacent to B boiler room on the starboard side. The explosion was deafening and the blast lifted the ship, causing it to heel over to port. We

138

were lucky that the Italian commander had not fired his spread of torpedoes a few seconds later as two hits would have finished us.

Having been asleep when the torpedo struck, the blast immediately woke me to find myself being propelled through the port rail and over the side into the sea. The sudden shock of immersion in water quickly brought home the realisation that we had been hit but, as I struggled to the surface for air, my immediate concern was of being left behind in the dark. Fortunately for me, the ship had quickly lost power and Bill, realising what had happened, had already grabbed a rope and was running back along the port side to where he could hear me shouting as I swam towards the dark outline of the ship. It was a great relief when I finally felt that rope in my hands and, with me climbing and Bill pulling, we were finally able to link arms and he hauled me back on board. I lay on the deck to get my breath back, still somewhat bewildered at the sudden chain of events.

A number of my shipmates were not so lucky. One of the marines who was also sleeping on deck had been thrown into the air by the blast and had come down on his chest across a bollard causing massive internal injuries. The pain was so bad he kept asking

139

to be thrown over the side to finish it. He clung to life for several hours but there was nothing that could be done and sadly he finally slipped away.

Inside the ship the torpedo had claimed more lives. The Petty Officer of the watch in the boiler room had just completed his check that everything was running normally and told the rest of the watch that he would go up topside and make the drinks. At the top of the ladder he stepped through the watertight door, closed it behind him and, just as he opened the hatch, the torpedo exploded. The compartment that he had left seconds earlier was devastated by the blast and his watch were all killed, either in the explosion or drowned by the inrush of water.

By the time I was hauled back on board, the injured were being taken care of and damage control parties were already checking out the ship and reporting our condition, although we all knew that we were in bad shape. There was no panic during the incident, and the discipline and organisation was first class, but there was still an air of disbelief that this could have happened to us. After about an hour of lying dead in the water, the Captain came on the speaker system and advised that we had no power but that the Australian sloop HMAS Parramatta was going to put a line on board and tow us to Port Sudan and we were to be escorted by a K class destroyer, *HMS Kimberley*, to provide protection.

As the condition of the ship was critical and the risk of further attacks was very real, the tow was to take the shortest and quickest route possible, which meant passing through shallow water between the coast and a series of offshore islands near Massawa. If the enemy spotted us and opened up with shore batteries or sent out their fleet, the Captain was going to return fire although in our weakened state with a hole dangerously near the keel, the shock of our own guns could possibly have broken the ship's back.

Within a few hours we secured the line from the *Parramatta* and she started to tow us northwards with *HMS Kimberley* providing the escort, criss-crossing our path as we went.

It was a relief to be moving again, even if we could only manage about eight knots. Even so, all three ships were vulnerable to further attacks and we fully realised the risks that our rescuers were taking on our behalf. We succeeded in slipping past the shore guns at Massawa during the hours of darkness and were well north by day-break. During the voyage a large section of the ship was sealed off as its structural integrity was unsure. Consequently I was unable to reach my locker or any of my personal kit but most of us preferred to stay on deck just in case the ship broke in half and went down quickly.

We then heard more news of our attacker. After the MTB had fired its torpedoes and taken off into the darkness, several of our accompanying destroyers had given chase and had captured it. It subsequently transpired that, unknown to us, the Italian forces at Massawa were to surrender later that day and, in anticipation of this, the MTB had left the port for one last mission, it now being the last Italian MTB operating in the Red Sea. As it was now low on ammunition and fuel, and did not have a base to return to, the Captain surrendered without a fight. He was pleased with his success and claimed that he had sunk a destroyer. To prove him wrong, our Captain had him brought on board the *Capetown* to show him that we were in fact a light cruiser and still very much afloat!

Welch finished the last four years of the war on HMS Mauritius where, after escaping from Singapore before the Japanese invasion, he subsequently served in the Sicily, Salerno and Anzio campaigns in the Mediterranean, followed by the D-Day landings during the

142

Normandy invasion. After the war he married Esther and worked for the Ford Motor Company in Dagenham until retiring in the early Eighties. His son, Ken, has helped him commit his memories to paper and Albert Welch now lives with his family in Hainault, Essex.

MAY 1941

The Germans invade Crete in the largest parachute and glider landing that has ever been undertaken. After 11 days of battle the Germans gain control of the island and on 29th May the Allies begin evacuating their troops.

HMS DORSETSHIRE
AND THE BISMARCK
Walter Fudge

Walter Fudge was born in 1920. In the Thirties he was working as an office boy in Ravensthorpe but joined the Navy when war broke out and served on HMS Dorsetshire.

Going north west of Gibraltar, in the last week of May 1941 *HMS Dorsetshire* was escorting a large convoy when news was suddenly passed around that *HMS Hood* was sunk and we assumed the *Bismarck* was responsible. Our skipper, Captain Pincher Martin ordered full speed ahead and announced to the crew that we were going to intercept *Bismarck* and if necessary go in and ram her!! Those of us who had come off watch found an increased speed as we left the HMACA Bulolo in charge of the brood of chickens. At approximately 9 a.m. on 26th May we joined the units of the home fleet and found, as one writer eloquently described it, the *Bismarck* had been delivered into our hands. This reference was to the aerial tinfish (torpedo) dropped by a plane from the carrier *Ark Royal* which had damaged *Bismarck's* steering, making her move in large circles unable to steer a course for Brest. Although surrounded by units of the home fleet, *Bismarck* continued to fire and scored a hit on *HMS Rodney*. The battleships were finding their target and *Dorsetshire* contributed by making several accurate hits. Our B turret accounted for 81 salvos whilst our X turret jumped off its bearings! *Dorsetshire* had moved in close and due to *Bismarck* listing she could not depress her guns low enough to record any hits on *Dorsetshire*. My friend in the crowsnest ducked each time the shells went over as though the plywood box would have offered any protection! This friend, by coincidence, survived the sinking of *Dorsetshire* with me

145

one year later. The Admiral of the home fleet instructed *Dorsetshire* to sink *Bismarck* with torpedoes and pick up survivors. We were the only ship with tinfish left, so we fired two into *Bismarck's* port side and the third into her starboard by going around 180 degrees. There was no way *Bismarck* could have scuttled. She was a flaming wreck and those who could, jumped into the Bay of Biscay and swam toward *Dorsetshire* and the destroyer *Maori* in that very cold water. The *Maori* rescued about 25, whilst we on *Dorsetshire* pulled about 87 out of the water. There were hundreds maybe a thousand we had to leave because lookouts sighted a U-boat whilst *Dorsetshire* was a sitting duck.

My activities during the *Bismarck* action could be described, simply, by saying that it was hard work keeping those eight inch guns roaring. At one time our turret was firing twin eight inch projectiles every eight seconds with no misfires. Our spotters recorded many important hits. My own personal feelings were many and varied. The biggest thought was to do it to them or they will do it to us. Like others I was somewhat on edge waiting for the 'wipe out' which never came. I never saw the *Bismarck*, as the sinking was over when I eventually set foot on deck.

Subsequently, when we got permission from the Captain to bring in survivors and leave our stations, we found our ship was rolling so badly it was difficult to keep one's footing on the deck, which was often awash.

County class cruisers were known to be very stable in heavy seas unless stationary, at which time rolling is very noticeable and such was the case that day in the Bay of Biscay. More *Bismarck* survivors would have been rescued otherwise. Ropes, with lasso looped bowlines at the end were thrown over for *Bismarck* survivors to slide into and this helped to haul the dejected men aboard. On the way to Newcastle one of the *Bismarck's* crew died and he was given the appropriate burial-at-sea service. One *Dorsetshire* crew member, a fine, large, well-muscled South African Afrikaner was put in charge of the *Bismarck* prisoners. They sang Deutschland Uber Alles until they were silenced by the South African who yelled for them to shut up or he would fill them all with lead. He was armed with revolver and ammo!

On arrival at Newcastle the prisoners were handed over to army officials. One prisoner gestured to me by assuming a boxing position and pointing out that Churchill and Hitler

147

felt that way about each other whilst British and German sailors had friendship for each other and he shook his own hands to illustrate his meaning.

Walter Fudge tells the story of the sinking of Dorsetshire in April 1942 on page 210.

JUNE 1941

On 22nd June the Germans launch their long planned invasion of the Soviet Union — over 3,000,000 German soldiers march eastwards to confront 2,000,000 Russians and a further 2,000,000 who are protecting Moscow and Leningrad. Finland and Hungary also declare war on the Soviet Union but Romania still hesitates. As the Germans advance the SS Special Task Forces murder thousands of Russian Jews. On the 1st of June the British complete their evacuation of Crete. However 4,000 troops are left behind and taken prisoner by the Germans.

CAPTURED ON CRETE
Tom Barker

Tom Barker was born in 1921 in Scotland and worked for the Norwest Construction Company in Liverpool before joining the Argyll and Sutherland Highlanders. Having

149

trained at *Stirling Castle* he was based in Palestine when war broke out. He fought in the desert as part of the 4th Indian Division, and having taken *Sidi Barrani*, his battalion was sent on to *Sollum* to guard thousands of Italian POWs. The battalion were subsequently sent to *Alexandria* to board the destroyer *HMS Glenroy* bound for Crete as more troops were needed in May 1941 to defend the island against German paratroopers. The battalion landed in TLCs(Tank Landing Craft) unopposed at *Timbakion*. After a while the Argylls were sleeping rough on Crete as they began patrols towards *Heraklion*. Barker was used as a sniper, free to range at will and watch out for German motorcycle troops. Hit by a German sniper and knocked unconscious, he missed evacuation with the rest of his battalion.

It began about the 1st June, a group of mixed remnants of regiments, about 200 were on the beach. Also, amongst the rocks were a lot of wounded. I can vaguely remember two Australians taking me to the beach; my head was bloody so they washed me off in the sea. Somebody had heard from a mate who had been told by a signaller that a submarine was going to take us off Crete. Because Stukas would come over without warning, the wounded were hidden among the rocks and caves. Anyone who could move under his own steam had to forage for food, water was no problem and I was surprised one day when I saw a bloke going into the sea with water bottles tied round his middle. I found out later there was a fresh water spring about 100 yards out; one could clearly see a patch gurgling up in the salt water.

We slept on the beach every night, the reason for this was the sub. If it did come it would not surface in daylight because of the Stuka threat. So we had a lookout system organised, also we would sleep within easy reach of the next man, so if the sub signalled at night the whole mob could be awakened in total silence and be ready to be taken off in small boats. Sound at night carries a long way, and we were not going to give a roaming sniper a chance to pick us off one by one.

We had a lookout posted on top of a hill and he would signal with his shirt because, although he could whistle pretty well, if the wind was blowing the wrong way we wouldn't hear him. He would let us know if any Stukas or anyone hostile approached. He was also a target for a Jerry sniper. When I pointed this out somebody quietly said, 'Better one than all of us, he knows that.'

On the third morning somebody pointed

down the beach to two figures approaching in the distance. I had a long barrelled Canadian Ross with a telescopic sight and confirmed they were Germans, one officer and an orderly. Somebody yelled, 'Don't shoot, they are carrying a white flag.' When they reached us the officer saluted and said, using his orderly as interpreter, 'I salute you all not because of military protocol but you are obviously front line troops and you have put up a hell of a fight. You are to be admired among fighters, with German officers you could rule the world. I will return tomorrow at dawn with a company of men and you will be treated as honourable prisoners of war,' and he added, 'Crete is now ours.'

Next morning the Germans arrived. Most of us had already thrown our guns into the sea, so when they collected us we had only identity tags and the rags we were wearing. They marched us off the beach and we arrived at Heraklion, a small town on the coast where an officer looked us over. I was picked out along with about nine others who all had a bandage on and we were escorted to a hospital. A bloke in a white outfit took off the bit of shirt that had been wrapped round my head for three or four days, and with a lot of tutting and a smile he dabbed some stuff on and said I was very fortunate because now for me the war was over. Then we were marched to La Canea [Chania]. This was a forced march of about 140 miles. During the march we were rested ten minutes in the hour. Being an infantryman and having marched in Palestine on different skirmishes against Syrian bandits and the Palestine Liberation Organisation since early 1939, it did not affect me as it did some others like clerics, signallers and tank men. But on a low food diet it makes a big difference, and lack of water didn't help. Jerry was also smart because at certain places along the route he had placed a new set of guards so that every day we had different guards.

The German paratroopers whom we had been fighting were the English public school sort, well-educated and with good manners. But the guards were different and brutality took over from orders. There was the rifle butt in the back, a savage kick or a fist in the face, and while some who fell by the wayside would be picked up in a truck, some were not seen again. Some blokes took off their boots because of sores and could not get them back on. Sometimes if a bloke straggled behind the main group he would be kicked to keep up. But this only served to add to his misery and if there was no truck handy and he got too far behind, one of the guards would turn round and shoot him. We were too tired to care any more and the thought crossed my mind, 'Well it's quick.'

When we arrived at La Canea we were locked up. I was with about 20 others and looking through the window, I could see the sea. One thing that stood out during that long week's march was that no matter where you were the smell of death was everywhere. Somebody got bitten by a snake during one rest period and he died.

We were put on Greek boats under heavy guard and I discussed with another bloke the possibility of leaving the boat before it got to Greece. The conversation suddenly changed to sharks and possible damage from a propellor and the chance of being shot in the water. I lost interest and consoled myself with the fact, 'There is always tomorrow,' and a tour of Germany would not come amiss.

We arrived in Greece and were taken straight to Salonika POW camp. The vermin in this camp had to be seen to be believed. The guards all had the same cap badge, skull and cross bones. They were the SS POW guards. These animals were recruited from doss houses, brothels and black marketeers. Then there were the permanent residents — rats, bed bugs, lice, and a lot you could not see in the dark. I sometimes think about that officer on the beach, 'I give you my word as a German officer.' That promise ended when we stepped into Salonika Camp.

Barker's account of what happened to a German guard when his POW camp was liberated can be found on page 442 in April 1945.

155

JULY 1941

The Germans advance across Russia. Meanwhile the British intensify their bombing raids over Germany.

TOBRUK
Alec Barthorpe

Barthorpe's accounts appear in September 1939 on page 4, January 1941 on page 116 and July 1941 on page 156. Having arrived in North Africa he had fought at Massawa; he then suffered a bout of yellow jaundice and was treated at the base hospital in Asmara. In June 1941 he was back with 144th Field Regiment and we take up his story as they move back to Egypt.

We duly arrived in Alexandria and pulled up at the docks at about 5 p.m. Alongside was an Australian destroyer, *HMAS Nizam* which we boarded. It was July so the weather was hot and the nights were balmy. We sailed before dark and were told by the Australian crew that we were headed for Tobruk to relieve the Australians who had been there since the siege began in April, and were now being removed for rest and recuperation at the special request of the Australian Government. We would be taking over their guns and equipment. The idea was to arrive in Tobruk at about midnight, so that most of the run would be made in the dark of night, as we were within range of Axis bombers for most of the way and Axis submarines were present in the Mediterranean. As the harbour was the Axis bombers' favourite target we were asked to be quick off so the ship did not waste time before commencing her homeward journey with her load of Australian troops. The journey itself was nice, quiet and free of bombs or torpedoes, and we were landed on a wreck to await the lighter which arrived after daylight and took us to the harbour from where we were taken by truck to the Australian gun position we were to take over. The Australians themselves were as good a bunch of guys as you could wish for; they were friendly and cooperative and full of stories of Tobruk from April to date. They were all Melbourne men and although we remained together for only a week or so waiting for the next convoy to arrive we were very sorry to see them go.

Tobruk itself was open and very sandy. The focal point was the harbour and everything revolved around it, including the bombs. There seemed to be no shortage of drinking water but this had all come from the sea water which had filtered through the sand into pockets similar to artesian wells, so tasted slightly salty, which affected all hot drinks like tea and coffee. It was an acquired taste which you would spit out when you had the first sip, but after a time you got used to it and eventually, like me, you might even get to like it. The harbour itself was fairly large and shaped rather like an egg, with the north and south sides being protected by high cliffs, the east side was the narrow entrance and the west side being the way out towards Derna and beyond. On the northern side between the cliffs and the harbour lay the town itself stretching westwards alongside the water to the end where the intersection of the road from Derna met the road from Bardia, to the east of Tobruk. Inside the harbour were more than 50 wrecks resting on the bottom. Most had their superstructures above the waterline, they were dwarfed by the wreck of the Italian battleship *San Georgio* which had been bombed and sunk at her anchorage just inside the harbour entrance. I never did find out how it was sunk as the Army claimed their artillery had shelled it and the Air Force stated it was their bombing, anyway the mighty ship was sunk when Tobruk was taken by the Australians in General Wavell's advance in 1940/41, so either story could be right!

The guns we had taken over from the Australians were old 18 pounders made in about 1912–1916, similar to the ones being fired in Sudan when we had first gone into action at Gallabat, and were badly worn out, however they were still usable so we fired them although never at maximum range. The Aussies had left us with very nice dug-in gun positions and sangars to live in which were all about five foot deep by about four foot wide with, of course, a raised portion left as a bed.

For a period I was detached from the guns and posted to the specialist section as their driver/relief number, and my job, which I enjoyed doing, was keeping communications between our Observation Post Officer with the Infantry Unit we were supporting, and our own troop gun position. The OP Officer and his assistant were changed every three days or so and I was to organise all supplies and changes by driving the relief up to the post and the relieved members back to the gun position. The time of the change was dependant on the ground situation at the time, as the guns could be called into action any minute, day or night, and the truck had to be parked at the OP position at all times; so I virtually lived there with the infantry. During my slack periods I used to help the OP assistant as I had been through the course and just needed some practical experience, and instruction. Meanwhile the infantry had been changed and the Polish Brigade had taken over the position. I am sure the enemy found out about this, or maybe the Poles were more aggressive than the Aussies because the activity on this particular part of the front seemed to increase for a while. I was always up early. One morning I heard a plane above us and saw a Focke Wolfe which appeared to be on a recce mission. I watched it swoop down very low and deliberately fly at only a few feet right along the infantry position. The Poles by this time were stirring and started firing at the aircraft with rifles and other firearms but they had been taken by surprise and their aim was bad. The machine passed about 200 yards away from me over the infantry, and I clearly saw the pilot having a good look at the layout of our position, so I gave him the usual army greeting. It was not long after this when our position got 'stonked' hard by the enemy, and I was very pleased to have such a secure sangar. I think the shelling was in retaliation by the pilot for my giving him the good old 'two's up' salute as he flew past that morning! It was shortly after this when the Poles were reinforced by the arrival of their artillery men who took over our position and guns, so we were moved to a new position nearer the centre of the line.

Barthorpe was wounded in the middle of 1942 in a freak accident with a leaky can of petrol which caught fire and burned his legs and hands. He was hospitalised for four weeks. In March 1943 he was commissioned, becoming a 2nd lieutenant in the 149th Anti-Tank Regiment. He joined the Free French Brigade and served with them in the final push for Cape Bon before returning to Algiers for a new posting. We catch up again with Barthorpe in April 1944 at Monte Cassino on page 341.

AUGUST 1941

The Germans advance to within 25 miles of Leningrad and Moscow is under continuous German air attack. Roosevelt and Churchill sign the Atlantic Charter which demands that neither Britain nor the USA seek territorial gains from the war.

RECOVERING BODIES AFTER THE TORPEDOING OF HMS PHOEBE
Silvester Macdonald

Silvester Macdonald's account of Clearing up after Dunkirk can be read in June 1940 on page 73. After serving with the Naval Brigade, Macdonald was assigned to HMS Phoebe in late summer 1940 as a member of the medical staff. During late 1940 and into the spring of 1941 HMS Phoebe joined the home fleet based at Scapa Flow and performed various duties in the North Atlantic. In the early summer of 1941 HMS Phoebe had sailed around Africa to reach the

Eastern Mediterranean and was involved in evacuating troops from Greece and then from Crete.

While the war was not going too well for the Royal Navy, it was going even worse for the British Army in the Libyan desert. All the gains that the army had made across Libya, had been reversed by Rommel's drive towards the Egyptian border. The only bright spot in the military picture, was that during the British retreat, they had left a garrison in the port city of Tobruk. This eventually proved to be a brilliant stroke of military ingenuity, for, without this thorn in his side, Rommel and his Africa Korps would probably have been in Egypt itself. To enable the garrison in Tobruk to survive the constant barrage and assaults by the German Army, there was a continual need for supplies and ammunitions, and the only way that these could be replenished, was by ships coming from the eastern end of the Mediterranean. Since these ships were subjected to everything that the enemy could throw at them, only extremely fast ships were selected. Another requirement was they had to have a good escorting force, and even then the most dangerous part of the trip was conducted under cover of darkness. I believe that the ships carrying the supplies were mostly very modern mine-layers, which had the speed capability that was required. While the supply ships were inside the harbour being unloaded, the *Phoebe* and other escorting vessels patrolled the sea outside, until the convoy could be re-assembled for the wild dash back to Alexandria. We had made several runs of this type to Tobruk, when our luck ran out and we were hit as we patrolled outside the harbour.

Again, it was either a guardian angel, or the fickle finger of fate, that put me some place other than where I should have been. When the ship was at battle stations, my duty area had always been in the sick-bay, in the forward part of the *Phoebe*. The other medic always manned the auxiliary first aid station in the after part of the ship. There was usually a double set-up for most operations, so if one place suffered damage, coverage could be given from the alternate site. The only time this was changed, was when my opposite number was sick, and was confined to the sick-bay. That was the one occasion when I was assigned to cover his station, so he could remain in bed, but that was also the one occasion when the ship was hit.

We had escorted the supply ships to Tobruk harbour, and were doing our patrol routine outside at the time. Since I was deep down in the ship below the water-line, and all water-tight doors between our group and the open deck above were tightly sealed, we knew little of what was going on. We heard the guns firing, and felt the ship taking the usual evasive actions, but it seemed just a normal type routine. That is, until we heard a loud explosion, and could feel the ship give a tremendous shudder. At the same time, the ship went way down on one side and only partially righted herself. We were all thrown into a heap on the starboard side, and because all the lights had gone out, it took some time to untangle ourselves.

In a reasonably short time, the auxiliary lights came on, but we had to remain at our stations until we had orders to do otherwise. We heard through the loud-speaker system, the various orders being given for the lifeboat crews to assemble on the upper deck, which gave us the impression that some personnel were getting off. We later found that boats, torpedoes, and other gear on the starboard side were being jettisoned to lighten the ship on that side so she would not list so much. Shortly after, I received orders to report to the sick-bay and leaving the after station went forward.

It seemed that the *Phoebe* had been

making a fast turn to avoid a torpedo that had been fired by an attacking airplane, when she was hit by another torpedo fired from a different quarter. The torpedo had hit the ship below the water-line, and had ruptured one of the fuel tanks; as well as an ammunition magazine compartment below one of the main armament gun turrets. These compartments had then filled with sea water, which was responsible for our heavy list to starboard. The hit on the ship was not too far from the sick-bay, and although there were no casualties in the sick-bay itself, the place was evacuated. Personnel entered the place at their peril, owing to the fumes from various chemicals that had been released from the shattered containers. Some medical supplies were obtained later by personnel equipped with gas masks, but these were not always in a usable condition. My opposite number, the other medic, who had been minding his own business in his sick condition, had gone through a very traumatic time. Even though he had personally felt so lousy, he had been putting splints on broken limbs, trying to stop severe bleeding, and generally doing his best for those who had been injured. By the time I arrived to assist, he and the doctor, and the others who were available, had pretty well accomplished all that had to be done on an immediate basis. It was more a matter of cleaning up, making those who had been hurt as comfortable as possible, and trying to get the sick-bay back into a usable condition. The ship then spent many hours limping back to Alexandria at a reduced speed, but fortunately we did not experience any further attacks in our weakened condition. At Alexandria, we were immediately placed in a floating dry dock, so the water could be pumped out and the ship made seaworthy. There were to be no repairs made to any inside parts of the ship. The plan was simply to cover the damaged hull with steel plates so we could steam under our own power to a place where complete repairs could be made. However, the first order of business once the pumping had been completed, was to remove the bodies of those unfortunate crew members who had been in the ammunition magazine when the ship was hit. For some inexplicable reason, although the pumping had ceased, there were two or three feet of a mixture of diesel oil fuel and sea water left in the bottom of the magazine. It was still there when I was ordered down to assist the doctor in the recovery.

A naked electric light had been hung from the upper deck, and was suspended into the bottom chamber some three decks lower. A line on a block had also been made available so the bodies could be hoisted up to the deck above. Both the doctor and I wore shorts when we descended, for we knew that slopping around in a black mixture of diesel oil and sea water would ruin any clothing we wore. When we reached the bottom compartment, we had to go down the last remaining rungs of the ladder, and get used to the slime that was almost to our waist. To say that the scene that met our eyes was awful, would be a gross understatement. This, too, was after our eyes had adjusted somewhat to the darkened conditions down there. There was the constant sound of the drip of oil and water. There were shells and cordite charges hanging perilously out of their storage slots, and the wreckage was strewn on the deck below our feet beneath the oil. We had to shuffle along each aisle, feeling with our legs and feet, until we encountered something that could only be a body. Then we had to take a deep breath, so we could reach beneath the oil, so that he could be lifted and carried back to the point where he could be hoisted above.

In a very short time, we were both covered from head to toe in a black, pungent, oily mess, and in that state, and in that gloom, we even had difficulty in seeing each other. Most of the bodies were recovered fairly soon, but there were a couple that we had some problem finding, and a bigger problem recovering. I paused at that point to give the utmost credit to the doctor. I saw him venture into places, where I was extremely concerned for his safety. At one point in the search for the last remaining body, we knew that it could only be at the far end of one of the aisles. This aisle had shells hanging out on each side and were resting against each other in a mass that reached from the ceiling to a few inches above the oil. The only way to get past this obstruction was to hold your breath, duck your head under and go forward a distance before you came up again. I knew that this was extremely hazardous, for the whole mass could have come down on him, and could have crushed him, or pinned him under until he died, or maybe both of the above. Fortunately, he did make it and returned back to the obstacle with the last of the dead, and with him pushing from one side, and me pulling from the other, we finished the most unpleasant task.

Only then were we both able to climb out of that depressing place, and rejoin the living in the sunshine above. We both felt that the bodies were much more than just shapeless and inert masses that had to be removed. We did not have to be reminded that a few short hours before, they had been as much a part of the ship as we were ourselves. We thought of those who had died, and related that person to the many memories we had of them when they had been living. One was a fellow that had a terrific sense of humour, and used it to make the ship a far more pleasant place to be. Another was a fellow that was a part-time barber, and had given me a haircut just two days before he died. One was a fellow from New Zealand, accompanied on the ship by his brother, but the brother was uninjured and one could feel his grief for the rest of the time he was aboard. The bodies were cleaned to remove the diesel oil, dressed in clean clothing to restore some human dignity, and taken ashore. They were given a military funeral by the ship's company several days later, before internment in a cemetery in Alexandria.

In February 1942 Maconald joined the crew of HMS Delhi. After docking in Plymouth he had two weeks' leave. Having asked for a transfer several times, he couldn't face the future as a medic responsible for the dead and dying and went AWOL. Macdonald gave himself a new identity and joined a merchant marine cargo ship, the Dutch SS Bodergraven, on which he stayed until she was sunk by a German torpedo in July 1944. Picked up by *HMS Pict*, he then volunteered to man a cargo ship, *SS Charles H Cramp*, sailing to the US. It was while he was based in New York that he married an American girl. On attempting to join the US Navy, he was found to have illegally entered the country. Macdonald confessed to having unofficially discharged himself from the British Navy. He was imprisoned on Harts Island and at his Court Martial was given a 30 day suspended sentence and shipped straight back to England. Macdonald was at last able to transfer and joined the NAAFI as a Petty Officer Canteen Manager. His wife was allowed to come to England and lived with his parents in London until Macdonald was discharged at the end of the war. The Macdonalds now live in New Jersey, USA.

SEPTEMBER 1941

The Germans reach Leningrad and cut off all rail connections and therefore any hope of supplies reaching the city for the winter. Thus the siege of Leningrad begins.

LIFE IN LINCOLN
May Wedderburn Cannan

May Cannan told her story in January and August 1940 starting on pages 37 and 80 respectively. She moved house several times following her husband as he was posted between appointments. They now move to Lincoln and Percival Slater becomes a Brigadier.

PJ had been given a Brigade, the 50th Anti Aircraft Brigade, which had its Headquarters at Digby, a large RAF Station near Lincoln, a place and a part of the world unknown to me. My first sight of the town, with that magnificent cathedral on its hill was on a sunny, cold afternoon in September when I went to find somewhere to live and was cheered by a Company of young soldiers from the local training camp marching and singing 'It's my delight.' . . . I found a house in the cathedral yard which an old lady wished to let and in which I eventually had three rooms with use of bath and kitchen — the most horrible words in the English language. I settled in and looked for work. PJ seemed to have a very large number of troops — it was a double brigade with guns in Derby and Nottingham and ran as far north as the Humber — and, 'I might,' he said, 'come in useful, if I worked for the Citizens Advice Bureau' — so I found out about them — offered myself as a worker and started at a rather dismal office down in the lower town in rooms belonging to the Baptist Chapel. We were the creation, it seemed, of the National Council of Social Service and existed to give advice and help (but not money) on all and any problems brought to us. I remember saying earnestly to a grateful client in a later day when I was the assistant secretary that we reckoned we could always do something about everything, given a little time — and mostly we did.

We had a waiting room like the waiting room of a Doctor's Surgery which we frantically tried to keep warm with a very small allowance of coal; we had a large office with tables for interviews and filing cabinets for the regulations and the case sheets and a small secretary's office in which one could conduct the more private enquiries, generally about marriage, divorce and once, a suspected attempted murder.

About a dozen of us worked there — all unpaid volunteers working so many shifts a week although the assistant secretary worked all shifts and the secretary got a small honorarium.

I was also the representative on the local information committee set up by the Ministry of Information and chaired by the Archdeacon and ran what we called the Flying Squad — a team of four of us. We could be called out by any CAB within a wide radius for help in a raid or other emergency, so that we did indeed see life.

There was a shortage of iron, and following collections of saucepans and anything metal that it was thought the long suffering housewife could spare, we gave up our garden railings and louts with hacksaws appeared grinning with the joy of destruction and sawed them off leaving gaping teeth and open ends to gardens which made them unsafe for small children and dogs.

The food shortage got worse. Lord Woolton quietly performed miracles and won the trust and respect of everyone so that there were no food riots. However, he could not prevent the under-the-counter racket that the tradesmen worked for the benefit of customers. Babies, expectant mothers and the old were, very properly, given priority, but growing teenagers serving in the Officer Training Corps, the Fire Fighting and other services went short. One would give them one's sweet or butter ration till they realised what was happening and refused it. Then they would ask, 'Is there anything at all to eat in the larder?' which was heart breaking. Meanwhile the army complained that recruits were coming in underweight!

Into my office came wives of service men with their men in North Africa, Italy, Greece, Egypt, or lost in Crete; and of course men serving in remote parts of the British Isles all in trouble from one thing or another: the army allowance was not coming through, the husband was going with another woman; the wife was going with another man and the husband was due home on leave; the children were involved with the police; they had become homeless for one reason or another; they couldn't make ends meet on service pay and if they went to get supplementary allowance the neighbours, working down in the town, jeered that they were taking charity.

Then there was the Grimsby Raid to which the four of us, who were the flying squad, were called out in the cold drizzle of a first light. Mercifully transport was provided. I remember waving to a friend who was head of the Women's Voluntary Service (WVS) and was seeing off her food vans to the same place, and then all I remember is a table in the town hall where I worked non-stop till it was lunch time and the long queues faded out and Boy Scouts brought in trays of tea and sandwiches.

It was a rather special raid because, apart from the quite appalling destruction, the Germans, it seemed, were trying out a new bomb, the Butterfly, and we were all asked not to talk about it as it was hoped that if there was no outcry they might think the bomb a failure and not repeat it. It says much for everyone concerned that nothing did apparently get out. These bombs were timed, sinking a short distance through pavements and going off later with vibration as you walked over them; we were told to walk carefully — and we did.

I remember an endless queue of white faces as I dealt with their needs: house door blown up or jammed needing immediate

176

repair because of looting; loss of furniture; loss of everything including clothes (we sent them on, with a Scout to lead, to the WVS Clothes Store). One girl when I asked 'Clothes?' opened her mackintosh and showed me her nightie. We dealt with houses made uninhabitable; with changes of addresses; children evacuated to relations or friends; with possible compassionate leave for husbands in the Forces; with claims for compensation. Padres wandered around waiting to take charge of a case of shell shock, or someone needing hospital. Boy Scouts stood ready to act as guides and distributed food. There was a deluge of rain and it came through the roof — the town hall had been hit — and dripped down our necks, and we had to keep on shifting our papers to keep them dry.

When I got back in the late evening I went to collect a loaf and thought that they looked at me oddly. My voice had gone cracked and when I reached home I found I was deep in dust including my hair. PJ, when he found out where I had been was furious, but I said I had my job as he had his, so he kissed me instead . . .

May Cannan wrote her autobiography in two volumes, before she died in 1973. The first part — **Grey Ghosts and Voices** was published posthumously in 1976. The extracts in this book are from her second unpublished volume of memoirs. **The Tears of War**, published in 2000, tells the story of her relationship with Bevil Quiller-Couch.

OCTOBER 1941

On 19th October Stalin declares Moscow under siege. American sailors die in the first U-boat attack on a US battleship.

TRAINING
Charles Hanaway

Charles Hanaway was born in Paddington, London in 1923. He left school at 13 and was employed in a variety of jobs before the war including working for a local engineering company and for J Sainsbury the Grocer delivering orders. Hanaway enlisted in the 70th Middlesex Regiment in 1941. This was a young soldiers' Battalion which included a number of ex-borstal boys who had been given the option of joining the army. These soldiers were being trained in airfield defence against any possible German invasion.

Our next move was to Hounslow Heath where we spent another boring time 'Square-Bashing.' There were all sorts of comings and

179

goings, some of the lads were sent to the Middle East to join the Desert Army, others went to other regiments. The only good thing about this place was that it was near to my home, which I could reach by tube from East Hounslow station.

Mainly because of boredom I seemed to get involved in petty disputes with NCOs, I certainly disliked some of them, likewise I suppose they had a similar opinion of me. On one occasion, returning from a 24 hour pass, I was late. Put on a charge, I was sentenced to seven days 'Pack Drill' punishment which in effect meant that every evening at 6 p.m., I paraded on the Drill Square wearing full marching order kit. The kit weighed about 25lbs. The routine was to be marched up and down reversing every 25 yards to march back again, on the instructions of an NCO, who barked out orders to us. This went on for one hour non-stop. One particular evening I was marching with another poor soul who had been given the same punishment. It was a very warm evening and we were sweating profusely, we were instructed to don gas-masks, which we carried in a pack on our chests. This was a stupid order and cruel considering the circumstances. Both feeling all-in we continued to march up and down. Suddenly my companion collapsed to the ground, unconscious. The drilling stopped and my companion was carried to the sick-bay for treatment. Unfortunately, shortly afterwards he died; a post-mortem was held and the unfortunate victim was found to have had only one lung. The gas mask folly, had killed the man. After this tragedy all further punishment of this type was abolished. The NCO was in my opinion guilty of manslaughter. The punishment and the way it was carried out could have killed a healthy man with two lungs.

Hanaway survived fighting as an infantryman for the last nine months of war in Europe, having joined the 6th Royal Scots Fusiliers in May 1943. His battalion was disbanded shortly after the war. Hanaway is married and lives on the Sussex coast.

NOVEMBER 1941

Churchill orders a new military offensive in the Western Desert, Operation Crusader and the British 8th Army drive Rommel westwards and link up with British troops in Tobruk.

PRISONER OF WAR
Jack Durey

Jack Durey was born in 1920 and worked as a cabinet maker before the war. He joined up and was sent out to France as part of the 1st Guards Brigade of the 1st Division in September 1939. He was stationed near Templeuve through the winter of 1939/1940. In May 1940 he was captured and spent the rest of the war at Willenberg Stalag XXA.

We valued our weekends in the camp, for pleasure activities, washing clothes, cleaning the place and some elaborate attempts at cooking that usually failed. There were still a few lice about but they were losing the battle.

There was a steady arrival of nutritious items in the food parcels, changes of clothing and, of equal value, better news of the war. To top our improved circumstances and attitude, we received a complete new British battledress uniform. I already had new boots, which I took great care of by keeping them standing on two sticks when not being worn so the snow and wet could drain off completely. I had been issued with a light Polish cavalry overcoat during the first winter which, although long, had already seen better service and was thin, little protection against the severe winters. The Germans were quick to cash in on our good fortune and had us photographed as a group for 'sending home', but envelopes were never supplied. The photograph did appear in their newspapers to 'show how well we were being treated'. In the early days they had not cared at all and treated us like dirt, but the pendulum was swinging with a vengeance.

A guard saw me having a scratch one day and asked if I was lousy. I said I was and, reaching inside my blouse, asked if he would like one — he leapt back a foot but we believed they also were lousy. Their situation was little better than ours. Their uniforms were a joke with us because they were partly made of wood pulp and fibre, so that when they unfolded their overcoat after being compressed in their packs, it creaked and squeaked like an ill fitting door!

Life was certainly getting more difficult for the Germans in many ways. One Sunday we were all taken to a farm where vast quantities of cabbage had to be converted into sauerkraut. The cabbages were taken into a building where there was a very old fashioned machine like a mangle. Two of us turned a large wheel each side whilst the cabbages were thrown into a hopper to emerge shredded and fell into baskets which were transported into another room. Here the shreds were tipped into enormous barrels. Either side a prisoner stood on a box to gain height, armed with heavy poles to beat the shreds until the sap floated on top. Salt and herbs were sprinkled over the cabbage and the process continued until the barrels were full. Left to ourselves much of the time, I thought I would get a laugh by tapping my cigarette ash into the barrel. That started something. Another spat in it and we all followed suit, then one of the lads pissed in it. About three months later we heard, and saw in a newspaper that the Poles showed us, that a large consignment had been condemned.

The Red Cross parcels that had been kept there were transferred into the guards' quarters. A beady eye was kept on them so they were not tampered with. Soon after, there was a general rule from Stalag that all tins and packets should be opened and inspected. This meant that we could no longer keep our own weekly parcel and use it as we wished, sometimes sharing for better economics. The parcels stayed in the guards' quarters and at 6 p.m. each evening we had to queue up, select what we wanted from the parcel with our name on and then a guard would open the items. It was a bloody nuisance but some revenge was possible. After a while they got a bit lax, only opening one in three tins. It so happened that occasionally one would be 'blown' (gone bad), and this could be seen by looking at the end which would, in that case, be curved outwards. This one would be put forward for opening with the result that as soon as it was pierced, the contents would hiss out spraying all over the guard with a horrible stink!

Durey now lives in Tunbridge Wells, Kent.

DECEMBER 1941

On the 7th December the Japanese attack Pearl Harbour. Battleships are sunk and their airfields are also attacked. 2,403 Americans are killed. The United States immediately declares war on Japan and on 11th December Germany declares War on the US. Meanwhile off the coast of Malaya where Japanese troops had landed at Kota Bharu, Japanese aircraft sink two British battleships *HMS Prince of Wales* and *HMS Repulse* killing 840 men.

THE SINKINGS
Ralph Robson

Ralph Stobart Robson was born in 1917 in Northumberland. He worked as a Post Office Telegram boy until he was called up into the Royal Navy when war broke out and trained as a signalman. In October 1941 he sailed down the Clyde on the battleship Prince of Wales which was heading for Singapore to supplement the Far East fleet.

On Monday, 8th December *HMS Prince of Wales* and *HMS Repulse* sailed north up the east coast of Malaya hoping to intercept enemy transport ships. I had been transferred from the *Prince of Wales* to the *Repulse* to take the place of a leading signalman who had been involved in a dispute with a fellow rating.

The miscreant had been allocated a cooling off period on the *Prince of Wales* and I have often wondered whether he survived. Perhaps this incident inadvertently saved my life.

Next day we continued to head north. Since we had no fighter protection we were glad of the low cloud and mist which screened our progress. But at about 5 p.m. visibility improved and we were spotted by three enemy aircraft carrying out a reconnaissance. As soon as it was dark the battleships altered course and proceeded south to Kuantan where, it had been reported, Japanese troops were landing.

As a clear day dawned we stood off Kuantan only to find that the information was incorrect and all was quiet. Admiral Phillips set course for Singapore. At 11.08 a.m. on that sunny day, nine bombers in close formation attacked the *Repulse* scoring one direct hit which started a fire. By 12.27 p.m. the *Repulse* had been struck by five torpedoes and began to sink.

During the attack I was on duty in the Signal Office. Since I wasn't normally part of the crew I was given spare jobs to do (one of which was typewriting). The Yeoman of Signals ordered me outside to close the big square steel covers in front of the portholes. These gave the Signal Office some protection but hadn't been used for many a long day, if ever. Consequently I found them very stiff and almost impossible to move. While I was struggling to accomplish my task, Japanese twin-engined bombers were swooping down low and machine-gunning the ship. As soon as I had finished I turned back towards the Signal Office. Taking a quick peep at the upper deck I saw a dead gunner bisected by machine-gun fire, his lower torso on the deck below. Blood was spattered over a wide area. I dived into the Signal Office, too numb with shock to even mention it. About 20 minutes later the first torpedo struck and 20 minutes after that we were ordered to abandon ship. The *Repulse* was listing badly to port. I stood with one foot on the rail and one on the deck. Men were scrambling down as best they could. Some slithered on their backs. I managed to walk and eventually reached the water and walked into the sea.

It was vital to swim as far away from the

ship as possible in case we were sucked under when she sank. There was no panic. Fortunately it didn't occur to us that we were in shark-infested waters. Strangely enough, no sharks ever appeared, nor were any reported.

After we had swum about 100 yards, I turned to watch *Repulse*, waiting for her to go down. It was an awesome sight. Nearly an hour later we watched the *Prince of Wales* as she too foundered about three miles away.

The destroyers, *HMS Electra* and *HMAS Vampire* began their rescue work. Their sister ship the *Express* was alongside the *Prince of Wales* rescuing as many of the crew as she could. I noticed a seaman thrashing about in the water and swam over to help him. Later I always thought of him as 'The Blackman', because the poor bloke was smothered all over with fuel oil. He must have jumped off the ship into the middle of a swelling pool of oil. He didn't hear me approach and gave a startled gasp as I touched him. I did my best to calm him and convey to him that we were heading towards rescue. Grabbing him under the armpits I started to swim towards the *Electra*.

I seemed to have been swimming for miles before I got alongside the destroyer which was crammed with survivors. Thankfully I grabbed hold of the rope netting above which sailors were helping people on board. One sailor told me to climb aboard too. 'I can,' I called, 'But this bloke can't.' Two sailors immediately climbed down the netting and with some difficulty hauled 'The Blackman' aboard. Wearily I followed.

Once on the deck of the *Electra*, I realised how limited my vision had been while swimming below. I gazed at the surface of the sea, covered with the detritus of sunken vessels. There were dead men, Carley floats, launches, pieces of wood and other debris. 'The Blackman' was lying near one of the deck houses and I slumped down beside him, totally exhausted. Presently the nets were pulled on board and we got under way. I didn't realise it at the time but it was the end of an era. No longer would battleships be considered the masters of the ocean. They had been conquered by machines a mere fraction of their size. Aircraft were now masters of both air and sea.

The crew of the *Electra* had been engaged all this time in rescuing the survivors. 'The Blackman' had been taken below by a sick berth attendant. I went to the rail and saw the same attendant coming back along the deck. I asked him how 'The Blackman' was and he said, 'Sorry mate, but he was dead when he was pulled aboard.'

It was nearly 2 p.m. before the search for survivors was called off. Commander May of *Electra*, who was now commanding officer, ordered *Express* and *Vampire* to make a last sweep and then proceed to Singapore. An hour later, dangerously loaded with survivors, they departed. Commander May took his ship on a last sweep and then we took off for harbour. I found out later that the three ships had landed 2,081 survivors plus those who died on board. We left behind boats, Carley floats, lots of oil and all kinds of floating debris as well as many dead bodies.

While the rescue was taking place, Japanese planes could be seen high overhead but they made no attempt to molest us. In view of their behaviour before the sinkings and subsequent behaviour as the war progressed, this inaction seemed inexplicable. They were reputed to have returned the next day and thrown a wreath where the two British ships had sunk. We made our way south in the Gulf of Siam on a smooth oily sea, eventually rounding the Anambas Islands and steering west to the naval base harbour. We tied up at around midnight preceded by *Vampire* and *Express*.

On the quay there was great confusion. Dazed survivors stumbled ashore in a motley collection of clothing. Many had discarded garments before abandoning ship so as not to be weighed down in the water. Few had footwear and what clothing they had was oil-stained and filthy like the overalls I wore myself. The little ships were littered with blood-stained bandages and oily clothes.

Men gathered on the quayside under arc lights and beneath the shadow of a gigantic crane. Some had been given rum aboard the destroyers and were now offered more. It had been discovered that the rum made them vomit, thus bringing up any oil they had swallowed. Some of the helpers who welcomed us ashore were under the impression that we had been in action against a large Japanese battle fleet. They were stunned when we disillusioned them. Indeed it seemed incredible that such a disaster had been caused by a few aeroplanes.

Some semblance of order was restored and the dead bodies taken away. We were led to a series of tables and chairs where details of our names, service numbers and rank were recorded. When asked for the name of the ship from which I had survived, I naturally said, 'Repulse.' I had only been on board for three days before setting out on that fateful voyage but assumed that I had been listed as a member of her ship's company.

We were then marched along the dockyard and up the hill to *HMS Sultan* where we were given accommodation and a meal. *HMS Sultan* was quite a large barrack complex which, I was told, was a gift to the British Navy from a previous Sultan of Johore. As soon as I lay down, I went out like a light. It had been the longest day of my life. For 840 of my shipmates it had been the last.

Robson remained in the Royal Navy through-out the war and was land-based in Italy, South Africa, India and Singapore. He married Monica Flynn at the end of 1945 and settling in Newcastle they had two daughters. Robson worked as a pensions auditor for the Ministry of Health and Social Security. He died in 1994.

JANUARY 1942

Senior German Officials meet at Wannsee outside Berlin to prepare a plan for the continual destruction of European Jews — The Final Solution. Rommel begins a new advance through Cyrenaica towards the Egyptian frontier.

ON THE RUN IN THE DESERT
Bob Mallett

Lawrence Robert Mallett was born in 1912 and joined the RHA in 1933. Mallett fought at Tobruk in May 1941 and, as a 25 pounder gunner, saw a lot of action. Having become separated from his battery during a sandstorm he was captured by Germans. He was handed over to the Italians along with other prisoners and while on his way to Tripoli, their convoy was attacked by fighter planes. In the ensuing confusion he managed to escape and was to spend over a year alone in the desert.

I used to lay up all day but go out all night looting. At first I went only a short distance to see what I could find but soon I got bolder and made sorties out to the main road, where the convoys were going through to the front line. I used to prowl until I had found an Eyetie, or Jerry lorry parked for the night. Usually the crew would be asleep in a dugout yards away. I used to climb into the back and throw out anything I could lay my hands on. I acquired, in this manner, everything that a man could wish for. I had matches and cigars, newpapers, gelignite, beans, a beautiful little Eyetie Breda sub-machine gun and ammo to match, blankets and a petrol camping stove, even chocolate and biscuits. I did get shot at a few times but shooting at something in the dark desert is like firing with no eyes.

One night I climbed into the rear of a wagon, and trod on the face of a Jerry who was sound asleep there. I left hurriedly amidst a burst of rifle fire, but the shots were wasted on the desert air. I then started jumping lorries; I would hide near the road, let them go past, and then jump in the back. After a quick inspection of the contents I would throw out anything I fancied before jumping out and following the tracks back to my loot. After a time the Jerries realised there was someone in the district, and I heard patrols out at night. I often heard their footsteps on the rocks at night and once I had just returned to my cave when I heard boots on rocks. I sat in my cave with my eye glued to a little pinhole in the wall, smoking an Eyetie cigar, as I watched a little procession of 12 Eyeties stagger past. My water supply was still holding out. I started to collect explosives. I had a large supply of Italian grenades which had a rubber tag on the side. If this tag was pulled off they would then explode when dropped. So I conceived the brilliant idea of putting a few prepared grenades on the chassis of lorries I looted before I left. Quite a few of the drivers must have got a real kick when they drove off in the morning after spending a night in the district. Then I went one better: I stole a load of electrical detonators and started fixing them to the spark plugs of parked lorries during the night. I figured that when the driver started up in the morning the detonator, snugly embedded in a nice large stick of gelignite, would really start the day with a bang. I returned later, on several occasions to observe the result of my labour and found the results quite impressive.

I had been searching the coast for a boat, hoping to make a sail and return to

Alexandria, but had no luck; then fate took a hand. One morning I sat outside my cave sunbathing and three Arabs suddenly came round a corner of the rock. I had no chance to hide and knew the game was up but smiled and told them in bad Italian that I was a German on coastguard duty. They hurried off and as soon as they were out of sight I grabbed a sack of food and my little Breda and went off in the other direction. I knew they would be back with the Jerries before long. I hid up again two miles off and saw several patrols during the day not to mention a spotter aircraft that kept zooming along the coast. Nightfall came and I was off. Going by the stars I tramped eastwards all night and many nights after that. I was carrying a little grub, my gun and my original two gallon can of water. I knew there were frequent wells on the road where I could fill my can. Food was no problem as it was dumped everywhere. My boots however fell to pieces. Fortunately I found a dead Eyetie in the desert. He was really ripe and I had to hold my breath while I took off his boots. One boot came off easily. The other one came away with his foot still in it and I had to pull it out, bone at a time, but they were good boots, nearly new and I was grateful to him. I dumped my gun as it was getting very heavy. My boots rubbed my bare heels and raised a large blister. I laid up for a few days in the hope that it would heal but it got worse and the flies would not leave it alone. I had to push on and as my foot was swollen I dumped one boot and wrapped my foot in an old sack. So I kept going and then one morning I inspected my foot and saw some maggots crawling about in it. There was also a blue streak going up my leg. I knew that if I did not get some treatment for it soon, it would be my lot. So I turned north for the sea. I found a deserted wadi, with ripe prickly pears, fig trees and water. I laid up there for a while, living on fruit, dead fish and winkles that I picked off the rocks and boiled. I bathed my foot in hot salt water and it gradually returned to normal.

Not a soul came near me during this time — I could have been on the moon. Several times I heard the roar of half-track vehicles in the distance and at night often saw flashes out to sea, so I assumed there was a battle going on somewhere.

Mallett's story continues in July 1942 on page 225.

FEBRUARY 1942

Singapore surrenders to the Japanese.

EVACUATION FROM SINGAPORE
Charles C Weston

Charles Clifford Weston was born in 1908. He joined the RAF in 1940 and was serving in Malaya when the Japanese came.

During the small hours of Sunday 8th February the enemy made a landing on the west coast of Singapore Island and fierce fighting ensued. They were at first repulsed in places but superior numbers and air superiority told against us. Louder grew the sound of guns and more columns of smoke roared into the sky as the scorched earth policy of destruction continued.

As various people evacuated Singapore they were obliged to leave their cars on the docks as the ships could not take them. Had we so wished each member of the embarkation staff might have acquired a model to suit him. A lorry driver told us that the enemy were advancing on Tengah RAF Station and that it was being heavily shelled. For some days we had been expecting orders to proceed to a ship that would take us to the Dutch East Indies. That night the Flight Sergeant gave orders that we must be packed and ready to move at short notice.

The enemy began to shell gun positions somewhere beyond Mount Elizabeth and one or two shells exploded. The Flight Lieutenant phoned Air Headquarters and then ordered us to go to the docks and board a ship. And so we left, while sounds of machine gunfire could be heard in the distance and clouds of smoke suggested where trouble was taking place. Broken telegraph wires were mute evidence of flying shell splinters. We all squeezed into the various lorries and cars and started for the docks. The roads were practically deserted except for a group of bedraggled and weary looking Indian soldiers returning from the battle front. We entered the dock gates and drove to the quay where the *Empire Star* was moored. Air raid warnings were sounding and all was chaos on the quay. The pilot stood talking to us, he said, 'Young men — today you see one of the blackest days in the history of the British Empire.'

All day long parties of airmen, civilians a

few soldiers and a party of Australian nurses kept arriving until the ship was absolutely packed. The forecastle was originally for the embarkation staff but many other airmen had to join us. The holds were full of airmen or nurses while the civilians occupied all the cabin and stateroom space amidships.

By 6 p.m. the loading was completed, the mooring ropes were cast off and the ship slowly moved out into mid stream and then sailed towards the harbour mouth. When the ship reached the roadsteads it dropped anchor. Darkness was now falling quickly but it was not to be dark that night as the sky was illuminated redly by the leaping flames of a dozen fires. In one direction the blazing hulk of the *Empress of Asia* was reflected in the calm water. It had been heavily bombed and set on fire while bringing reinforcements to Singapore. Many troops had been killed but the majority were taken off in tugs and barges. In another direction the most gigantic fire I had ever seen was raging. It was the Shell petrol installation on a nearby island. It was not less than a quarter of a mile long and many flames were dancing and leaping to great heights lighting the sky for miles and casting their reflections across the water. Added to these conflagrations were the great fires of the Naval Base, Bukit Panjong.

By 8 a.m. the next morning our ship was steaming well out to sea. Then a sudden movement occurred and an airman looked round and said, 'Get under cover, aircraft are sighted.' We all crouched in the passageways leading to the crew's quarters in the stern. A few minutes later the aft ack-ack gun spoke and was followed by the patter of machine gun fire and the roar of aero-engines as the planes dived down towards the ship. Then came the explosions of bombs — they dive bombed again and this time I was crouching in the corner of the passage wondering if I and others were shortly to find ourselves on a sinking ship. Someone said, 'The ship is making for the islands.' This was not so but it was zigzagging which probably gave the fellow this idea. When the aircraft roared down the second time a bomb hit the ship on the starboard side of the poop deck. The concussion shook the vessel heavily at the stern. Someone shouted, 'The ship's on fire.' Being crushed among the crowd in the corridor, I could see no flames but the fire was actually on the deck outside a few yards away. A couple of airmen seized extinguishers and quenched the flames in less than five minutes. Two bombs had also fallen amidships, one having smashed a port lifeboat and blown a gunner into the sea. The other fell into a port cabin and killed the occupants.

We were not the only ship being attacked that day. The *Empire Star* was one of a convoy of three including *HMS Durban* a cruiser and an armed auxiliary vessel the *Kedah*. The *Empire Star* was the largest vessel and together with the cruiser bore the brunt of the attack.

Sometimes the enemy came over in squadrons of 18 or more. The suspense was awful as we waited in the fetid atmosphere of the forecastle. Again and again the bombs whistled down and yet they seemed to miss us. Each time we just crouched down in the semi-darkness and hoped for the best. The ship was most certainly in the valley of the shadow of death but a divine providence placed a great power in the hands of the Captain that day, for it was he we have to thank for the fact that the ship was steered from danger. He stood at the wheel watching every move of the enemy and when the bombs were released he swung the wheel that the ship turned from the jaws of death. The raid continued all morning. The biggest shock of all occurred when 21 bombers dropped a whole load of bombs which exploded in the sea about 20 feet from the port side of the ship. Everyone in the forecastle stood up in consternation as the vessel jumped madly up and down in the water. The detonation of the bombs was terrific. It was estimated that 100 bombers in waves took part in this raid and yet they did not succeed in sinking any one of the three ships. This was due not to the lack of skill on the part of the enemy but to the helmsman of the ships. The sad note was the fact that eight were killed and 22 were injured on the *Empire Star*. I was told later that the *Empire Star* was normally a meat carrying ship that plied between New Zealand, Australia and England. It was lined with cork to aid the refrigeration of the meat and thus would sink less quickly if torpedoed; also it had accomplished 12 crossings of the English Channel in the evacuation of Dunkirk. And in addition it had taken part in the evacuation of Crete. The Captain said, 'The Jerries and the Italians bombed us and could not sink my ship and I'm damned if any little yellow . . . are going to do it!' The enemy did not trouble us any more and it was a relief to steam towards safety that afternoon. . . .

On Friday 13th February land could be seen in the distance and in the evening the ship dropped anchor in Batavia Roadsteads. The mainland of Java appeared fairly green and flat but a lofty cone-shaped mountain reared its summit to the sky.

MARCH 1942

The Japanese drive forward into Burma and approach the capital Rangoon which is rapidly evacuated. The Dutch High Command on Java surrender to the Japanese and 100,000 Dutch, British, Australian and American troops are taken prisoner. The British step up bombing raids over Germany specifically targeting factories.

INITIAL RELIEF AT BEING TAKEN PRISONER
Charles C Weston

Evacuated from Singapore to Java, Weston now becomes a POW at the hands of the Japanese.

Our journey by train continued until Tasikmalaja was reached. We now began to get thick sandwiches of bread and bully beef or cheese that was being issued slowly owing to the crowded state of the trains. At 11a.m.

205

on Sunday 8th March sudden orders were given by the officers that personnel parade on the platform. Gradually we did so and squeezed outside the station where airmen assembled in the various units. The news of the capitulation was true — we were to embark on a different adventure, that of becoming Prisoners of War. No one present looked very sorry. The adventures of the past few weeks had led us into danger on several occasions and we had not at any time been of much use to the war effort. Nor on the other hand had we enjoyed comfort or good food apart from that bought privately in Batavia. None knew whether more hardships or dangers were in store but the majority were willing to take a chance. It was a good thing that the distant future was not unveiled. Airmen from many directions had arrived at Tasikmalaja. Consequently my friend, Percy and I met several of our former Kuantan room mates all glad to think that we were finished with the active side of being chased about by the enemy.

After a considerable wait, the different sections of airmen were marched off, some to a race course and others, including us, to various schools in the town. Here we stayed for a few days. At 9 a.m. on 11th March everyone was packed up and ready and the officers led the party in sections each with a white flag on the mile and a half march to Tasikmalaja aerodrome. As one of the airmen had a white Pomeranian dog I thought he should have led the way. This little dog, Peggy, had been given to him in Greece and had been evacuated to Crete and again to Egypt in a Sunderland flying boat and later had come over to Sumatra and finally to Java.

We had been told to look as smart as possible and to march as well as we could. Considering that many still suffered with blistered feet caused by the long walk before becoming Prisoners of War, a remarkable display was put up and the party remained in step the whole of the way, a feat usually impossible in the RAF. Most of the population seemed to line the roadway to watch us pass and they could by no stretch of the imagination think we were in any way down-hearted. The mile and a half seemed more like three miles and I for one was relieved when just beyond the outskirts of the town we approached the aerodrome and marched through an entrance to a partially completed runway where a temporary halt was made. On looking around it was apparent that the aerodrome was only in the stages of construction. One or two hangars were completed on one side of the field but vast buildings works were visible far away on the opposite side. A row of small Dutch civil biplanes that had probably been used for reconnaissance stood before a hangar that was being used for airmen to sleep in. Groups of fellows could be seen clearing up around the hangar.

In a few minutes we began marching up the long runway that was well-rutted and scattered with stones. Near the end of it we turned onto the field, marched past a damaged Hurricane that stood on its nose and by several damaged Dutch aircraft to a spot where several huts were huddled among trees and shrubs. The huts were constructed of woven strip bamboo with roughly tiled roofs and concrete floors. We swept them out and spread our kit into our respective bed spaces.

The next morning a parade was held on the runway, where all airmen on the aerodrome assembled. Afterwards we were marched back to our section and the CO informed us that we were definitely Prisoners of War and not internees of the Dutch as some seemed to think. Also that in a few days we would proceed to a tea plantation in the hills where we would build ourselves a proper camp and would be free to move around in an area of some miles and while we observed various regulations we would be left to ourselves by the Japanese.

Weston's account concludes in August 1943 on page 295, revealing that life as a POW was very much contrary to his CO's expectations.

APRIL 1942

**Japanese aircraft sink four British war-
ships including cruisers, *Dorsetshire* and
Cornwall.**

THE SINKING OF
HMS DORSETSHIRE
Walter Fudge

*Walter Fudge whose life on HMS Dorset-
shire was featured on page 144 in May 1941
recounts how she went down.*

On Saturday 4th April a group of us were
sitting in a movie house in Colombo, Ceylon,
(now Sri Lanka) when on the screen,
appeared 'MEN OF H.M. SHIPS RETURN
TO THEIR SHIPS IMMEDIATELY' — so
out we scrambled to our liberty boats, back
aboard ship and out to sea we went. It was 11 p.m.
and not until the next morning did we notice
being in company with *HMS Cornwall*. Further-
more we had some of *Cornwall's* crew and
Cornwall had some of our crew. At 11 a.m.

210

Sunday 5th April, a single Japanese plane was spotted astern and at 1.40 p.m. *Cornwall* and we were attacked by some 80 planes. In less than ten minutes *Dorsetshire* was sunk and within five minutes more *Cornwall* went down too. Two shipmates went down in the mess and refused to leave the ship — they were non-swimmers. At a time like that it is every man for himself. I recall seeing our new Captain Agar VC giving a salute on the fo'c'sle intending to go down with the ship; but Cassier, another shipmate would not allow that!! He bundled him over the side. A yell from the bridge to the 4 inch AA guns crews — 'Why aren't you firing?' Reply — 'All dead except me!'

The masthead lookout scrambled down a rope, which had been secured there, and I was right behind him. We both smiled at the water's edge and we exchanged words 'After you!' 'No, after you!!' At that time, much of the ship had gone under and only the fo'c'sle was out of water.

There was no vortex — just ear-splitting noise from the bombs (these were responsible for deafness in my right ear). The water was warm. I felt happy to have had a tot of rum earlier.

We swam away and a few low flying planes machine-gunned swimmers and I found a bullet in my ankle but only under the skin — the depth of water must have slowed down its velocity.

So there we were for over 30 hours — one man taken by a shark — 1,222 officers and men from the two ships — with a total loss of 425. Tropical sun and thirst were problems but the wounded obviously had the worst time. Only one whaler boat survived and this was filled with the wounded and those badly burnt. The remainder of us clung to floating objects like Denton rafts and Carley floats. I recall two Marines who were wearing necklaces of precious stones mostly made of rubies. They were the richest pair out of the whole bunch. The rest of course lost all they had to the bottom of the Bay of Bengal. Early on Monday 6th April a single Allied plane flew over and signalled-'HANG ON- HELP COMING'. Well, help did come later that day; the destroyer *Paladin* threw down her scrambling nets and we struggled aboard.

After the war Fudge, his wife Elizabeth and their baby daughter emigrated to Canada, where he worked for 30 years for the federal government. He has been retired for the last 20 years and lives on Mayne Island, British Columbia.

MAY 1942

The Battle of the Coral Sea takes place in which the Americans are victorious over the Japanese. The RAF launches its heaviest bombing raid yet with Cologne as its target, incurring enormous damage on the city and factories. Meanwhile the Japanese complete their conquest of Burma.

BROTHELS I KNEW
AS A BACHELOR
Alastair Gordon
(The Marquess of Aberdeen)

The Marquess of Aberdeen was born Alastair Ninian John Gordon, in 1920. He was the youngest of five children and the fourth son of Lord Dudley Gordon. He was educated at Harrow and the Gray School of Art, Aberdeen. In 1939 he was commissioned into the Scots Guards and sent to the Middle East and then North Africa. Here he was shot in the shoulder *accidentally by an Irish Guardsman and sent to Syria to recuperate. On leave with fellow officers the Marquess of Aberdeen recounts:*

First, Madame Jannette's in Beirut in 1942. Her establishment was a convenient two minutes' walk from the St George's Hotel. She was a benevolent but strict Madame.

You entered a large room comfortably furnished with sofas and armchairs, in which she invited you to sit and have a drink or a cup of coffee. Strolling about or draped deliciously on sofas were attractive young girls wearing figure-hugging ankle-length silk dressing gowns. You were invited to take your time in making your selection. I made mine quite quickly — a quiet beautiful brunette.

You paid Madame and the girl then led you to her own bedroom in which was a large double bed; leading off behind a screen was a bathroom complete with bidet. Over Olga's bed were colour photographs of her as the cover girl of Belgrade magazines.

Poor Olga — she had fled Yugoslavia ahead of the German invasion, landed in Syria and perforce joined the only profession available. I tried to be as kind as possible to her then and on subsequent visits, and I believe she was grateful, regarding the urgent attentions of a sex-starved subaltern as a necessary panacea.

More from Alastair Gordon can be found on page 422 in January 1945.

JUNE 1942

Rommel finally takes Tobruk from the British who hastily retreat into Egypt.

THE LOSS OF THE PUTNEY HILL
Alan Shard

Alan Shard was born in Radcliffe, Lancashire in 1922. He went to sea in June 1940 and served for four years as an Apprentice Deck Officer with Counties Ship Management Company.

The date was 25th June. The merchant vessel *Putney Hill* of London was en route from Cape Town to New York to pick up a cargo of military equipment for Russia. She was approximately 500 miles north of San Juan, Puerto Rico, proceeding independently on a zigzag course at ten knots. Lying in wait for just such an opportunity, (convoys had not yet been established by the Americans on the US Eastern Seaboard due to Admiral King's aversion to British tactics) was Kapitanleutnant Rolf Mutzelberg in *U-203* a Type VllC

216

U–Boat, surface speed 17 knots, submerged speed seven knots.

The time was 11.25 p.m. It was a brilliant moonlit night, warm, with little breeze and slight sea and swell. The lookout in the port wing of the bridge was a young apprentice from Lancashire, who was scanning an area from right ahead to right astern on his side. I was that young apprentice. The Third Mate was keeping a similar lookout on the starboard side and an Able Bodied Seaman at the wheel. The fourth member of the watch, on standby, had just made the coffee for the Middle Watch coming on at midnight. (Coffee on a British ship in wartime consisted of throwing a few handfuls of grind into a converted 5lb jam tin with a wire handle and letting it stew on the galley stove). The Standby man came up on the bridge to check the time before he called the 12–4 a.m. watch at 11.30 p.m. As he left the wheelhouse to go below, I asked the time. With a slap on my back, the standby man replied 11.25 p.m. and simultaneously both of us were blown into the air from the blast of a tremendous explosion at the waterline in Hold Number Three, slightly aft of the bridge structure. I struck my knee on the after bridge rail and fortunately did not fall over to the deck below. The reverberations echoed through the empty holds like a giant hammer blow from Thor and *Putney Hill* went dead in the water. Neither of us was hurt and we donned life-jackets immediately. Smoke from the explosion hung over the decks. The Captain came running out of his cabin on the lower bridge deck and as the ship had now taken a heavy starboard list, he ordered 'Abandon Ship'.

I wondered why I had not seen anything out there on the port side and figured the torpedo must have come down a moonbeam reflection in the tropical waters. It was later discovered from the U-boat War Log that the first torpedo (also unsighted) missed. The two life-boats on the portside of the ship were useless, having been blown inboard against the funnel, so everyone ran to the starboard side which was almost at sea-level. I was carrying an old army gas mask case made of canvas known as the 'grab bag' in which I kept my Merchant Navy Identity Card, a Mars Bar, extra pair of socks, some private papers and my camera. I threw them in my designated Lifeboat Number Three which was already in the water and swarmed down the falls to join 15 others.

The lifeboat was a clinker-built wooden craft which had not been in the water since I joined *Putney Hill* two years earlier in June

1940. Consequently, the seams were open to the sea and she soon settled to the 'gunnels'. Everyone baled furiously, and I even used my shoes as a container. Several men from the smaller Lifeboat Number One, which had capsized, now endeavoured to climb into the waterlogged boat which also capsized throwing all hands into the 'drink'. The 'grab bag' was lost in the exodus. The ship was now down by the head, but without the heavy starboard list. The torpedo must have struck in the port deep tank amidships, which held several hundred tons of ballast. This ballast was released in the explosion causing the ship to list immediately, but now, due to the fact that the starboard deep tank ballast was flowing through to the port side and in effect equalising the situation, the ship eventually became upright. This new state of affairs was not lost on Mutzelberg who surfaced in order to execute his next move. No shots had been fired from *Putney Hill's* 4 inch stern gun as the acute angle of list had rendered it useless and all hands had already left by the time she righted.

I had never swam more than 50 yards in my life, but wearing my life-jacket, struck out for a life-raft floating a short distance astern. Several others had the same intention and eight clambered on board. During this short swim I was stung by a 'Portuguese man-o-war', but felt nothing at the time. It later developed into a rotting hole and needed hospital attention in New York. The life-raft was about eight feet square and consisted of wooden planks enclosing metal airtanks with a depression across the centre for survivors to set their feet whilst facing each other. Someone pointed to a man hanging on to the propeller which was clear of the water. It was the mess room steward and he was later rescued.

The *Putney Hill* was lying like a ghost ship on the gentle sea, the silence punctuated by occasional loud bangs as various bits of the structure gave way under the increasing pressure. Without warning an incendiary shell hit the funnel and started a fire. It was followed by a further 63 shells into the hull, counted by those on the life-raft from their grandstand position. Well at least Mutzelberg had allowed the crew to leave the stricken vessel before opening up with his deck gun. At approximately 1.30 a.m. on 26th June *Putney Hill* became almost vertical and, still burning, slid beneath the sea bow first.

We were left alone with our own unspoken thoughts. I was thinking probably the same as the others. What next! We were not left in doubt very long. *U-203* eased out of the gloom and approached the life-raft. A voice from the conning tower, in perfect English, enquired of the whereabouts of the Master. No one knew which was just as well as he might have been pointed out, such was the life of misery he had led us.

The U-Boat picked up a lifebuoy and moved off into the darkness after establishing where the ship was from and the nature of her cargo, which of course was nil, being in ballast. Then suddenly she reappeared and to everyone's amazement we saw on the foredeck one of the apprentices. 'What the hell is Hancock doing on board the sub,' said the Second Mate who was the senior officer on the raft. By now the wind had risen and the sea was a little choppy, so the U-Boat could not get too close. The Commander called from the conning tower and requested that someone should come and assist the apprentice back to the raft as he could not swim. Without hesitation John McKenzie, the Second Mate dived in, swam to the submarine and escorted the youth back to his fellow crewmen.

He was besieged with questions and basked in the 'limelight' in the middle of the night as he told his story. When the lifeboat capsized he was able to grab and hang on to an oar. He was apparently joined by a young Royal

Navy gunner, Jeffrey Banks, but the oar would not support both and in the ensuing squabble the gunner was lost. After some time in the warm waters, Hancock found himself in the direct path of the U-boat as it searched for the Master. As it cruised by him at a couple of knots, the apprentice grabbed the ballast intakes, was sighted by sailors on the deck and hauled on board. The Commander quizzed him at some length, but as a mere apprentice he knew nothing of the codes and naval orders, so arrangements were made to return him to his shipmates. The Commander told him that if he was eventually rescued, he should not return to the Merchant Navy, for if he was caught again the ending would not be as pleasant. Needless to say, all four apprentices were back at sea again within 14 weeks of the sinking of *Putney Hill*.

When dawn broke, we saw at some distance the two lifeboats which had been righted and sails rigged. After some arm waving our raft was sighted and the largest of the two lifeboats came alongside with the Master on board. Heads were counted and the Second Cook, James Campbell of Liverpool and the Naval Gunner were amongst the missing. The Master then set sail for the West Indies towing the smaller boat, because its rudder pintle had been damaged and she would not steer. The time was spent keeping a lookout, sleeping and discussing what we would do if we made a deserted island. Strangely enough we young apprentices appeared to accept the situation with a spirit of high adventure, little doubting that we would eventually make it, but the older, more sober members of the engine department were very morose. Rations consisted of an ounce of water three times a day, a spoonful of pemmican (dried meat pounded into a paste and melted fat), two Horlicks malted milk tablets and a spoonful of condensed milk. One day it rained a tropical downpour and water was collected in the sail and funnelled into the tanks. It was pink from the red sail and the lads pretended it was a strawberry drink. I was dressed only in a singlet and a pair of naval bell bottom trousers, but the nights were bearable in contrast to the broiling daytime temperatures. A piece of torn canvas from the lifeboat cover was utilised to cover three of us until the Third Mate, a hulking Dane, decided to take it for himself. He was big so he kept it. After a few days the Fourth Engineer, Kenneth Cowling, died in the Master's boat. His brother, the Third Engineer, was also in the same boat. The Fourth Engineer had been on watch in the engine-room when the torpedo struck and he was burned by hot oil from a burst pipeline, the burns covering two thirds of his body. With whatever prayers the shocked group could recall, his body was put over the side after his brother had removed his gold wedding ring. Someone said they saw a shark. The next morning a puff of smoke was sighted on the horizon as HMS *Saxifrage*, a corvette heading for her West Indies Station, revved up to full speed and bore down on the boats, at first mistaking their sails for a U-boat on the surface. All hands clambered up the scrambling nets to wild shouts of joy. Again another coincidence, one of the corvette's sailors came from the next town to Radcliffe and he gave me his own bunk for the night. Next day *Saxifrage* arrived in San Juan, Puerto Rico where we were taken ashore and rigged out in a motley selection of donated clothing.

Alan Shard met his German wife while serving as Navigating Officer on Canadian Pacific's Beaverbrae transporting immigrants to Canada. For the last 30 years he has worked as a marine consultant and nautical inspector to Foreign Flag Administrations in Canada. He now lives in Vancouver, British Columbia.

JULY 1942

PQ 17, one of the British convoys taking supplies to Russia, is destroyed by the Germans. The first battle of El Alamein begins.

TOBRUK AND RECAPTURE
Bob Mallett

Mallett's story, which appeared in January 1942 on page 194, continues. Eventually Mallett met up with some South Africans from the 5th Transvaal Horse Artillery and was told that Rommel had just started a big drive and that all Allied troops were falling back on Tobruk. Mallett joined up with a disorganised Service Corps unit in Tobruk but there was chaos. Rommel had broken through the perimeter and Tobruk fell in June 1942. Mallett became a prisoner once more, along with thousands of others but soon managed to escape again, driving off in a German staff car which he later crashed as Germans were in hot pursuit. Taken prisoner *he was returned to Tobruk, transported from camp to camp and finally put on a ship with fellow prisoners bound for Italy.*

A motley crowd was herded onto the quay. We were now on our way to a prison camp, somewhere in Italy. Guards stood around us, dirty and unshaven, leaning on their rifles. We numbered about 400 English, South Africans, Indians, Australians and a collection of nationals from almost every European country. We were all dirty, hungry, lousy and miserable. A freighter was tied up in front of us, lifting gently in the light swell that was rolling across the harbour. This was our ferry for the trip across the sea to Italy. We were going back to Europe, but not the way that we would have wished. At last, we got the signal to embark and as each man reached the gangway he was presented with a packet of Italian cigarettes and a tin of corned beef. This was to last us until we reached Taranto and together with a quantity of rusty water all we had until we landed. We were packed into the holds of the vessel and given to understand that nobody would be allowed on deck in any circumstances. A number of buckets were then passed down and the Italian interpreter indicated that these were our loo for the trip. Some of the men already had dysentery and after two hours below, the atmosphere could almost be leaned upon. The ship had been carrying barrels of tar, and some had leaked as the whole floor had about an inch of tar over it. We had about two square feet of space each and when the ship got out into the heavier swell, sickness added to our troubles.

One of the guards lounging above the hatch shouted. We looked up and saw an Italian army padre peering down at us. He had a poor command of English and not a lot of tact. 'Englishmans,' he called, 'You have been conquered,' and got no further. From somewhere in the hold a tightly knotted tarry rag rose and caught him fairly in the face. Exit padre. We never saw him again.

For over two days we sat in that hold. The floor was soft and slimy. I had laid an overcoat on the floor, but the tar oozed through. Most of the men had nothing but shirts and shorts on when they were captured and the state of them can best be left to the imagination. Once anything was placed on the ground, it was impossible to remove it. The men's watches had all been taken off them when captured so we had no idea of time. It just got light and it got dark; that was all we knew. After what seemed a lifetime in this hell, one of the guards above shouted. We looked up. He waved his rifle, pointed and yelled 'Taranto' so we took it that we had not much further to go. The ship stopped rolling and slowed. The activity on deck increased and we guessed that we were through the boom into Taranto harbour. We just sat, sweated and stank while waiting our destiny.

The Italian interpreter arrived at the hatch. 'We are now mooring at the dockside,' he said. 'Soon you will be allowed up and marched off the ship. Those who need it will be given medical attention, the remainder are going to a temporary camp and will be given food and fresh clothes. You will be well guarded. Do not try and escape or you will be shot. That is all.' The dockside workers lowered a set of steps into the hold and we slowly climbed out. I never before realised just how sweet fresh air is, until I gulped it in on the ship's deck. About 100 prisoners were left below, some feebly waving an arm, others apparently dead.

We were formed up in threes on the jetty and the guards fell in on all sides of us. These were much older than the ones who had escorted us from Africa, and all seemed to have a sense of personal grievance against us. They did not miss a chance to hit with a rifle or kick anyone they thought a bit slow. We were marched off through the docks and across the town to the cages. A bit of propaganda to boost the Italian morale — Prisoners from Tobruk — all captured by Germans but who cared? The procession was lead by an officer and a squad of guards. Then came the prisoners covered in tar and excreta, some in rags, flanked on either side by a file of more guards; and a bunch of carabinieri bringing up the rear. The locals all turned out to welcome us with jeers and catcalls. We got bad cabbages and soft tomatoes tossed among us and other filth. From some of the upper windows came pots full of muck. The only consolation we had was that our guards were getting their full share of rubbish. And so we passed on to our destination at Taranto.

From Taranto Mallett was moved from camp to camp until in September 1943 the Germans took over in Italy and he managed to escape. Heading south he hoped to join the Allied troops who were moving up through Italy but met up with a band of Partisans and spent three weeks ambushing and looting German vehicles before being caught once again by the Germans. Herded onto a train heading for Germany he managed to hack a hole in the door with an axe and escaped once more. He headed south again and at last met up with a British unit based at Foggia, who had been reinforced with fresh troops — 'They had just been served with a meal when the Orderly Sergeant and myself walked in. All talk ceased and they looked at me in horror. They saw a very dirty, bearded, emaciated individual with bloodshot eyes and a little hair, covered in boils, and wearing tattered rags. 'Who's he,' they asked the sergeant, edging away from me. 'He is the escaped POW from up North, my lads, he's come from hell where you lot are going.' They all turned extremely white.' After the war Mallett bought a smallholding and was involved in gold mining. He lived in North Devon and died in 1997.

AUGUST 1942

Canadian and British forces raid the French channel port, Dieppe and incur heavy losses. In North Africa Rommel attacks Allied forces but is driven back.

THE BATTLE OF ALAM HALFA
Ernie Huntley

E (Ernie) W H Huntley was born in 1919 in Scotland. He left school at 14 and in 1936 joined the Royal Corps of Signals. He was posted in 1938 to No 2 Company Egypt Command Signals, Cairo, which became the Signals Unit for the newly formed Desert Division which eventually became the famous 7th Armoured Division.

Late July of 1942 found me back with my unit in the desert after a short leave in Cairo only to learn that Lieutenant General Straffer Gott, who had been selected to lead the newly formed 8th Army and the Desert Forces into battle, had been killed in a plane

231

crash. This news came as a very hard blow to us all, especially to the chaps like myself who knew him as Gentleman Gott for that was what he was, a true gentleman and he treated his subordinates likewise. His place was to be taken by a chap directly over from England. Now we had a saying to fit most newcomers, it was: 'They haven't got their knees brown yet' or in other words, they had a long way to go to 'learn the ropes.' What most of us were not aware of, was that this new commander had in fact spent a great deal of time in the Middle East some years before. This new man was Lieutenant General Bernard Law Montgomery.

Unfairly or otherwise, this was the attitude most of us forward troops had towards this new commander. He just wasn't one of us

— Yet! Firstly he had to prove himself. Unfortunately he hurt himself when he addressed many of us in the field. His attitude seemed to be so overbearing. He appeared to be 'putting us down' and various comments he made about some of our previous actions, left no doubt about the little respect he held for some of our present and former commanders. He appeared to be the 'Great I Am', for it was 'I this', 'I the next thing' and very little of 'we' or 'us'. We therefore felt the loss of General Gott even more.

As a member of the 7th Support Group, I provided rear link communication between the Battalion of the Rifle Brigade under command of Lieutenant Colonel Vic Turner and Support group HQ. We learned that we were to be part of a defensive action between Ruweiset and the Alam Halfa Ridges and were told that our function would be to entice the enemy forward; regardless of what happened, we were not to engage him. Now that order didn't go down too well with most of us for it was something we had never done, turn tail and run. We had always stood and fought for as long as we could before fighting a strategic withdrawal action. But being soldiers, we obeyed.

We were located between two low ridges about eight miles south of Ruweiset and about the same distance SW of Alam Halfa Ridge, with the 8th Armoured Brigade and the 7th Armoured Division, some five miles to our rear (or to the East). During the night of the 31st August, the enemy sent his 90th Light Division in our direction and to their south the main thrust of the DAK. We saw them coming, they in turn saw us, as they were supposed to. We allowed them, in fact encouraged them, to advance by making ourselves a prime target which they immediately engaged. We as ordered, turned and ran, hiding in whatever protection we could find, thus we found ourselves wedged between the 90th Light and their main thrust as both turned northwards towards El Alamein, in other words we were completely surrounded by the enemy! What most of us weren't aware of, was that false maps of the area had been allowed to fall into enemy hands which indicated certain routes between the Qattara Depression and the two ridges as being 'safe', whilst others were dangerous, meaning soft and treacherous sandy going. This ruse worked causing many of their tanks, field guns and vehicles to become 'bogged down' in the soft sand and we were trying to find a safe place in whatever craggy places we could hide.

The advance into that area was part of

Montgomery's plan to give Rommel 'what for'. Our armoured troops then came forward and engaged the enemy who, after a few days, fell back. We were then given the order to engage those in our area. We didn't need much persuading and did so with great gusto. We realised that we had in fact been used as bait and, regardless of the outcome didn't like it one little bit.

The enemy lost 50 tanks, we 68. There were 3,000 Axis casualties, we suffered 1,500. He lost 58 guns to our 18. Statistically we were the victors. Upon retreating, Rommel was allowed to retain possession of some high ground which we learned much later was also part of Monty's plan to allow the enemy to observe certain scenes of activity behind our lines meant also to deceive him.

The Battle of Alam Halfa isn't too well known, but was in fact a very important one, mainly because the enemy lost the last chance of breaking through to Cairo and the Suez Canal. It also gave us a chance to build up stores and equipment. Even more importantly a chance to train new arrivals and allow them an opportunity 'to get their knees brown'. It also proved that the Air Force and Army could work well together and I suppose to a certain extent it did serve to raise the morale of those in action for the first time as they took part in a victory.

Speaking as one of the forward elements, although we didn't like the idea of being used as bait, we had to grudgingly admit we had a commander who was efficient and had knowledge and skill. However, this one battle didn't endear him to us, he still 'had to get his knees brown'. It was and still is our opinion there was more than one Battle of El Alamein, and Alam Halfa was the first.

Huntley recounts events leading up to the Battle of El Alamein in October 1942 on page 239.

SEPTEMBER 1942

The Germans reach Stalingrad but the Russians put up fierce resistance. The RAF launch another sustained bombing offensive against German cities.

YOU'RE IN THE ARMY NOW
Michael Bereznicki

Bereznicki who told his story in September 1939 on page 1 and in February 1940 on page 41 continues:

Our family had spent well over two years in Arkhangelsk, but little did we know that outside events were rapidly spinning out of control. Rumours circulated. The Germans had double-crossed the Russians and had actually invaded the Soviet Union. This proved to be a very momentous event for our family and for all Poles exiled into Siberia. After the Germans attacked, the Russians steadily needed greater and greater numbers of soldiers. Stalin (out of the goodness of his heart) decided to release all able-bodied men (and their families) from slave labour and to conscript them into the armed forces instead.

All prisoners were called out into the courtyard in early September to hear an announcement from the Camp Commander, Major General Sakalov. He told us to line up for a medical examination. We stood there for hours waiting our turn to be examined by the camp doctors. The actual examination took about five minutes. Afterwards, we showered, got a change of clothing, and received a new set of identification papers. If anybody was ever stopped by the NKVD, all he had to do was show the police his new ID and he could not be arrested. These documents showed everybody that we were now soldiers and, therefore, had to be respected.

My family gathered our belongings and assembled on the train platform, where we each had to pay 50 rubles for the train ride to the Army Training Centre. As our rail car pulled out of Arkhangelsk, I felt happy. At last I could wave goodbye to Siberia.

Bereznicki's account continues in December 1943 on page 324 and May 1945 on page 451.

OCTOBER 1942

The Second Battle of El Alamein begins.

EVENTS LEADING UP TO THE BATTLE OF EL ALAMEIN
Ernie Huntley

Huntley's account of the Battle of Alam Halfa was told in August 1942 starting on page 231.

It was the 23rd October and we were on a 30 mile stretch of desert a few miles to the west of Alexandria in the north and down to the Qattara Depression in the south. The desert to many newcomers seemed like a very hostile place, but not to those who had become well seasoned Desert Rats long before the start of hostilities in North Africa. We had learned to accept it for what it was, we didn't try to change or adapt it to suit our needs but rather lived with what it offered. We grew to know its whims and little tricks and made it our home.

We were awakened at about 5 a.m. with 'stand to'! It was dark and cold, as it usually is at that time of year in the desert. Many men wore their greatcoats and others had thrown a blanket over their shoulders to ward off the chilly air. One could hear the merits of 'standing to' every morning and this brought the shout — 'Put a sock in it!' Some chaps lit up a cigarette and this resulted in the shout, 'Put out that fag!' Then came the advice, 'Better keep a sharp lookout for Jerry, chaps, he might surprise us this morning.'

When the sun started to shine it signalled 'stand down' and the start of the day's activities. Breakfast for some was fat greasy bacon, porridge, bread and jam and for those not so lucky, it was the usual bully beef and biscuits and of course in both instances the ever ready hot sweet strong tea. With the sun and the breakfast came the never ending scourge of the desert: the flies. They came in their millions getting into the eyes, noses, ears, and mouths of the men; anywhere they could find moisture.

The infantrymen made themselves as comfortable as they could in their narrow slit-trenches which gave a certain amount of shade from the hot daytime sun, but was of little use in the fly situation, rather the reverse and the cramped positions in the slit-trenches didn't help much either.

Activities were kept to a minimum. In the slit-trenches the men looked at their watches, checked and rechecked their weapons and equipment, keeping an eye open in the direction of the enemy lines. Then repeated the procedure over and over again.

During the afternoon the desert changed its character. Today it was the Sand Devils, a type of twister which blew loose sand into the eyes, noses, mouths and even the ears of the men and got into the cracks and crannies of everything not completely sealed.

Further back at the gun positions, the gunners were a little better off for, being in gun-pits, they had more room to move around, but even here it was check and recheck and keep under cover.

As usual in the desert, twilight fell very quickly. It was the time when all the Desert Force seem to come alive. The transport columns started to make their way forward from the rear echelon, over various tracks, Sun, Moon, Star, Springbok and many others raising as they did clouds of choking dust which completely blackened out the sky. Each evening they brought up fresh supplies of food, petrol, ammunition and the odd item from the canteen, letters, replacements and for some, the ever welcome hot evening meal.

Supplies unloaded, the men sat down to eat. Those with letters read them very, very slowly. Then it was back to check, recheck, and keep under cover. Some of the replacements were surprised to learn they wouldn't be needed this evening and when they asked the reason, were told they would find out soon enough. By now, the dust had settled and the moon was exceptionally clear amongst millions of stars. At the gun positions final checks had been made. Some of the men took off their coats, others took off their shirts for they knew before the night was over they would be wet with sweat as they were to be part of a large battery of 882 field guns which were to lay down a barrage of shells, the like of which hadn't been seen since WW1 and those guns still firing as daylight came, would have fired more than 600 rounds each. At 9.30 p.m., the preliminary orders were given and at 9.39 p.m. the gunners were ordered to 'Take post!'

Meanwhile in the forward areas, the infantrymen were waiting with bayonets fixed ready for the order to advance; with them were men of the Royal Engineers, the Royal Corps of Signals and the Corps of Military Police who formed part of the mine clearing squads. At 9.40 p.m. the command 'Fire!' was given. The whole area seemed to light up and explode from the sea to the Qattara Depression. The sky lit up like an elongated ball of flame and as each round left the guns another flash helped to keep that flame alive. Everyone, except the gunners, stood with their mouths wide open wondering how anyone could possibly remain alive under such a barrage.

As the guns were rumbling, the supply columns were making their way back to rear echelon and some were passing the guns as they opened fire, scaring the daylight out of the drivers and passengers. Now the chaps who had been told they wouldn't be needed knew the reason; it was no longer a secret.

Suddenly there was silence! Our guns had stopped firing. The combined efforts of those guns and the Desert Air Force had effectively kept the enemy from replying. And they were still silent!

At the gun positions new commands had been given. The gunners knew that this time they had better be 'on target' for their infantry comrades would be going forward under the next lot of shells. The infantry now left their slit-trenches and were nervously waiting, everyone alone with his own thoughts. Many expressed out loud: 'Thank God I'm not on the receiving end of this lot!' They looked at their watches, for some time stood still, for others it went by far too quickly for they knew that as soon as our guns opened fire again it would be their time to move forward.

Just before 10 p.m. at the gun positions, the order 'FIRE' was given. The infantrymen and the mine clearing squads moved forward. The Battle of El Alamein was on.

After his experiences in the desert Huntley was repatriated to Scotland where he joined the British 1ˢᵗ Corps and took part in the D-Day landings, before serving in France, Belgium, Holland and ending up in Germany as part of the Control Commission. In 1945 he married and had two sons. After the war Huntley transferred to the Royal Canadian Corps of Signals and served in various posts in Canada, retiring from the army in 1967. He then met the President of the Polish Government in exile and having fought alongside Poles in North Africa and in Holland agreed to enrol in the Free Poland Movement. Having held numerous Honorary Diplomatic Offices for the Government in exile he became a member of the Polish Independent Volunteer Reserves in which he started as a Captain and rose to Lieutenant General. Sadly his wife died in 1989; Huntley currently lives in Ontario, Canada.

NOVEMBER 1942

The second battle of El Alamein lasts from 23rd October until 4th November. It proves a decisive victory for the British and with the Anglo-American landings in Algeria and Morocco on 8th November (Operation Torch) any hope for the Axis powers of retaining domination in North Africa are dashed.

LETTERS FROM THE DESERT
Sidney A Wigglesworth

Sidney Arthur Wigglesworth was born in 1916 in London but grew up in Suffolk. He worked with his father as a pig breeder but didn't enjoy it and was glad to join up in 1940. He went out to North Africa as a Lance Corporal with the 9th Queen's Royal Lancers. He writes to his sister:

10th November

My Dear Kay

Have just received an air mail letter from you, posted during August. I had a budget of four letters, as owing to the recent action, we haven't had any deliveries. I expect you are most relieved at our success out here, and I can tell you, we certainly are most delighted with our effort. The whole thing was wonderfully organised, and we had some marvellous equipment and bags of it. I can't tell you really very much more than the radio or newspapers have already said, and certainly the former gives very accurate details. Those artillery barrages were just terrific and must be seen and heard to be believed — nothing could possibly exist under such a bombardment. It was a wonderful experience to witness it at night, while we waited behind, prior to going up the lanes through the minefields. The guns were some distance ahead of us while we waited, and we could only see the flashes and hear the continual roar and rumble which would die down for a few seconds and then return with apparent greater intensity. Most of the movement of the units took place within an hour or so of the zero hour, which is all the more credit to the management. At the appointed hour, we moved through the gaps and waited again till dawn, when immediately enemy tanks and guns were sought out and we got cracking. Until this time everything was horribly quiet and eerie, with a thick mist, which on clearing gradually exposed the enemy positions. We were most surprised, as no doubt you all were, to hear of the Anglo-American landings on the African coast; this will surely bring things to a rapid head, since these forces are moving fairly quickly. I don't think the French will resist very much except from a merely formal point of view.

I hope the torch etc arrives OK, but really you shouldn't have gone to this trouble; we are hoping to catch up with our mail now things are settling down a bit. Glad you enjoyed your stay at home, and were able to be of use on the farms. This photo of mine seems to have caused quite a stir; frankly I thought it awful — but so long as you are all satisfied, I must be content. I had a nice letter from Marjorie, with a photograph of the wedding. It is a pity that these newly weds have to be separated so soon. I'm glad you met her people — they certainly are very nice — I am quite fond of the old man. I used to enjoy spending evenings there, and we had some pleasant drinking and chatting times. I fancy he would go down with a bit of a bump if he were boozed!! Hope you are getting my letters all right — hope to get a telegram off as soon as possible. Do have a good time at Christmas — I fancy you might have a better do this year.

Much love to you both.

Your loving brother, Boy

20th November

My dear Kay

Thanks so much for your telegram received yesterday and for your most kind enquiry after my wants; but honestly I would not think of expecting you to send anything out here, owing to the risks — at any rate just now. Perhaps the only thing I might suggest is a few stamps — these are sometimes difficult to get and letters are held up . . .

It gives us all such pleasure to be able to write home now, feeling we have at long last done something worthy of note. I'm sure you must be feeling somewhat relieved, knowing of our success. It has all been so rapid, and we have travelled so far these past few days, that it seems impossible that we have retaken all these places. We have seen quite a lot of the havoc caused by the air force on the retreating Germans, but in many cases he has adapted the scorched earth policy. I think we can really finish him up pretty soon now, with the Americans the other end. It came as a great surprise to us, to know of this great landing. It was a marvellous feat. The French seem in a bit of a mess, what with those up here fighting with us, and those in Europe against us; I hope they soon realise that to be with us will be better for them. I would not mind betting that the Italians soon change their ideas — especially with the prospect of huge bombing raids.

The weather has changed somewhat now, and I expect you are feeling the full force of winter — thank goodness the Russian winter has set in at last, this will give the Germans a big headache! How is everything your way? I fancy you will be having a good do at Xmas, with all your variety of friends. I do hope you all have a good time; and that the conditions permit this. Perhaps you can induce Mother and Pop to spend a day or so with you. Perhaps it would be a good idea for you to get hold of my letters to them, now and again, as I try to vary everyone's as far as possible. Above all try and keep sending reading matter — I find the Argosy Magazine very good — even such things as True Romances go down well when in the mood

— by the way the crosswords are most acceptable. Love to you both.

Your loving brother, Boy

Wigglesworth was wounded in 1944 in Italy and sent back to England. After the war he emigrated to New Zealand where he married, settled down and ran beach stores and cabins. He died in 1995.

DECEMBER 1942

The war in Russia continues — Germans are trapped under siege in Stalingrad. The Russian Red Army overwhelm the Romanians, Germany's Allies.

CHRISTMAS AS A POW
George Sweetman

George Sweetman was born in Wiltshire in 1910 and was in the TA in 1939. He served as a Private in the Royal Wiltshire Yeomanry. This is an extract from Private Sweetman's diary. He was captured at El Alamein and wrote: '2nd Nov — went into action at dawn. B squadron first in. We shot up ATG lorries and tanks and then Jerries' main armoured force came and we lost. B Squadron lost all its tanks — we got wiped out and I was taken Prisoner of War.' Sweetman was transported via Athens and through the Corinth Canal on a journey which took 12 days. He was taken to M-Stammlager IVC in Germany. His diary for December reads:

251

1ˢᵗ December — Concert in the afternoon with band.

2ⁿᵈ — I received my first Red Cross parcel, it was very good.

3ʳᵈ — Just rambled round.

5ᵗʰ — Went to B . . . to get de-liced and took all blankets and clothes. Had hot bath. We were lucky we had a ride each way but many had to walk each way — nine or ten miles.

7ᵗʰ — Sing song in evening. No lights.

8ᵗʰ — Draw for Xmas card. I won and sent it home.

9ᵗʰ — Had a game of cards.

10ᵗʰ — Very cold wind.

11ᵗʰ — Spelling.

14ᵗʰ — Cup of ovaltine.

15ᵗʰ — Red Cross parcel. Concert.

16ᵗʰ — Talk in evening.

18ᵗʰ — Had first letter card and wrote home.

19ᵗʰ — Played Housey Housey.

20ᵗʰ — Won second round of draughts. Band concert in the afternoon.

22ⁿᵈ — Played Housey Housey in the evening. Only had three fags each.

23ʳᵈ — Went to bed early; fed up; no fag issue.

24ᵗʰ — Played basketball in the morning. The team never turned up so we were given the points. In the afternoon we played an Aussie team and lost 9 — 3. We had a neat meal in evening and had a concert in our hut. It was very good, finished up with a blind boxing match so that ended Xmas Eve — of course we missed the beer and food, just went to bed.

25th — We had tea in the morning and two or three biscuits out of our Red Cross parcel. Had a church service at 9 a.m. It was a lovely sunny morning. We had dinner just the same as any other day. The Red Cross Xmas parcel which we expected never turned up — a great disappointment. The Eyeties had a big surprise for us — an orange for each man. We had our hot meal at 4 p.m. just the same — no extra. We had a sing song etc in evening in our hut and so to bed, hungry and that was how we spent Christmas Day 1942. I thought of home and all the good food. That's all we think about here — food.

26th — Started to rain in the morning. Stayed in hut all day, food just the same; had Housey Housey in the afternoon; raining all day; had a talk in evening and so to bed.

29th — Went to concert in afternoon in Eyetie concert hall.

30th — Great excitement in camp. The Eyeties gave us 70 fags each — fags that they owed us. A talk in the evening on bull fighting in Spain.

31st — The Jocks in our hut gave us Scottish songs. Then we sang Auld Lang Syne and three cheers and end of 1942.

Private Sweetman remained in captivity until 1945. As the war ended he walked through Czechoslovakia before being picked up by a Dakota. After the war he married Doreen, working and living in Wiltshire until he died in 1997.

JANUARY 1943

In the Pacific the Japanese begin to retreat — Japanese forces on Guadalcanal are overrun; in New Guinea the Japanese are defeated and in Burma the British begin a counter-attack. At Casablanca Roosevelt and Churchill meet to discuss war strategy.

AFTER EL ALAMEIN
Harold Limer

Harold Limer was born in Jarrow, Durham in 1919. Having left School in 1936, in early 1940 he joined the Royal Corps of Signals. Selected for officer training he volunteered for the Royal Armoured Corps and went to Sandhurst OCTU from where in early 1941 he was commissioned and joined the 23rd Hussars. He was posted to the Middle East in 1942 and joined the 40th Royal Tank Regiment, fighting at Alam Halfa and El Alamein.

We joined 51st Highland Division in the several battles along the road to Tripoli, which we entered on 23rd January. During this advance against time, troop leaders had to take it in turn to lead along the road at night until contact was made — an onerous task and Bob Leon, in his first action with us in A squadron, was doing this when he was killed. What is now an amusing incident happened when I was waiting to move off in the moonlight, taking my turn to lead up the road. The leading tank (mine) carried no infantry but the two remaining tanks in the troop had a section of infantry mounted on them. I was waiting for them to arrive when, in the dark, a jeep came to a screeching halt about 50 yards away and an angry voice shouted, 'Who is in charge here and why the hell haven't you moved off?' I replied (we were all very weary from lack of sleep by this time) 'I am and I am waiting for the bloody infantry to arrive.' The jeep turned round and screamed off and the infantry arrived very shortly afterwards. Someone called out, 'Do you know who that was.' I replied, 'No.' Answer: It was General Wimblerley (Commander 51st Highland Division). I asked if he knew who had answered him and the reply was, 'No.' So I said 'Thank God for that!'

Harold Limer was wounded in April 1943 at Wadi Akarit. On return to his regiment he was promoted to Captain. He took part in the landings in Salerno in September 1943, was in Eygpt and Palestine in June 1944 and in Greece in October 1944 as the Germans withdrew. He remained with the regiment until it was disbanded in Salonika in June 1946, by which time he was a Major and remained in the army until 1959. He now lives in Hertfordshire.

FEBRUARY 1943

In North Africa Rommel is driven back across the border into Tunisia.

FULL OF INSOLENCE
Andrew Sewell

Andrew Sewell was born in 1921 and educated at Marlborough College in Wiltshire, leaving in the summer of 1939 to enter the Woolwich Royal Military Academy. He was posted to Larkhill and was commissioned into the Royal Artillery in February 1940. He was sent to join the Lanarkshire Yeomanry who were still horsed but were under orders to be re-equipped and he soon found himself out in Malaya equipped with 4½ inch Howitzers. The Japanese had deployed their elite Imperial Division to seize Malaya and the Lanarkshire Yeomanry suffered substantial casualties at Slim River. Here Sewell was promoted to Acting Captain to take over F Troop. Acting as a guide for an advance by the 3/16ᵗʰ Punjabis he was hit in both legs and had to withdraw. *In due course he was awarded the Military Cross. He was evacuated to Alexandra Hospital in Singapore which was attacked by the Japanese a few days before the general surrender. Taken prisoner, he went, with what was left of his regiment, to Taiwan where he became camp tailor.*

In February 1943 we were all ordered to work, I, of course, was already tailoring and was classed 'unfit' due to my legs. It was suggested that we might like to go down to the mine and make ourselves helpful clearing a space for recreation. Very shortly, this turned out to be helping in the extraction of copper from the water coming out of the mine. It ran down a kind of inclined wooden staircase filled with scrap iron. The copper rich water reacted to deposit the ore as a mud, which could then be refined. I rather enjoyed a day out seeing how this worked and collecting some odd bits of scrap, in particular a traditional crowncork opener!

However when we got back to the camp we examined the position rather more carefully with the benefit of the Manual of Military Law which one of us had brought with him. This made clear that the Geneva Convention allowed officer POWs to work, but not on tasks helping the enemy war-effort. Since the mine was virtually the only source of copper available to Japan our position was quite clear. So we downed tools and made our position clear to the Commandant. This resulted in all officers being shut up together in one hut without bedding or clothing other than that which we had on, until we showed repentance. Rather to the Japs' disappointment our soldiers, instead of being ashamed at our refusal to work, were more than pleased to do what they could by smuggling food through the lavatories and cheering us on. As our incarceration went on, it became a rather tricky question of how we got out of the situation. The Japs were in the same stew and tried to suggest ways of finding a solution using our Jap speaking officer, who continued to work in the camp admin. The idea that we would each write a letter setting out our views, and to an extent blaming the Geneva Convention, misfired. The Commandant arrived with an escort of armed guards and addressed us on the basis that our initial insult to the Emperor might have been rather school-boyish, but this new insult was too much. The rations were halved to three small rice balls a day and we were to keep silent and squat in the customary manner and at least in theory, woe betide anyone found not complying. Our one blanket was removed and we had to snuggle up on the straw platforms at night and be ready to stand to instantly, if a sentry came in during the night. At any rate the solution was to get hold of the Kempitai, the Japanese Army Police, to interview each of us about our backgrounds, where had we been to school etc — I gave the address of my long distant kindergarten. At any rate at last it was agreed that we would each write a letter judiciously saying we had not intended to insult the Emperor etc and we were finally let out after nearly three weeks. It was a real joy to be welcomed by all the soldiers in the camp who, much to the fury of the Japs, rallied round to get our bedding back in place and a supply of food. Indeed, I think this quite exceptional mutiny made our names and we were never really expected to work again outside the camp.

Sewell remained in captivity until August 1945 — it was only then that he could 'escape' as the Russian Army took over and made the Japanese Guards captives at last. He eventually made it back to England that September. After the war Sewell underwent surgery on his legs before returning to the Royal Artillery. He married and remained in the army, commanding his regiment before joining the civil service. He then worked as regional director for the Countryside Commission in the South West. He now lives in Aldbourne, Wiltshire and has one son, two daughters and five grandchildren.

MARCH 1943

The British step up their bombing campaign against the Ruhr.

A BOMBING MISSION
Alan Frank

Alan Donald Frank was born in Cheshire in 1917. He was educated at Eton and Magdalen College, Oxford where he learned to fly with the University Air Squadron and was commissioned into the Reserve of Air Force Officers. After war broke out he was posted to the advanced Air Striking Force in France. He married Jessica Ann Tyrrell in 1941 and was awarded a DFC that year. By the end of 1942 he was Flight Commander of a heavy bomber squadron. In early 1943 Frank is given command of No 51, a Halifax Squadron.

Yorkshire has some lovely scenery but No 51 Squadron has been planted at RAF Station Snaith which is situated in what should be

263

called the South Riding. It is flat country intersected by canals and usually covered in industrial haze. The scenery is not improved by the ominous shapes of Halifax bombers dispersed round the airfield. There is low cloud and drizzle, but at least our small prefabricated offices are easily warmed.

We are in a moonless period, when we should expect to be operating hard, but for the last two nights the weather has been too bad for flying. Tonight might possibly be better and I call on my three flight commanders to discuss how many aircraft and crews we can offer Bomber Command.

Charles Russell commands A Flight. Tall, slight, fair haired and gentle, he is a peace time entry. I know that he hates operational flying, but grits his teeth and carries on. Dinty Moor, who started life as a sergeant pilot, commands B Flight. Small, tough, a Jack Russell type, he is quite fearless and is apt to regard any training in flying by himself or his crews as a pointless and unnecessary chore. Since new crews arrive on the squadron with less than 200 hours flying, we tend to disagree on this. C Flight is commanded by Charlie Porter. Charlie, a navigator is, at 30, the oldest of the four of us. Small, square with a handle-bar moustache, he is completely laid back and seems to look upon our world war as a slightly humorous but minor inconvenience.

Of our 30 crews we can expect to lose perhaps 12 a month. The high replacement rate makes it extremely difficult to assess the new crews and almost impossible to break them in gently on the easier targets. After discussion we select the most experienced 22 crews available to man the serviceable aircraft on the assumption that the target will be Germany. Should it turn out to be Italy or occupied territory we will change the list to blood the new boys.

While thumbing through a new intelligence

summary, I hear the teleprinter start to tick. Pretending an indifference I am far from feeling, I stroll across to look at its output — Whitebait (which means Berlin) and Goodwood (which means maximum effort). Berlin is Germany's most heavily defended target, and with a churning feeling in the pit of my stomach I remember that squadron commanders are supposed to set an example. I ask the airmen on duty to tell my crew that we are flying tonight.

The Met Office is my next port of call. Clear skies are forecast over Berlin, but there is a vigorous frontal system approaching this country which looks likely to interfere with our operations. The timing is uncertain but my guess is that we are heading for that most frustrating of experiences — a late cancellation — this means all the tension of pre-flight nerves with nothing to show for it.

My crew consists of the bomb aimer — Flight Lieutenant Minchington — squadron bombing leader, quiet, competent and confident. It is he who, looking down through his Perspex transparency, has a perfect view of what is going on below and what is coming up from below. During the bombing run his voice never alters. My navigator is Toddy, alias Warrant Officer Todd. He's at least ten years older than the rest of us. He came into the RAF as a boy entrant and trained as an instrument fitter, converting to air crew shortly before the war. As for the other members of the crew, Vic Harris is the radio operator and Jona Jones the tail gunner (both sergeants) — both are quiet, pleasant characters, good at their job, calm in an emergency and never showing signs of the fear we all feel. The Flight Engineer, Sergeant McCann, is different. Mac is an excitable Scotsman who holds no particular grudge against the Germans but God help any fitter who skimps his work on his aircraft. Apart from the old man, Toddy I was, at 25, the oldest member of the crew.

Briefing at 4 p.m. for a 7 p.m. take off follows its normal course. But then I am summoned to the telephone. As ever it has all changed, but not by the cancellation we have expected. Take off time is put back to 1 a.m. The logic is obvious. We can take off in filthy weather and by the time we get back the fronts will have gone through and the weather will be fit for landing. I retire to bed with a book. Then a bang on my door, '11 p.m. Sir,' and with a sinking feeling in the pit of my stomach, I return to reality. Coffee and sandwiches in the mess and then out into a filthy night with cold rain belting down. I arrive in the crew room. Here is chaos as 22 crews — 154 men — sort out the paraphernalia which goes with the well-dressed airman. Miraculously everybody seems to find all their bits and pieces and crew by crew we disappear into the darkened buses to be ferried to our aircraft. F for Freddy is dispersed in one of the furthest corners of the airfield and we are the last to leave the bus. Mac and I follow the rest of the crew on board with minimum light to help our night vision. I put on my parachute harness, strap in, plug in the R/T and the oxygen and we are ready for the check list. One by one the four Rolls Royce Merlin engines splutter into life and settle down to a gentle rumble. Then we must check each at full power. With 2000 gallons of petrol and five tons of bombs F for Freddy is at maximum weight and our lives depend upon all four engines behaving on take off. Five minutes to take off. I wave a torch to signal 'chocks away' and follow two faint blue torches directing me out of dispersal. The hooded taxi-way lights are minimal at the best of times and in belting rain are the devil to see. We get to the runway and a green light allows us to line up for take off. And now comes the first nerve jangler. It is pitch dark, the countryside is blacked out and beyond the dim runway lights there is nothing.

Gently open the throttles, check all four engines, hold her on the brakes till she starts to move, brakes off — full throttle and painfully slowly with her heavy load she starts to accelerate — 80 knots, 85, 90 at the same moment the last of the runway lights disappear under the nose. Slowly both our speed and height increase till at 500 feet and 125 knots I can relax — the first hurdle is over and we swing east towards the North Sea and the Third Reich. The next hour or so we are controlled by the weather. Heavy icing is forecast in the frontal cloud so we are routed across the North Sea where we can fly below freezing level, then the forecast claims the weather will clear before we reach the Danish coast so that we can climb to operational height before meeting any defences. This means a long stint of instrument flying but the auto-pilot is for once working and so can take the strain. Crossing Denmark we pass into the Baltic and swing towards Berlin. Now we are in the thick of the fighter defences and bursts of horizontal tracer show that the Luftwaffe is active. Over to port an aircraft bursts into flames and descends seemingly amazingly slowly to earth. It is impossible to see the aircraft type nor whether any parachutes have emerged.

Suddenly straight ahead the darkness is transformed. A single search-light sweeps the sky, then another, then in virtually no time hundreds — the flak follows and the sky ahead is a continuous mass of flashes from bursting shells. Intelligence told us of 400 heavy AA guns in the city's defences, but that looks like an underestimate!

Then the flare droppers get to work and perhaps a hundred parachute flares hang in the night sky. The target markers will be dropped by radar but the master bomber will try to assess their accuracy visually. The target markers resemble clusters of brilliantly coloured chandeliers bursting a couple of thousand feet up and continuing to burn on the ground.

The first markers down are red. The master bomber now picks the most accurate and directs the back-up marker force to aim green markers at it, and that is our target. Finally comes the main force — some 2000 aircraft each carrying many tons of high explosives and sticks of incendiaries and the scene below passes belief. Continuous flashes mark the burst of high explosive and sticks of incendiaries draw incandescent streaks across the city where fires quickly appear to complete a picture which Dante could hardly have visualised.

By this time we are entering the Berlin defensive ring — about 80 miles across. So long as we are only subject to barrage fire, the best bet is to grit one's teeth and fly straight to get through as quickly as possible, but this time we are unlucky. A searchlight picks us out and almost at once we are at the dazzling centre of a cone with predicted flak coming up at us. Dropping 2,000 feet to keep clear of the incoming bomber stream, I turn through 180 degrees and fly north out of range of the defences. Then I swing south again to join the tail end of the attack and try again. This time we are luckier. A searchlight picks us up and we have only the barrage and the ever present danger of night fighters to cope with.

Fragments of bursting shell rattle against the fuselage and in the general tension I suddenly realise that my mouth is quite dry, but it is now as safe to go forward as back. As the inferno that is Berlin disappears under the nose, I tell Minch, lying on his stomach in the nose studying the scene below, to take over. With a voice of absolute calm I hear, 'About two minutes to run, Skipper, left, left, steady, steady — bomb doors open please — all bombs gone. Camera has operated — close bomb doors.' Now F for Freddy, less half her fuel load and five tons of bombs, feels positively skittish! 'Course for home please, Toddy,' and we swing westward. Ahead is the frontal cloud which caused us worries on the way out. Now it offers protection from the ever present fighter threat and I fly towards it. Once into cloud we can all relax except Toddy. From him I get the usual steady grumble about the unreliability of forecast winds, the lack of pin-points and the uselessness of the radio bearings but it does not stop me from opening the thermos and enjoying some indifferent coffee. However we are not home yet. Over the Zyder Zee we run out of cloud and this is a notorious area for night fighters. Everybody wakes up to peer into the darkness. Nothing is seen but suddenly Monica starts to emit a stream of excited squeaks (Monica is a device which warns us that we are being tracked by a night fighter radar). Reaction must be quick and I go into a corkscrew — a violent diving turn which spills the coffee and throws loose objects round the flight deck. An equally violent climbing turn to starboard presses us all into our seats. Thankfully Monica has relapsed into silence. We have shaken the fighter off.

Now comes the best moment of the flight. Minch tells us that we are crossing the Dutch coast and gives Toddy a pin-point. As usual Toddy's pessimism is proved to be unjustified

272

as we are only a few minutes off track. On reduced power the four Merlins produce only a gentle rumble as I push the nose down to get out of enemy radar cover as soon as possible. Dawn overtakes us as we cross the North Sea and it is a lovely spring morning. Ten miles out — the control tower clears us for a straight in approach. Wheels and flaps down, throttle back till the only sound is a gentle rumble. A great feeling of well-being spreads through the aircraft and, with the engines at low power, we slip towards the runway. I close the throttles and, with a squeal as the tyres meet the tarmac, our night's work is done. Once more the team has done it and we are thoroughly pleased with ourselves. The euphoria only lasts for a short time. I am told that nothing has been heard from two aircraft. They may have landed elsewhere but experience tells me that that is a vain hope. Statistically two losses are about what one might expect but these are people, not statistics, and I start to wonder about any failure of mine which could have caused their loss. But this only leads to intolerable worry so from long practice I bring down a steel curtain to shut out such thoughts. The two missing crews are fairly new to the squadron and I hardly knew them — but somebody did.

Frank was awarded a DSO in 1943 for his attacks on important targets in Germany and Italy. In the autumn of 1944 he moved to Bomber Command HQ. After the war he remained in the RAF serving at the Air Ministry and commanding the RAF's first Avro Vulcan nuclear deterrent V-Bomber Squadron. He was appointed CBE in 1962 and CB in 1967. He was senior Air Staff Officer at Air Support Command and was made Air Vice Marshal before retiring in 1970. He and his wife had two sons and two daughters. Sadly, Alan Frank died in 2001. Jessica Frank's account of waiting for the Bomber Squadron to come home in February 1941 is told on page 121.

APRIL 1943

Allied bombing raids continue against German cities with attacks on Frankfurt, Stuttgart, Mannheim and Stettin.

LETTERS TO MOTHER
Terence C Irvine, MC

Terence Carlyle Irvine was born in 1897 in West Hartlepool in Durham. He was educated at Wellington College but ran away to join the army when he was 16 and enlisted as a trooper in the 19th Hussars. He fought in the First World War, was awarded the MC and became a Captain in 1920. He retired from the army in 1921 and worked in the race-horse business. In 1940 Irvine was granted an emergency commission and joined the Military Police. In 1942, now a Lieutenant Colonel, he was appointed Deputy Provost Marshal (DPM) 9th Army in Syria and later was based at El Alamein as DPM on the Staff of General Montgomery.

8th April

Still plodding on, as you can see, we seem to be the only people who move and I am the person who moves more than anyone — traffic takes me here, there and everywhere and I am beginning to become weary. The fact that we are going the right way, however, helps and the country is at last getting a bit greener ... I am very busy dealing with the large proportion of the Italian Army which is at present giving itself up as no doubt your papers tell you. They are a poor lot and all lousy. I scratch every time I look at them. Our soldiers are ridiculous, as usual, and treat them as sort of pets. My desert wardrobe is becoming very dilapidated and I shall be quite pleased when we get to our destination. I am afraid no more goodies can be sent off by me — The Boche has not left much behind, you may be sure, and what he could not take, he destroys so that any more hampers for home must be cut out, I am afraid. Brian Robertson has been promoted to Major General and is in command of Tripolitania. I get on very well with my new branch head — Brigadier Miles Graham of the Life Guards, so I am lucky again. The police are very busy and take on more and more duties every day, making my responsibilities larger and larger with all its abundant worries. I use Tommy Sutherland as a sort of Secretary — ADC! He is a great scrounger and we do not live too badly.

Love T

18th April
Still on the move and getting nearer to our destination. I'm now very busy occupying French towns. The French people are giving us a tremendous reception and flowers and embraces are the order of the day — I think you will be seeing me in the pictures one day as I have been in charge of many shows of pomp and often am in attendance on Monty. I am in a house once more! Some very charming elderly people of a very good French family own it and do everything to make me comfortable, flowers all over the room, towels, sheets, soap and two eggs each morning for the 'Breakfast a L'Angletaire'. My French is improving and I get along quite well when people talk slowly, which they rarely do in spite of my requests to parle doucement! This country is very restful, lovely flowers everywhere, not too hot. French cooking

once more and plenty of fresh vegetables and salads . . .

Love T

A further letter by Irvine can be read in April 1945 on page 436.

MAY 1943

The Allies capture Tunis and Bizerta and the Axis troops are forced to surrender. Approximately 270,000 troops are taken prisoner.

TALKING WITH THE ENEMY
Valentine J Wrigley

Valentine Wrigley was born in 1915 and educated at Uppingham School and Queen's College, Oxford. In the spring of 1943 Wrigley was serving in North Africa as Section Sergeant of 52 Wireless Intelligence Section, Intelligence Corps, attached to the short-lived IX Corps and 1ˢᵗ Army. His task was to intercept, decode and identify enemy radio traffic.

11ᵗʰ May
We moved up to Grombalia. We didn't go into Tunis unfortunately, but joined the main road south from Tunis by an aerodrome which had some German aircraft damaged on

the ground still on it, and went through Hamman Lif, where there were a good many signs of fighting. From there on the road became an amazing sight, with three streams of traffic. On the far side was a stream of carts and conveyances of all kinds, carrying Arabs and other refugees and their families and laden high with household goods, back to Tunis. On the near side was our convoy, and in the middle was a constant crowded stream of Axis prisoners, hardly escorted, driving their own vehicles packed with their own men, down the road and into captivity. It was a remarkable scene, not to be forgotten; someone counted 164 vehicles in this convoy. They were of all types — officers in requisitioned French private cars, huge Italian lorries with trailers and German Schutzenpanzer. Everything was there. The Italians seemed happy and waved to us; the Germans were more sullen. The stream went on all day and through the night by moonlight, and for several days to come. How they were all fed and accommodated at all was a mystery. However, though the Axis supply system had broken down, big dumps, presumably including food, were captured.

We arrived at an olive grove just north of Grombalia, recently abandoned by German Signals, who had burnt their tents. No sooner had we settled here than we were amazed to hear shells whistling quite close and then coming closer still. A German battery in the hills had seen the convoy coming along the road and was trying to get the range. A bit of shrapnel landed near, so we ran from it and dispersed behind trees. We were reassured to see the Corps Commander, General Horrocks, a fellow Old Uppinghamian, sitting unconcernedly behind his tank. Some people got very panicky, but the shells did not last long and none were really close. I think the battery's ammunition failed and I believe they surrendered soon afterwards. Anyway, it was nasty to hear those shells whistling and to have no idea of their direction; also it seemed incongruous to get shelled at this stage when the battle was becoming a rout.

Soon we started work again and very interesting it was, as the enemy got more and more rattled and units gave themselves up. Some were ordered to fire their last rounds and to come over in their sections, which apparently they did. Others didn't bother with the last rounds or the sections! By now most groups were surrounded and there were very few gaps left by which any could escape to the coast, and we all began to feel a holiday spirit coming on us. In the evening we slipped up to the main road for a few minutes to watch the constant stream of prisoners. We felt like truant schoolboys. Some Eyeties who were quite pleasant, offered me cigarettes and wine.

As everywhere now, I slept in the open, under the canopy of the van. The day had quite staggered us, the work we did, the sight of all those prisoners driving past unescorted, the shelling — all created a feeling of amazement. Opposite us were some toughs of 8th Army who stopped nice vehicles that they saw, crowded the prisoners into other ones, and went off joy-riding in the ones they had pinched! Not very good behaviour, but they got some nice cars!

12th May

Work still went on, but at greatly reduced pressure. In the afternoon, I was able to get off for the first time for weeks and several of us walked into Grombalia, where we were able to fill several bottles of wine — our first in Tunisia. If we don't have more luck it may be our last! I had quite a chat with the proprietor. Most of the inhabitants had not got back: in any case they seemed to be Eyeties. We hoped to come back for more wine, but later our troops disgraced themselves by breaking into a wine cellar and getting drunk. After this the town was closed to troops and we got no more wine.

13th May

Defying the ban on Grombalia, I went in the back way to see the Prisoner of War camp. It was hardly a cage in the strict sense of the word, and one could easily talk with the prisoners. The Germans were at one end — the Eyeties at the other. I worked round the Germans and soon was in conversation with a typical blond Nazi. Soon a whole crowd of others gathered round, including a couple of fanatical Feldwebel (sergeants). This was rather unfortunate, as the others, bar the Nazi, didn't dare speak. Soon, too, Eyeties crowded round the back of me and I was the centre of a big circle! We went through the standard political arguments: I had a feeling that some of the rank and file agreed with me, but only the two Feldwebel and the young Nazi did the talking. It was like talking with fundamentalists. They trotted out many of the old arguments and it was amazing how they had excuses for each new Hitler aggression. I kept stressing the fact that it was curious that all the nations of Europe were against him. They tried the blood brotherhood business with me too, and said how different were the Arabs. I got in a good reply in asking why did they then make friends of the Arabs for political purposes to stir them up against us and the French. This they did find awkward! I also talked to an Eyetie schoolmaster in French. Then two British officers turned up and wondered what it was all about. The Intelligence Corps badge seemed to satisfy them, but as I was already late for tea, I left, after a most interesting afternoon.

A further account by Wrigley appears in May 1944 on page 346.

JUNE 1943

The Allies move forward from their base in Tunis capturing four Italian islands between Tunisia and Sicily: Pantelleria, Lampedusa, Linosa and Lampione.

A LETTER HOME
Louis Johnson

Louis Johnson was born in Stafford in 1920 and educated at King Edward VI School, Stafford but left early due to lack of money. He went to work in the office of Dorman's, a firm of engineers in Stafford. When war broke out he joined up and was in the RASC from 1942 serving in North Africa and then Italy.

To: Mrs F M Johnson
58 Grey Friars
Stafford
England

10678946 Cpl Johnson
W/S Platoon, 490 GT Coy, RASC
BRITISH NORTH AFRICA FORCES

All at home,

Yesterday while I was in the middle of writing an airgraph, a letter from Bill arrived, dated 18th June. He is neither right when he says we see no newspapers at all, nor when he suggests that we are in a position to give him the news about the war out here.

Of course there is no war out here today, only the aftermath and the preparation and the air attacks. The lorries move ceaselessly to and fro and most days a heavy dull roar heralds the passage overhead of massed formations of 'Flying Fortresses' and from this we know that Italy or what is left of her island possessions are in for another 'thunderbolt.' They made a fine sight, 100 at a time, in perfect formation.

But, apart from the rumours we hear and which we must not repeat, this is about all of the war that we get first-hand. When the

Tunisian campaign was being fought we heard nothing definite for days on end. You, thanks to the BBC, were kept immeasurably better informed.

This was partly due to our own movements and unsettled conditions generally which prevented us availing ourselves of the news facilities that do exist here for the troops.

These facilities largely centre around the British Forces newspaper 'The Union Jack' which comes out three times a week, to provide us with the latest news. For a field publication it is quite good. This we supplement with the French papers which, thanks to old 'Spot' Howard of Kes I am able to read. One of our fellows has a wireless set, which goes occasionally, and this is an additional help.

For the rest, rumour plays its part — rumour, incessant rumour that exists, rumour that is difficult to kill. At home the six o'clock news puts an end to the rumour of the afternoon. Here the rumours last indefinitely. At least six times we have heard that troops from England have invaded France. We have heard that Italy has capitulated, that Sicily is in our hands, that the Russians are on the move again.

The strange thing is that however many times the rumours are shown to be without foundation they still find plenty of adherents, especially if they are of the comforting variety.

That is the end of the news. It is now time for dinner.

Louis.

Demobbed in 1947, Johnson went back to work at Dorman's. Later he trained as a teacher and taught in South Birmingham until his retirement. Johnson died in Wolverhampton in 1996.

JULY 1943

The Battle of Kursk, the largest tank battle in history begins on 5th July with the Germans attacking the Kursk Salient — on the 5th day of battle the Allies launch their invasion of Sicily. Hitler is facing onslaught on two fronts — Sicily is taken by the Allies and the Russians hold on to Kursk.

THE INVASION OF SICILY
Ted Gumley

Ted Gumley was born in 1919. He served in the 6th Battalion, Seaforth Highlanders during the war and married his wife Kathleen during embarkation leave.

We left Port Said on 5th July and, once clear of land, were told our destination — Sicily. We were issued with a booklet — *Soldiers' Guide to Sicily* — detailing the customs and traditions of the Sicilians, places we should see if the Germans let us and any Italian

289

phrases we might need. I was at the Ops Room today and saw air photos and a model of the beach where we are to land and our fighting objectives. On the ship we had received instructions about our kit. We had to dump all photos, letters etc in case we were captured. We had to have a field dressing in our pockets, sun goggles, and wear our identity discs with our blood group. As well as our rifles and assault respirators we had to carry in our pack one spare set of clothes. Our greatcoats, shorts and one shirt were to be carried in transport which would land later. Midnight 9th July — only a few more hours to go; this is the worst time — waiting and wondering what lies ahead. I've just been up on deck; it is a lovely night. During the day I could see the outlines of the ships in our convoy steaming slowly along and I know that other convoys are also steaming towards Sicily. We've had a very quiet voyage; one enemy recce plane flew over but that was all.

Zero hour is 3 a.m. — 10th July. Having reached the shore we were told to prepare to disembark. I trudged down the gangway and then said impolite things about the landing craft and its crew — I could see water between the ship and the beach — and knew I'd get my feet wet. I stepped down and moved forward into water up to my shoulders. I plodded on and my sodden clothes and the weight of the equipment made the going worse; if there had been any deep holes, I doubt I could have surfaced again but we made it to the beach. We followed a path between white tapes which indicated it was clear of mines. Every now and again flares went up and we stood still till they died down. Progress was slow but we made our way inland and as daylight broke we reached a grove where we rested. We then started towards Cassibile and Syracuse. As we marched up the road an Italian plane came over, machine-gunning, probably aimed at troops still on the beach but I took no chances and dived into a ditch. When I stood up I noticed a dead Italian soldier lying in the ditch on the other side. There was sporadic machine-gun fire ahead but so far no heavy stuff. We captured Cassibile, stayed for a while then moved forward to take Casa Nuova. We carried on towards Syracuse until we reached woods and stopped for the night. Low flying enemy aircraft came over machine-gunning but we were well hidden and didn't seem to be the target. There were lots of tomatoes but nobody fancied picking any. The Italians and Germans had planted red-coloured antipersonnel bombs called red devils among the tomatoes so nobody was taking any chances.

Early the next morning we marched towards Augusta bypassing Syracuse which had been captured. There were early morning attacks by enemy aircraft but our planes were now in evidence and it began to show. We saw some terrific dog-fights and quite a few enemy planes coming down. One Italian baled out as his plane came down in flames. A German plane after righting itself twice finally nose-dived and thudded into the beach near Priolo scattering sand in all directions. That night we spent in Priolo.

The next day a group of Italian soldiers came in, hands in the air, only too glad to be captured and out of the war. They had no arms and we could do nothing about them so we directed them back down the road to base. One of them came out with the whining patter of the kind we were to get to know so well — 'Me Americano, born in Messina, fascista niente buono.'

We finally contacted the rest of the Battalion outside Augusta where a sniper was holding us up. High above the town we had a grandstand view of our naval ships firing shells into the town and sailing back out before the Germans could retaliate. With 2 RSF [Royal Scots Fusiliers] our Battalion captured Augusta but sustained quite a few casualties. We then carried on up the coast passing Villasmundo and dug in on the Lentini Plain. Our trench was in the middle of a field and although it was camouflaged I felt quite conspicuous. But the Germans didn't see us or were too busy looking after their own skins to worry about us.

One day a farmer near where we were camped reported that one of his labourers was an Italian soldier; he was brought in for questioning and, as he was coming in, he said to his escort, 'morte?' The escort had no idea what he meant but to be friendly agreed, 'Morte, yes, yes.' 'Morte' in Italian means death and the poor man was asking if he was going to be killed. However he was soon chased back to the farm. All Italians had to do a period of army service and the labourer had been a soldier at one time. It transpired that a British soldier had given him a pair of boots in exchange for cigarettes or vino or farm produce. The farmer had seen the boots and wanted them but the labourer refused and so he concocted the story.

We kept on moving forward until we reached Misterbianco where we stayed for the next few weeks. Monty sent us a message to say we were the cream of the 8th Army. Of course he had sent the same message to all the troops.

Ted Gumley had not seen his wife once in four years when war ended but their marriage survived and they have now been together for over 60 years. They have three children, seven grandchildren and three great-grandchildren and live in Perthshire, Scotland.

AUGUST 1943

The Germans evacuate Sicily and withdraw from Kharkov in Ukraine. The RAF launch a new campaign, the Battle of Berlin.

DYSENTERY, DISEASE AND DEATH
Charles C Weston

Weston who recounted his story in February and March 1942 starting on page 199, has now been a Japanese POW for 17 months. He writes in note form:

Rumours of another move. We are formed into new sections and companies. This time we are going by boat and arrive at an island, one of the Amboine group called Haroekoe. We learn that we are to build a runway. Dysentery breaks out on board. At Haroekoe there are huts but no bali bali [straw]. We sleep on the ground. Rain pours along the ground. We get soaked. There is no cookhouse. We get organised. Four cookhouse staff build a cookhouse but can only make pap. Mud is everywhere. On the second day we get soup. After three days we start work on the drome. What a sight — two hills of solid coral that we have to level. We work in two shifts — 750 men — 6 a.m. until 12 p.m. and 750 men — 12 p.m. until 6 p.m. Diarrhoea increases. Dysentery starts. Men going down right and left. After ten days, work at the drome is abandoned. Deaths several each day. The camp is split into two. One half a hospital, all men with dysentery and diarrhoea are taken in. The other half of the camp who are the fit men, work in the camp, grave digging, making lavatories, looking after the sick and generally cleaning up. Men begin to die like flies. The rainy season is on. Food is fair, pap for breakfast, rice and soup for dinner, vegetables are pretty good, and pork occasionally. After ten days work begins again. This time only 100 men available out of 2000. Natives are also working on the drome. Shop opens but only the fit can buy. Deaths are five to ten a day. The workers' food is good. Dysentery and beri-beri are still rife, about 1000 patients. Shop sells bananas, tobacco, other fruits and coconuts. Rain every day. Working party pushed up to 200. Camp more like a camp nowadays. Maize and kidney beans used for soup which is poor and indigestible. Shop now sells dried fish, biscuits and cigarettes, ketchup, peanuts, pineapples and occasionally papaya. We have boxed meat but very little fresh meat is available. We keep our pay for our food, make own tea and hot water is supplied. Then I get beri-beri which is a disease caused by deficiency of vitamins; it affects the nerves of the body and the tissues and usually begins in the ankles which become swollen and lose their sense of feelings. It may spread to other parts of the body and becomes dangerous if not treated in time. Death roll is now 250. I am moved into the beri-beri ward. Those who are sick but can walk have to collect stones to make a road around the camp. Rough bali gives me hell but despite swollen legs I hope for the best.

Weston died on 14th September 1943 aged 35, from beri-beri while a Prisoner of War in Japanese hands on the island of Haroekoe near Ambonia. After the war his body was exhumed and is now buried at Galala War Cemetery, Halahera Island, Dutch East Indies.

SEPTEMBER 1943

The Italians surrender and the Allies land on Italian soil.

THE ITALIAN ARMISTICE
Alexander H Smith

Alexander Smith was born in 1920 and was at St Andrews University until 1942 when he was commissioned into the Welch Regiment. He served with them as part of the 1st Army HQ in Sicily and Italy.

One of my outstanding memories of the Italian Campaign is the signing of the Italian Armistice at Cassibile South of Syracuse in Sicily on 3rd September. General Alexander had established his headquarters in an olive grove and as HQ Defence Company we were required to mount a Guard of Honour for Marshal Badoglio. The Italian appeared looking like a tramp in contrast to the smart Allied Officers and after the short signing they also appeared outside the marquee. The

Marshal and General Alexander each plucked a sprig of olive from one of the trees and the party then broke up.

Smith was serving with the 2nd Battalion Somerset Light Infantry when he was wounded in June 1944 in the advance on Florence and lost his left arm. After the war he worked as a lecturer in modern languages at the Dundee College of Education. He retired in 1981 and lives in Dundee.

ESCAPE FROM CAMPO PRIGIONERI DI GUERRA
Bob Walker Brown

Bob Walker Brown was born in Scotland in 1920. He was commissioned as a reserve officer in the Royal Engineers, was mobilised in August 1939 and was posted to Egypt in 1940. Transferring to the Highland Light Infantry in 1941 he joined the 2nd Battalion of that regiment at Tel-el-Kebir, Egypt before moving with the battalion to the Western Desert. Wounded and captured by the Germans at the Battle of the 'Cauldron' in June 1942, he was taken to Naples on the Italian hospital ship, Viriglio. Before embarking the wounded the Viriglio had in full Red

Cross markings spent two hours unloading ammunition. Arriving at a military hospital at Caserta, Walker Brown was then sent to a Prisoner of War hospital at Lucca where his wound was at last treated. Many wounded British prisoners died there, the same parish coffin always being used, sometimes being placed in view of the dying prisoner; this was the standard treatment of the local poor by the nuns who ran the hospital and no unkindness was intended. After three months Walker Brown was sent to a prison camp.

Disappointed by the discovery of three attempts to start tunnels in early 1943, a number of obstacles to success had been identified. Camp PG21 was a typical Italian Army barracks; that is, several accommodation and administrative blocks surrounded by an 18 foot high wall for the benefit of the less enthusiastic Italian soldiery. For our benefit wall-mounted sentries, searchlights, wire on both sides of the perimeter wall and trip wires had been added. The barrack blocks were single-level affairs with a floor of about 18 inches of concrete, topped by tiles . . .

The barrack blocks were surrounded by flagstone and cement paving. It had been spotted that one flagstone, facing the perimeter wall, close to lavatory and ablution windows, had a small central depression. Under a covering of dust a small lifting ring revealed itself. Cautious investigation indicated that we had found the lid of a storm drain sump giving access to a brick chamber about four foot deep and about 15 inches square. It was out of the line of sight of the two nearest wall sentries but was close to the perimeter track that was patrolled frequently by armed Carabinieri. This seemed a promising site; plans were made to begin work using the top of a fig tree, just visible above the perimeter wall, as an aiming point.

Eventually after four months and in early September, our measuring string indicated 140 feet. The large volume of spoil was first packed into the 'hollow' walls of the ablutions, a risky operation and later, into a very active smelly sewer found just above the shaft. The construction of the break-out chamber, from a depth of seven feet, was the most difficult operation of all. The soil became drier and drier, as we were near the fig tree, and threatened to collapse from the top. A risk was taken; a complete bunk was stripped and the four posts were dragged up the tunnel to support a sort of canopy with a central hole. Through the hole soil was scraped by hand; the height of the canopy was slowly raised by a system of wedges and a lever, all from the bunk. At last, by pushing up a home-made periscope, we realised that we had made it; but at the same time we prayed for no observant eyes.

Preparations now went ahead for escape proper. Rations and escape aids were stored below. We suspected, but did not know if, the Italians patrolled outside the perimeter wall. The break-out point was visible by day to at least one of the wall sentries.

Events in Italy were now very difficult to assess from inside the camp as we had no source of news. However we could hear the sound of moving columns of transport and tracked vehicles on the main road just outside the camp. We knew that the Allies had landed in Italy, but had no knowledge of the battle situation. In view of the nervous behaviour of the Italian camp staff it was decided to wait for a short period; an additional reason was that the Senior British Officer (SBO) refused permission for escape attempts. Two or three days later, after hearing rifle shots during the night, we awoke to find that the camp had been taken over by a company of German parachutists who presented a very different picture to the low-category Italians. The German company commander ordered an assembly for the evacuation of the camp. Although the SBO refused to rescind his ban on escaping we decided that it was time to go.

As the prisoners formed up we went below, the lid of the tunnel being sealed by a few of our companions who, at the last moment decided not to use the tunnel. The break-out was somewhat of an anti-climax; after waiting underground for several hours we assumed that the camp was empty, and made a trouble-free break out at night. I, with two companions, moving only at night, headed along a long spine of hills some ten miles from the Adriatic. German patrols had to be avoided while fording some of the wide, fast-flowing rivers; of Germans in strength, however, there was no sign. We lived on figs and peaches which also kept us on the run!

After walking for ten days the sound of gunfire could be heard which became louder and louder. Eventually, armour was seen on a crest at first light. As we pondered if it was friend or foe we were surprised and captured by a section of German infantry, complete with machine gun and an ammunition-smothered mule. The section commander was suspicious, as well he might be, and ordered us to dig a slit trench while mounting the machine gun facing us. Unpleasant thoughts crossed our minds. However, luckily we all came under fire and the Germans departed — in very good order. Waiting, very uncomfortable for the tide of battle to pass us, we at last met the leading companies of a battalion of the Northamptonshire Regiment who were equally suspicious of us.

Arriving at Naples Walker Brown hoped to rejoin the 2nd Battalion Highland Light Infantry then in the line in Italy. Instead he and his two escape companions were ordered to make their way back to the UK. From Naples they travelled to Tunis by a US Navy landing craft then by rail to Algiers where a departing troopship was found and finally to Southampton in November 1943. Walker Brown's account of an SAS mission to France is told in July 1944 on page 366 and SAS Operation Galia in December 1944 on page 401.

OCTOBER 1943

The Allies are advancing up through Italy. In Yugoslavia Churchill has decided to give further consideration to the whole question of the British relationship with the resistance and arranged for new missions to be sent out. In April 1941 Germany had attacked and occupied Yugoslavia. The King and Government had fled to London and Hitler had divided the country amongst his allies. Croatia was handed over to Ante Pavelic; a puppet government was established in Serbia under General Nedic. However it was in Serbia that a group of officers, peasants and farmers had banded together and taken to the woods. Under a Yugoslav Army Staff Officer, Draza Mihailovic they were known as the Cetniks and were hoping to restore Yugoslavia under the leadership of Serbia. Meanwhile the Communist Party had appointed Tito as leader. He was also calling for Serbs to revolt and many, mainly peasants, intellectuals and workers joined him. This group called themselves the Partisans and their aim was to help the Soviet Union in their war against Germany. Churchill had already sent Bill Deakin to Yugoslavia to report back on Tito and the Partisans. Henniker-Major gives us an account of the mission he undertook.

TITO, THE PARTISANS AND WORKING WITH FITZROY MacLEAN
John Henniker-Major (Lord Henniker)

John Patrick Edward Chandos Henniker-Major was born in 1916. He was educated at Stowe and Trinity College, Cambridge. He served as a Major in the Rifle Brigade in the Western Desert before being deployed on a military mission to Yugoslavia.

The Military Secretary at British Headquarters told me that Brigadier Fitzroy MacLean wanted me to go with his mission to Yugoslavia. As he later put it, he thought my 'combination of military and diplomatic training should be very useful for our kind of job.' . . . Our brief, in Winston Churchill's inimitable style, was brief and clear: find out whether Partisan or Cetnik was the best resistance group to support; find out Tito's

agenda; endeavour to mediate between Tito and Mihailovic; gain Tito's support for the return of the King; supply resistance groups; co-ordinate resistance operations with our own in Italy; evacuate the wounded.

We were trained near Alexandria with many other SOE men who would be dropped elsewhere. Parachute training consisted of jumping off fast-moving trucks in the desert. As a preparation it actually did no good at all. If one was not crippled in this process, one was fit to go on a jump with a parachute. I was additionally handicapped by being told that I was to jump with a heavy piece of equipment; a beacon to attract other planes, from which on pain of death I was not to be parted. After other necessary training I climbed into an RAF Halifax at Bizerta. We flew in two planes to Bosnia, our heads filled with lurid stories about the fate of trainees before us, such as George Jellicoe, an old Cambridge friend, whose parachute had failed to open and who was dragged along behind the plane until he could be winched back inside . . .

Fitzroy MacLean and Major Vivian Street — a soldier who had been assigned by Winston as the mission's chief military adviser — went in the first plane with Colonel Peter Moore, a senior Sapper. They, at once, found the dropping ground properly marked by the Partisans, but we missed it. Our crew were Australians at the end of their tour, and were thoroughly cheesed off. After several hours flying across Bosnia and Serbia, the pilot realised we had missed the target, decided we were over Bulgaria and returned to Tunis. We tried again the next night and dropped successfully. My vital beacon, assiduously protected, turned out to be quite useless as no aircraft ever carried the counterpart equipment . . . We were found at once and there were several people who could speak German and a few words of English. The Partisans were recognisable as soldiers in serviceable uniforms and in familiar units; men and women together, for there was absolute equality in the army. We were whisked away to a small cottage with a spotless bedroom, large bed and a comfortable duvet and were given good food. Our baggage was collected and put onto an ox cart. Next morning we set off for Jajce. I had been told by Fitz that I was to be his number two and chief political adviser; I was in fact a sort of general bottle washer and foreign affairs adviser and became the bread and honey gatherer. Fitz like me was an amateur and was in need of someone who was militarily more impressive. Thus he picked Vivian Street, like me also from the Rifle Brigade, to be his actual second in command. In Jajce Fitzroy and Vivian, who had landed before us, had their first talk with Tito and were busy reporting to Cairo and London.

Our first task was to discover which of the resistance movements was fighting and killing the most Germans. This was really the sole criterion on which the Government in the person of Churchill, would decide which group to back and of course we could only report about the Partisans. We were deeply suspicious of most of the stories we had heard. At the first meeting, Tito gave a good and full account of the actions in which his troops had been engaged, but this obviously required direct observation by our mission.

As for Tito himself, there were many extraordinary stories about him, for he was always a very secretive figure. Some including Evelyn Waugh, who was later a member of our mission, insisted that he was a woman; others that he was of any possible and many impossible nationalities and backgrounds. Fitz's impression of Tito, which we confirmed, was very favourable. He was clear and decisive and unlike so few Communist leaders, gave an impression of having an open mind and of being prepared to discuss any subject with an appearance of spontaneity and frankness. He was able to talk to Fitzroy in Russian or to me in German.

We had to seek to persuade Tito to co-operate and make common cause with Mihailovic. Tito said that when he had gone into the woods he had been prepared to agree to serve under Mihailovic. This proposal had been rejected. Since then relations were further soured by a lack of co-operation and of trust, or even of information, as well as of frankness and what the Partisans saw as untrustworthiness and betrayal by the Cetniks. For the present Tito was not sure his followers would now agree to co-operate.

The main help we could offer the Partisans was in supply drops. If there was a wind during a drop the supplies could drift a long way. We were given gold coins as currency to buy the pack horses and any other supplies that we needed. Of much greater interest to the Partisans was the parachute silk which replaced non-existent material for clothes. Small red parachutes brought our personal mail and any other excitement. The main assistance the Partisans could afford the Allies was in distracting the Germans and Italians. The Partisans managed to keep 20 German divisions occupied in Yugoslavia; such was the size of the country and the nature of the resistance. We were charged with co-ordinating Partisan operations with our own in Italy. I tended to seek RAF help to attack small specific targets, such as a train in a station. The RAF would appear with one bomb strapped on to the plane, and they quickly learned and invariably managed to take the target out cleanly. On one occasion, before the liberation of Belgrade, I asked inadvertently for American support in Leskovac. The response from a friendly American General, Ira Eacker, was too large, less targeted, and would and did result in a quite unnecessary overkill. I was expecting one plane; they sent over 20 planes. They bombed Leskovac on market day. I had hoped that they would bomb the factories. In fact they bombed everything but the factories. It perhaps counts as my war crime.

The most important single function was perhaps the evacuation of wounded Partisans to Egypt or to Italy. Mobility was the key to guerrilla war, and Partisans could thus never carry a large, or indeed any baggage train. In the nature of things many people were wounded and could only be moved in great discomfort in bullock carts, with an almost complete lack of medicine. Most operations which were necessary were done with a swig of Slivovic. If captured by the Germans, the wounded were likely to be shot and the Partisans did the same to the Germans unless they were important enough to be exchanged. British officers were strictly instructed not on any account to have anything to do with prisoners taken by the Partisans nor to benefit from any intelligence they might bring, in case this might appear to condone the gruesome practice. In fact the RAF did marvellous work in evacuating many hundreds of wounded and this gave a great boost to Partisan morale . . .

Having completed our first contact in Jajce the next task was to see as much of the fighting as we could. Fitzroy decided that he and I should go to the Dalmatian coast and islands to arrange for supplies to be brought in by sea, as the retreating Italians had left a gap on the coast. On our way down to the coast, we met Bill Deakin returning in a farm cart from Split, where he had witnessed the handing over by the Italians of a very considerable accretion of arms to the Partisans. Their acquisition alone transformed the ability of the Partisans to wage war. In a crowded Split, with the Italians anxious to go and the Partisans anxious that they did, Deakin and Popovic (the first commander of the Partisans) took the Italian surrender. Deakin gave graphic accounts of the operations in which he had been involved with the Partisans and of their breaking their way out of Montenegro to Bosnia. It had been a very severe undertaking. It was the first time I had really spoken to Deakin, and from that moment we became close and trusting friends . . .

Fitzroy and I moved on along the coast to Baskovoda. From there we took part in the first liberation celebrations in Korcula. Over 50 years later I still have the hangover. We were taken from village to village, and in every village were offered a tot of the local brew to toast every good cause. We were very impressed at the first village by a guard of honour who was a model Partisan. He was a dramatic character with a thick, black moustache, riding a beautiful black horse, who drew a sword to salute us and shook our hands. We were even more impressed when a similar figure repeated the ceremony at the next village, though neither he nor the horse looked quite as mettlesome as those at the first village. It was a process that was repeated at every village, but each time the man and horse that greeted us looked wearier and wearier. Then the truth dawned on us, through the haze of the local plum brandy: we were welcomed to every village without a flicker of recognition, by the same man who was galloping ahead of us. I wondered many times whether he had survived the war. He had. Forty years later when I appeared on Fitz's *This is Your Life* the horseman had been discovered, living in Dubrovnik; his name was Malina Ante.

When a German flying boat bombed the harbour, and with Germans returning along the coast road and the Peljesac peninsula, we decided that, with telegrams arriving from the Commander in Chief and Churchill, it was time to return to Jajce and arrange for the dispatch of the first Partisan mission to the Allies. The Partisans had captured a small German aircraft which was to be used to take the party out. The Yugoslav party, Deakin and several British officers had come down from Jajce overnight and were on the landing strip at Glamoc. When the aircraft arrived and was, with engines running, about to take off again, Deakin and some others looked up, saw a small German aircraft fly over, and a bomb bouncing towards them. It did no harm to the first person out of the plane, Tony Hunter, but as it bounced on it blew up and killed Robin Wetherley and Donald Knight, an engineer. Deakin was so small that the blast went over his head and did him no harm and did the same to his wireless operator who was even smaller. The bomb also killed Lolo Ribar, an outstanding young communist and a close confidante of Tito. His death was probably the worst blow to the future of Yugoslavia, for he was unique, on account of his age and intelligence, in the Communist Party, and the gap he left was never adequately filled. The bomb also severely wounded the other partisan, Miloje Milojevic, a heavily decorated soldier. The party withdrew, and some days later the rest of the mission were picked up by the RAF and Fitzroy landed safely in Italy.

It was subsequently suggested that the betrayal of the plane's movements to the Germans was the work of the plane's Partisan wireless operator who was also killed by the bomb after he had passed a message to the German headquarters at Banja Luka.

Churchill subsequently decided to aid Tito and the Partisans, rather than Mihailovic and Henniker-Major was involved in putting this decision into effect in the spring of 1944. He remained in Yugoslavia until the end of the war. From 1946 to 1948 Henniker-Major was Private Secretary to the Foreign Secretary Ernest Bevin and from 1966 to 68 he was Assistant Under Secretary in the Foreign Office. At present Lord Henniker, who is married to his second wife Julia and has three children, presides over the running of the Thornham Estate in Suffolk.

NOVEMBER 1943

Roosevelt, Churchill and Stalin meet in Teheran for a conference.

LIFE IN ALBANIA
Fulvia Gent

Born in Gorizia, on the Slovenian border of Italy in 1927 and raised in Palermo, Sicily where her father was a bank manager, Fulvia Liliana Schiff Gent, of Jewish origin, spent the war years with her family in Albania to escape the Fascist Race Laws of her native country.

On the 8th September, 1943, Italy, under General Badoglio, had signed the armistice with the Allies, against the Germans' will. We were treated much worse both by our ex-Allies and the Albanians. No warning was given to the commanders in different areas of the war; the Italian troops in Albania and Greece found themselves in the middle of a foreign country surrounded by hostile

318

ex-Allies and occupied ex-friends. No orders were issued by Badoglio and several divisions of the Italian armies found themselves in a dreadful situation. Some surrendered to the Germans; some fought and were decimated by the Germans. Mussolini had been imprisoned and Fascism in Italy was declared finished. Badoglio appeared to be the saviour of Italy, many think that he caused much more bloodshed and destruction in our country. The carnage of our troops by the Germans continued and the Julia Division, the elite of Italian alpine troops, was decimated and treated as labour workers.

After the armistice there began an even more fearsome period in our lives and each day was worse than the previous. There was no food available for us, the bombing increased, there were more attacks on Italian nationals and there were more executions in Tirana's market square. Death became a way of life and we were not shocked by the continual violence around us. We were young, my sisters and my brother, and we did not fully appreciate what was happening. We used to go roller skating in a building which had been a Fascist ministry and was now abandoned; it had gorgeous marble floors and they were an ideal skating surface. Most days we went in the afternoons to play there.

One afternoon I thought I could see more people coming and going around the area and I said to my sisters and brother that we better go home earlier; I set off for what was only about five minutes' walk from the building. Luciana and Sergio said that they would follow after trying a new pattern they had learned on their skates. I had hardly reached the building when I heard the sound of shooting; I ran to the window (we were on the fourth floor) to see if my sister and brother had followed me, I could only see a great deal of armed men swarming all over the area and there appeared to be two different bands as they were exchanging fire; I found out later that a group of Communist Partisans had infiltrated the German lines and they had been attacked by pro-German Partisans. I was trembling and I was told off by my mother for not waiting for the others. While I watched I saw a young man dressed in a light-coloured jacket running towards our building, being pursued by a German on a sidecar. He was getting near when suddenly the German aimed his machine gun at the retreating man and I heard the rat-tat-tat of the gun. A red pattern appeared on his whitish jacket. He kept on running and he seemed to reach the entrance of the flats. By this time there appeared several armed men and many soldiers. There was a great commotion as they entered the building in search of the injured man; every apartment was searched and when a door was not answered it was smashed down. All the men found on the premises were collected and put in the courtyard. By the time they reached our door my mother had become hysterical but they searched in vain. The man was not found; he had disappeared as if by magic. Unfortunately, the troops and their followers were incensed and lined up all the Italian men in the courtyard, threatening to execute them in reprisal. All the women were crying and begging the soldiers to release the men; we were very sure that this was the end. Suddenly a group of German officers burst on the scene and I recognised an officer who was stationed near our home and to whom I had spoken twice in French. He came from Alsace-Lorraine and was not very much in agreement with Nazi ideas. Anyway, he was our saviour because he gave orders to release the hostages and leave us alone. We could not believe our good fortune and thanked him and his men for saving us. We never found out what happened to the injured Partisan; somebody in our building must have given shelter somewhere where nobody could find him. I hope he survived but the person that hid him endangered the lives of nearly 100 people. Thank God he was not found!

The morning after this I went to do the usual shopping in the market square; it was covered with bodies lined out in rows. The red [Communist] Partisans had all been taken and killed and their bodies were left for everybody to see so that they would understand not to defy the Germans; there must have been at least 100 men stretched out on the pavements and square. After all these episodes my father and mother decided to book a passage on the next ship to Italy. We were due to leave on the 14th November, 1943 and we sold all our possessions and obtained some gold currency, the only thing that would be worth something anywhere and was easy to carry. We were all ready when the wife of my father's cashier was taken ill with nerves; her condition was bad and my parents decided to let them go in our place and wait for the next sailing. The ship was within reach of the Italian coast when it was sunk by British submarines; my father's cashier was one of only three survivors who swam to the shore. Once again we had cheated death and lived to fight another day. I can only remember that we could not go on another boat because all sea crossings were stopped after this disaster and we had to resign ourselves to remaining in Tirana indefinitely.

Things became worse all the time and food was in even shorter supply. We were treated very badly both by the Germans and the Albanians. We had to use our wits to survive and I, being the eldest, had to do all kinds of crafty and dishonest things to help us. My father was the bank manager at the Banco di Napoli and he did not know that his eldest daughter was at the Ministry of Supplies (a few doors up the street) claiming to be a refugee from Koritza and asking for food coupons and obtaining them. I do not know to this day how I managed to convince them that I was Albanian and from Koritza!

Fulvia Gent continues her story in January 1944 on page 331.

DECEMBER 1943

The German battleship, *Scharnhorst* is sunk off the North Cape.

WELCOME TO THE FRONT
Michael Bereznicki

Michael Bereznicki whose story was told in September 1942 on page 237 continues his story. Having been trained in Tashkent in Uzbekhstan for six months, his Polish regiment was transferred, on Stalin's orders, to the British Army to make use of better training facilities and equipment. It became the 7th Polish Artillery Regiment operating under the British 8th Army and in late 1943 Bereznicki found himself in Italy.

I had arrived at the front in the autumn. I felt relieved to be back amongst old friends again. The regimental commander assigned me to supply and service duties. My job was to transport food, fuel, coffee and tools to the front line troops. This was more dangerous than it initially sounded. The Germans were only about 200 metres away from our front line troops and could very easily see us coming. They were always higher up, in the mountains, looking down at us.

About the beginning of December our supply column was driving up a hill, when a German gunner decided to open fire. One shell landed to my right, and another to my left. My windshield broke from the shower of rocks sprayed up by the explosions. I pushed the accelerator to the floor, but my truck was heavily loaded and barely crawled up a very steep incline. A third round whistled over my head and another volley of rocks pelted my canopy. Fortunately, I climbed over the hill and disappeared from the gunner's line of fire.

One night, I was driving through the mountains on my way to resupply the troops. I hated driving at night. I was under strict orders to keep my head lights off, so that the enemy couldn't see me or any of the other vehicles in our column. Not being able to see made me nervous. There were about 20 to 30 trucks in our formation and I was somewhere in the middle. Suddenly there was an explosion. A lorry three or four ahead of mine blew straight up into the air and then went tumbling into a ravine. The entire column halted. I asked one of the soldiers walking past, 'What happened?'

'Oh, nothing much. He just hit an anti-tank mine, that's all,' said the soldier.

'Are there any more mines ahead?' I asked nervously.

'Well, we've got a bunch of engineers further up the road trying to find out if there are any left.' The entire formation waited until the mine-clearing unit gave us the thumbs up, and we continued our trip. But as I drove along, I couldn't help thinking about how lucky I was. While the line-up of trucks remained motionless, it could have been an easy target for some German gunner. The easiest target is a stationary one. I thought the mine explosion would have attracted enemy attention but somehow it didn't.

Another night, I had to cross a bridge. There were two vehicles ahead of mine and both were already on the bridge, while I was just about to drive onto it. I heard the sound of metal grinding on metal. I hit the brakes. The noise grew louder, until I heard a loud crash. The entire structure collapsed. I stared in disbelief at a large, black chasm which had just swallowed up two of our trucks. Behind me I could hear loud honking and people yelling at me to get going. Obviously, they did not know what had just happened. I got mad and stuck my head out the window and shouted, 'Forget it. The bridge just collapsed.' The honking stopped and we had to find an alternate route back to the supply depot.

Bereznicki's account: The End of War in Italy appears in May 1945 on page 451.

JANUARY 1944

Leningrad is liberated. Allied forces land at Anzio, Italy.

ESCAPING WHILE WOUNDED
William Renwick

William Renwick was born in 1913 in West Lothian, Scotland. He was the ninth of ten children. When war broke out he became a guardsman in the 1ˢᵗ Battalion, Scots Guards.

In the first few days of 1944 we sailed from North Africa for Italy. I was in the advance party that landed in Sicily but the fighting was over. So the Battalion sailed to the Italian mainland; we went up and down the coast for three days landing each night at a different place, including a few hours on Capri. We finally landed at Anzio on 22ⁿᵈ January but still we saw no fighting, no sign of Germans anywhere.

We engaged in training exercises around Pompeii, Mount Vesuvius and Monte Cassino.

After that we did engage in heavy fighting in a mopping up exercise. The fighting was heavy and we were under so much pressure that it was only relieved by calling in a small detachment of five tanks. We were unable to call on any reinforcements.

During this fighting we ran into a very heavy mist. To help guide our positions the officer called for smoke — in misty weather! Instead high explosives were used so that we could follow the sound but in doing so we ran straight into a German position.

Then I was shot in the leg. My shinbone was shattered from the ankle to the knee. Along with the other wounded I was taken prisoner by the Germans but because I was unable to walk I was directed to make my own way to a small hut some way off. It took me more than four hours to crawl there.

Once there, a German sergeant used my own field dressing to dress the wound. There was also an officer and three young German soldiers who looked no older than about 17 who spoke excellent English. I was given wine, a cigarette and two oranges.

During darkness the British started shelling and the Germans disappeared into a dugout. This was my chance; I crawled away and kept going all night. I continued to crawl for three nights, resting during the day without food or water. On the fourth day I was in an olive grove when I spotted an English soldier and he alerted a medical team. I was treated by a doctor from Glasgow and stretchered to a first aid post. I was then shipped back to a hospital in Sicily. There I was cared for by a Nurse McLeod whose cousin had been my number two Bren gunner at Anzio. After several days I was due to be airlifted to Algiers but the last available place on the plane went to someone else. That plane crashed without any survivors. Instead I was sent by the next plane. Because of my condition I was shipped back to England and ended up in hospital in Bradford.

After his recovery Renwick was posted to Glencorse barracks near Edinburgh and married in June 1944. He rejoined his battalion later that year and spent the remainder of the war guarding Buckingham Palace, Downing Street and other public buildings. After the war he returned to work for the Midlothian County Council Roads Department. He had two children, a son and a daughter. Renwick lived in Renfrewshire with his son and family for the last three years of his life. Sadly he died in November 2001.

BACK TO ITALY
Fulvia Gent

Fulvia Gent continues her story told in November 1943 on page 318.

Time passed and, at last in January 1944 we were repatriated by the Germans. We left Tirana by truck one cold morning and the last sight of the square in Tirana will forever be in my memory: the last thing I saw was the body of a young Albanian Partisan hanging by his neck in the main square of Tirana. I remember his face, his blackened tongue hanging out of his mouth and the white shroud in which he was enveloped.

It was a very strenuous and hazardous journey; it lasted for two full weeks. We started the journey by lorry with three German guards. On reaching the border between Albania and Yugoslavia we met with thousands of Italian troops who had been taken prisoner by the Germans after the signing of the armistice. The majority were members of the crack Julia division of Alpine troops. They were in a pitiful condition both mentally and physically. They were clearing the snow in sub-zero temperatures and they were begging for bread. We managed to throw them some which often landed in the snow and slush but they retrieved it and ate it ravenously. They shouted messages, but we were not allowed to stop. One of the guards must have felt some compassion because he threw some cigarettes and food. We continued our journey on a long train which we shared with hundreds of soldiers going to Budapest. They travelled in the carriages but we had to manage in the animal trucks. We were very crowded and only had straw to sleep on. It was a very cold winter as we travelled through the barren areas of Montenegro, to Hungary, Austria and eventually finishing our journey in Venice on the morning of 19th January 1944.

Fulvia Gent met and fell in love with an English soldier towards the end of the war. Married in Manchester in 1946 she became the mother of six children, theatrical landlady and passionate supporter of Manchester City. She still lives in Manchester.

FEBRUARY 1944

The Allies bomb the Monte Cassino Monastery but the Germans hold on to it.

AN EPISODE IN ITALY
Allan Seggie

Allan Paul Seggie was born in Scotland in 1923. He was an apprentice grocer before joining the army in Derbyshire in February 1942. After training with 10 MAC, RASC he went to North Africa on Operation Torch in January 1943. Having spent a spell in hospital at the end of the Desert Campaign, Seggie landed in Taranto in 1943 having joined 134 Coy Armoured Brigade, RASC and served as a motor-cyclist in Italy.

We were allocated a task to collect an Indian Mule Pack Company in the Appenines, being given a map reference to rendezvous with the Indians. As was usual we, our Officer, MT Sergeant and myself as convoy rider, studied the map. We worked out that about three miles after crossing a Bailey Bridge, we would leave the main road, as 'main' as any road was in that area, and proceed up a country track to the left. I made my way through the convoy after seeing it over the Bailey Bridge. Very soon it was obvious to me that the Convoy Commander had turned off the road too soon. The Sergeant who was at the rear, as usual, agreed with me. I transferred to the back of the bike and we shot up the convoy as quickly as possible. I tried, to persuade the Commander to turn back, to no avail. Very soon things didn't feel right. It was very quiet and shell and mortar holes seemed suspiciously new. Then a scout car with a driver and officer from the RWK (Royal West Kents) came shooting up and stopped the 15cwt with the Convoy Commander. The officer jumped out and yelled, 'What the hell are you doing up here.' Our bloke said, 'We're looking for an Indian Mule Pack Company.' 'You'll get no mules here. Do you see that white house?' It was about a quarter of a mile ahead. 'That's a German Observation Post and we've been crawling on our stomachs, frightened to raise our heads, for the last fortnight.' By this time his driver had turned the scout car and our officer said 'God, what'll I do now.' The RWK bloke said, 'I don't know what you're going to do but I'm getting out of it,' jumped into the car and shot off. Now, the track was too narrow to turn a three tonner but that day 30 were turned as if they were on a huge airfield. We made it back to the main road safely, Jerry never fired a shot at us. He probably thought we were deliberately causing a diversion in the hope he'd give away the positions of his artillery batteries. Incidentally we got the Mule Company, crossed the Appenines via some hairy passes and delivered them to the American 5th Army who were in desperate need of them to supply their troops in the mountains around Cassino. The yanks were so pleased they gave our Company a special commendation — but we didn't tell them about getting lost.

Seggie continued to serve as a motor-cyclist until his Company reached Trieste in 1945. In 1946 his unit was sent to Greece to settle the civil unrest in that country. On leaving the army he returned to his trade as a grocer, but his passion for motor-cycles never left him and he ended up as manager of a motor-cycle company. He married, had four children and now lives in Blairgowrie in Scotland.

MARCH 1944

With the Soviet forces advancing towards Romania, Hitler decides to occupy Hungary. Meanwhile the Japanese begin an offensive towards Imphal and Kohima in India and the British begin operations behind Japanese lines in Burma.

TRAINING MULES IN BURMA
James Pearce

James Pearce enlisted in the army in 1940. He joined the Ox n'Bucks Regiment (Oxford and Buckinghamshire Light Infantry) and spent some time in training at Northwich before arriving in India for training in jungle warfare in Mysore. After periods in Salem and Madras he was sent with his regiment to Chittagong.

Our next move was a shock. All the transport was given up and in its place we drivers took over pack mules. How I wished I had my father's experience to hand, as a cavalryman.

336

All the mules were completely untrained and in most cases were completely unmanageable, and my pack mule worse than any we discovered. Nine of us were needed to load him and it was a big enough tussle to get bridle, bit and pack saddle on him. We would put a twitch on his nose and he would have his near hindleg caught up in a noose and hauled up under his belly and tied round his neck. We would then load the chargils (water tanks) onto his back. Once loaded, I had to grab the reins and twitch in one hand, untie his back leg with the other hand, then gently release the twitch. While the twitch was on, every move he made was painful so he stood still, but, immediately that twitch was loosened all hell broke loose. He would buck and kick, twirl round and round with me hanging on with the reins twisted round my hands. The mule did his best to get the load off his back, even to the extent of rolling on the ground and he would never give up until the chargils were off. By this time I'd given up trying to control him, court martial or no, I would be forced to let him go. I would then hare off, up the jungle trail after him, pick up the bits and pieces, carry them back myself, then go and fetch him from where he would be quietly grazing as if nothing was amiss. I would grab the reins and lead him back to camp to be greeted by 'Well done, Pearce,' from the transport officer, for persevering presumably and what was more important in the army's eyes, fetching the mule back to start all over again. I should explain that it was a court martial offence to lose your mule under any circumstances unless killed in action.

My mule behaved like this for weeks, while all the other mules had settled down to their normal duties. One thing we learned very quickly! Never approach a mule from the rear, especially a jenny or female. One of our lads did: walked up to his mule with a bucket of water to give it a drink from the rear and was kicked full in the face. He ended up with a broken jaw, smashed nose and broken cheek bones and it was some weeks before we saw him back in the regiment, with a face like a boxer's until the swelling subsided.

It took me almost three months in training to quieten my mule down, after he'd acquired a taste for army biscuits. This I discovered quite by accident one day. I had just received my army biscuit ration and popped them in the pocket of my jungle suit, then went forward to the mule lines to start grooming and cleaning the mules. My mule sniffed around my pocket and showing signs of interest in the contents, so I gave him a biscuit to sample while washing down all his bits and pieces, which he thoroughly enjoyed.

After that, I rewarded him with an army biscuit every time he did something right and, if he didn't do what was wanted, he didn't get a biscuit. Slowly but surely, he began to respond to this treatment and with biscuit bribery began to follow me about everywhere. In some ways this proved very useful to the army. For instance loading mules up a ramp on a landing craft proved a constant battle and was time consuming. So I was ordered to lead my mule, who followed me everywhere, first. As soon as the mules saw one mule walking calmly aboard more followed suit, with the awkward ones being rushed aboard by four men. I was made lead mule, which I didn't like at all, now that we were in the war zone, and as Jappy had a nasty habit of sniping at leaders, in the hope that they would pick off officers. However, as yet we were not in regular contact with the Japs, as we were waiting for the whole division to assemble.

So, came the first vet's inspection and to our complete surprise the vet discovered my mule was stone deaf, after looking down his ears with a light and snapping his fingers in his ears, so he was given a course of treatment by the vet's assistant who flushed out lumps of wax and dirt deep inside his ears despite all my grooming. At least the vet said it was too deep to see without his light. Now I understood why my mule never turned a hair during occasional bouts of shelling and mortar attacks while the other mules jumped and rolled their eyes and tried to get away from the noise. His deafness undoubtedly was the reason for his behaviour. It wasn't until we discovered my mule was deaf, that we realised it must be the bumping up and down of the empty chargils that frightened him — the full ones didn't move as he walked. So the empty chargils were very quietly and gently put on and with the occasional army biscuit, very slowly, my mule began to stand still, to accept bridle, saddle and load, but was still wary of the water tanks.

We were still not in actual contact with Jappy although we suffered the occasional bout of shell and mortar fire. It was not until some weeks later that we received information from villages that the Japs were preparing to move out, so patrols were set up to check and we were soon on the move giving chase.

Pearce fought with the Ox 'n Bucks as part of the 14th Army as the British regained control of Burma and made it to the end of the war in the Far East in August 1945. He lives in Cippenham in Berkshire.

APRIL 1944

The Japanese besiege the Indian town of Imphal.

MONTE CASSINO
Alec Barthorpe

Barthorpe now an officer in the 149th Anti-Tank Regiment and part of the 4th Indian Division arrives at Monte Cassino. His previous accounts are in September 1939 on page 4, and January and July 1941 on pages 116 and 156 respectively.

Due to the inclement weather, no casualties received from the bombing and to the subsequent unsuccessful assault on the monastery, although they had achieved partial success in fighting for the town of Cassino, the New Zealand Corps was reduced to virtually a holding unit. This delayed another planned assault on the monastery until our reserves, the 78th Division, arrived. Meanwhile the weather got colder, wetter and windier, and the troops remaining in their exposed positions suffered unnecessary casualties which mounted daily.

This was the situation when I arrived and despite the casualties suffered, the men had to be supplied and fed and that had to be done during the hours of darkness as daylight hours brought instant death to any man who moved unnecessarily into sight. We found out later that the Germans in front of us were paratroops, the toughest soldiers in the German army. Volunteers were always required to assist in the portering of supplies to those on Hangman's Hill and other exposed positions, as most of the mules used had become casualties to the enemy constantly shelling and mortaring the dark positions during the night hours. I volunteered for a few of these portering duties, in between my duties at the gun position and observation post. We got shelled occasionally but nothing serious happened and to see the gratitude on the men's faces when we arrived with their rations was, to me, thanks enough for making the effort.

Meanwhile the paratroops launched several attacks against our men causing many casualties, but invariably broke down in the face of heavy firing from our artillery and machine guns. Eventually the whole corps was relieved, our regimental position was taken over by units of the 78th Division and we were pulled out of the line and returned to where our guns had been temporarily parked, near a town called Benevento.

On our way to collect our equipment we camped for the night alongside the Volturno River which was high, full, and running fast. At the place where we camped the river had widened due to the heavy rains and had isolated a large tree which must have been on higher ground as it appeared to be a small island in the fast flowing water and was about five metres from the mainland, and about 20 metres in length. We paid no attention to it until we all heard the sound of a plane coming fast towards us down river, then I heard the sound of machine gun fire and the detonation of a small bomb, and realised it was an enemy on a hit-and-run mission and we were the target. I saw a group of four men behind me and shouted to them to get down. There was no truck near us so the only thing to do was lie flat on the ground, lie still and hope the pilot ignored us. The pilot did just that and having dropped his bomb upstream, was past us before dropping another beyond us downstream. It was after the plane disappeared that I heard a shout, looked around and saw that one of the men, who had been standing behind me, was now standing on the island next to the tree. The others shouted to him to return to the mainland, but try as he might he could not get back, as the current was too strong and he found he was out of his depth. So how did he originally get on to the island? He was the only man in our regiment to have 'walked on water'. We eventually got him back by floating a rope to him with the help of a two inch mortar and pulling him back. He never did explain how he got across in the first place!

Having recovered our equipment, we then proceeded to a position on the east side of the line between Cassino and the Adriatic Sea in the mountains. This was to be a holding position, as we badly needed a rest and the main force was to be concentrated around Cassino for the final assault on the monastery, which was to take place shortly.

In October 1944 Barthorpe, by now a Captain, was sent to Greece as part of the 4th Indian Division who were to police the country. Unfortunately he was captured by ELAS soldiers (Greek communist guerrilla forces). He and other prisoners were eventually released and Barthorpe arrived back in England in time for VE Day. After the war he and his wife Jeanne had six

344

children. He joined the police force and worked in Rhodesia, retiring as a Chief Inspector in 1973. He and his wife emigrated to South Africa in the Eighties and he worked for the Water Board until he retired in 1990. He died in 1996, three days after finishing his memoirs.

MAY 1944

Allied forces stage invasion rehearsals at Slapton Sands in Devon but are spotted by German U-Boats and over 600 Americans are killed.

WORKING IN INTELLIGENCE
Valentine J Wrigley

Wrigley whose previous account appears in May 1943 on page 279 is now Section Sergeant of 105 Wireless Intelligence Section attached to 105 Special Wireless Section (Royal Signals) working for one of the Corps making up 8th Army before the final battle for Monte Cassino. The section's work was to intercept and decode German messages.

5th May

I heard Odile [Wrigley's wife who is French and was a translator/announcer on the BBC French Service] several times during the week. It is very nice having a wireless in the Intelligence van.

7th May

I made progress with the wall round my tent, as we were daily expecting 'the big do' to start and as we were well up and in sight of the monastery of Cassino we were expecting some counter battery fire. Some excellent photos arrived from home, from Charles [Wrigley's twin brother, a Major in the Intelligence Corps] — most nostalgic especially one of the smokeroom.

9th May

I heard with pleasure that Geoff (an older brother — Major in the RAOC) had arrived in Italy. His letter had only taken 1¾ days. I guessed, rightly as it turned out, that he was in Naples. I got instructions today to fill in a WOSB (War Officer Selection Board) form and on 10th May I had to go for a medical exam to get the MOD signature on the form. I got two letters from Odile which made me very happy and were a great relief after so long without good news.

11th May

I sent off my 200th letter to Odile since I started numbering them on 17th May last year. The acting G(I) (Corps Staff Intelligence Officer) Captain Rawes gave us a talk on the coming battle for Rome and it began that evening. I listened to Odile at 9.15 p.m. and then went to lie down, fully dressed. My snooze was disturbed by the opening of the barrage at 11 p.m. I was awed, frightened, impressed and very sorry for the Germans — all at once. I went up by the red house where we worked and stood at the opening of the cave with Harry Martin (he had a very good degree in German and was a brilliant decoder though only a corporal). It was tremendous and the noise deafening and the light flashes almost blinding. The effect on us, the spectators, was stunning and it seemed impossible that anything could live at the receiving end. There were said to be 1,100 guns in the 8th Army sector and 900 on the US 5th Army Sector (on the left). However many there may have been, we could see only from one end of our viewpoint to another. It continued in waves, presumably moving forward. However, the chief fury was exhausted by midnight and we thought of the attackers going in blind, firing tracer shells to mark the boundaries of the attackers. I went into the Intelligence van. They were very busy, but there were ample people on duty, so I went down the hill, looking back at the scene as the guns flashed and made everything for a second or two as light as day. I went to listen to Odile at 12.30 a.m. on the wireless, wondering if the news of the attack had got through to her yet, but it hadn't. Then I went to spend another restless night sleeping on the floor of my trench.

13th May
Naturally we were extremely busy (analysing wireless traffic, identifying units and decoding German messages and passing them on to Corps) for the first few days of the battle and I had to do a very busy night shift.

16th May
Another night shift. Naturally we followed the news of the battle with terrific interest. Things seemed to go really well, especially on the French sector (to the left of US 5th Army) but the Jerries kept getting away, though they must have had heavy losses.

17th May
We finally walked into the much-fought-for Cassino without a struggle as it had been turned.

19th May
We packed all ready to move but it turned out to be a 'dry run'. However the rain came to make things more difficult and we were to get up at 3.30 a.m. for it, so I slept under a

temporary shelter and eventually about 5.45 a.m. we moved. It was not yet possible to go through Cassino, so we had to go round by the railway route (Speedy Express) and across the Rapido River. Then through a mistake in map-reading by our OC, we found ourselves only three miles from the front, blocking important traffic. We retreated and then blocked the Polish Armoured Brigade! However we eventually got to the chosen site: a damaged house on the Cassino-Pignataro road. It was infested with fleas from German occupation and smelly from nearby corpses. There were a good many knocked out Sherman tanks about. Then the guns whistled over our heads. There was talk, too, of enemy counter battery fire so Corps decided not to move forward again and set off through Cassino — a town more completely knocked over and flattened I've never seen. It is just a heap of rubble with some arches, cellars intact and the walls of such strong houses as the Hotel des Roses and Priory. The station area bore very clearly the marks of bitter fighting, for as the town is surrounded by what are practically marshes, the station with its solid base was obviously the key to the whole situation.

A day or two later Wrigley was called back to Naples for the selection board and was commissioned immediately after that. In his diary he could give no details of the work which was highly secret, but he remembers identifying the arrival of German 1st Parachute Division at Cassino — a unit kept in reserve to be deployed only in key sectors. 'On 1st May the section decoded a message from what we knew was an artillery observation post speaking to the guns, 'Can you see the 'Hackenkreuz?' (the Nazi flag). We looked out and saw it and we were able to give the exact position to Corps. On another occasion we decoded a message asking for firing on an Allied convoy below us in the valley, but the answer came back 'Leider, keine munition' — Unfortunately no ammunition.' Wrigley became a teacher in the Fifties and was Headmaster of Apsley Grammar School in Hemel Hempstead (later merged to become Longdean Comprehensive). Sadly he died in August 2001.

JUNE 1944

On the 6th June British and American troops land in Normandy.

D-DAY
Melvin Farrell

Melvin Barnett Farrell was born in 1920 in Georgia, USA. Before the war he was a civil engineer and surveyor and after war broke out he joined the US Army as a combat engineer.

At 1.30 a.m. on 6th June the order came through to board the smaller Landing Craft (LCMs), and at a given signal we were to rendezvous for the frontal assault on Normandy Beach. These boats were large enough to accommodate a full platoon, 41 men with combat gear and had a ramp in front which the operator could lower to allow fast exit.

Ours was the 2nd Platoon, Company B, 121st Combat Engineers Battalion and was scheduled to be the lead or spearhead

352

because of the nature of our mission.

This mission was to demolish a masonry wall about four foot high and four foot thick that ran parallel to the water's edge so that the Tank Forces could get in. We all carried 40lb satchel charges of TNT for this purpose plus a seven foot bangalore torpedo, full field pack and rifle.

A few yards from the beach was a barbed wire entanglement that we would encounter before getting to the wall. The bangalore torpedoes were for cutting huge holes through the wire.

I had been on the English Channel at least four times before and had never seen the water so rough. It was vicious. Waves would throw the LCM up out of the water and it would slam down with a bone-breaking jar. We were all seasick.

'H-Hour' or landing time was originally set for 6 a.m. This was changed, moved to 6.20 a.m. because of high tide and rough water. Our radio operator was so sick he missed the message so our 'H-Hour' was still 6 a.m. sharp. As we neared the beach we began to look about us. Never did I think there were so many boats and ships in the world. They were everywhere!

The Air Force had taken the paratroops in earlier in what appeared an endless stream of planes. Then about 5 a.m. they started bombing and strafing the beach to try and soften up the defences. The large battle-wagons behind us opened up with their big guns lobbing shells over our heads to the beach. It would seem that nothing could have withstood such a bombardment of shells and blockbusters but somehow the German personnel escaped serious injury. At least they were still very much alive and alert at 6 a.m.

About 200 yards out our LCM floundered, nosed up on a hidden sandbar and stuck fast. The operator seesawed back and forth but she wouldn't give. The machine gun fire rattling off the sides set up such a din you could hardly think. The operator threw the ramp down and yelled, 'Hit it!'

I was the third man out. We three wheeled left and jumped off the side of the ramp. Machine gun fire was now raking the inside of the LCM, and a high percentage of our men were killed before they could get out.

When the three of us jumped we landed in a shell hole and with all our luggage we plummeted to the bottom like rocks. We walked until we climbed out of the hole. It seemed an eternity before we reached the surface. We were then on the barren sand but there was another stretch of water between us and the beach. This stretch contained a maze of tank traps, mines and every object the Krauts could plant to thwart a landing attempt.

It all seemed unreal, a sort of dreaming while awake; men were screaming and dying all around me. I've often wondered if all the men prayed as fervently as I did. I remember going past one of the log type tank obstacles with 'legs' attached to the back end. I ran up beside it and got down as low as I could to rest a moment and find as much shelter from the hail of machine gun fire as possible. Looking over the log I discovered about half way up was a large Teller Mine with 'trip' wires running in every direction. Since some of the detonators are tension devices I knew that if a bullet cut one of those wires it would blow me to bits. But the question was how to get past? I knew I had to make it so without hesitation I angled off to the left and somehow made it through the maze of wires with all my gear.

I suddenly found myself confronted with what seemed a mountain of rusty barbed wire. I slid the bangalore as far under as I could, cut as short a fuse as I dared, lit it, ran back about ten paces and flattened myself out on the ground. It blew a gap about 20 feet wide in the wire.

This section was under intense fire from

the pillboxes that we could see on the hill. Every fifth bullet used in machine guns is a tracer, which you can see in the form of a glow. These looked so dense and criss-crossed that it is hard to believe anything could get by unscathed. With heartbreaking slowness I arrived at the wall behind which several of our men were already waiting for us. I threw my satchel charges onto the wall and attached the lead fuse to the primacord they had already stretched and started crawling down the beach for safety from the coming explosion.

When the explosion occurred, the first wave of infantry was about 100 yards out. At this time our initial mission was completed so we huddled behind the ragged remnants of the wall we had just blown. I turned my gaze toward the coming infantry and saw my Sergeant, Steve Kleman, not 40 yards from me. He was sitting down, having been hit through both hips. I tried four times to get out to him to drag him in. Each time I left cover a hail of machine gun fire would drive me back. By this time he had been hit so many times it was hopeless.

Company B sustained 73% casualties on this landing but lying behind the cover of the wall we could not tear our eyes off the infantry. They ran through and up the hill in a never-ending stream, the dead and dying piling up behind them. I honestly could have walked the full length of the beach without touching the ground, they were so thickly strewn about. Stark raw death in every imaginable form lay all around us. I remember a corporal, still walking, looking for a medic, with his whole chin and nose shot away, cut cleanly and evenly.

Farrell was captured by the Germans during the days that followed D-Day and taken to a prison camp in Czechoslovakia where he was employed in a coal mine; as the Americans advanced he was force-marched eastwards towards Germany. Once liberated he returned to the US and marrying in 1953, had three children. After returning to work for a few more years as a civil engineer, he became Director of Parks and Recreation for a large county on the outskirts of Atlanta, Georgia. He died in 1981.

D-DAY
Les Edwards

Les Edwards was born in 1920. Before the war he worked for a large firm of bakers and confectioners as a clerk. He was called up in

May 1940 and initially joined the Hampshire Regiment. Later he transferred to the RAC and trained as a driver mechanic at Catterick in Yorkshire, before being posted to Penrith and training on flame-thrower tanks. He was then transferred to the Royal Engineers 81st Assault Squadron (explosive experts) to drive tanks for them. He was the first British soldier to land on the beach at La Riviere driving a Churchill tank at 7 a.m. on D-Day.

We were about three miles off shore. The minesweepers had done their job — ours was to come. We were right out in front now. The remainder of the armada seemed to have stopped. Either that or we had speeded up, increasing the distance between us and the remainder as the shoreline became more distinct. There were fires and smoke and gun flashes all along that shoreline. The Royal Navy was hurling shells over the top of us into the defences. We could hear the big ones splitting the atmosphere with a low hum as they went above us. We couldn't hear the bang as they landed on target.

There was plenty of noise as I started to uncouple the chains securing our tank. I wondered if we would ever have to use our escape kits. These had been issued and consisted of a small compass, Horlicks tablets, tablets to keep us awake, tablets to make us sleep and other bits and pieces. We had been told what to do in case of escape on foot in circumstances of failure. Surely this operation could not fail. It was so big. There was so much at stake.

'Start engines' — the command came over the intercom from the Tank Commander. They started first go, and as I pressed my foot on the accelerator and felt the power I was at last occupied with the job in hand. I could drive that tank as well as any driver in the British Army. I could turn her on a sixpence. I could drive through a gap with an inch to spare on either side. I could balance her on the top of a bank and let her down gently on the other side. I don't think I was afraid, in fact preferred to think of the word apprehensive and I felt ill — it was the sea sickness. And then the ramp slowly moved down in front of me.

There were burning buildings, smoke, fires, tracer bullets, noise, spikes, mines, obstacles, sand, dry land and not a soul in sight. 'Advance Eddie' — before the command was finished I had the clutch in, engaged first gear, watched the rev counter move round to 1200, let the clutch out and we were moving slowly forward.

The coconut matting began to unroll and

everything was fine. We moved forward ten yards and the roll of matting went partially down into a hole and refused to unwind. The sea bed at La Riviere is not as flat as the golden sands at Bideford in Devon. I stopped.

'Move on,' said the tank commander, 'The tanks behind us cannot get off the landing craft. Drive over the bloody thing.'

In clutch — in gear — out clutch — over we go. The tank moved up at an angle. The frame was quite strong. We got half way up at an angle of 45%. The frame snapped — we bumped down on one side. I moved slowly forward towards the spikes, the obstacles and the mines.

What's that water doing all round my feet? There's water inside the tank — it's getting deeper it's up to my knees, now my waist. My co-driver and I are sitting waist deep in water. Must keep the engine going at full revs, mustn't stall. Can't steer!

The bump, as we had gone over the coconut matting roll, had dislodged the air louvre extensions and part of the English Channel was now in our tank. A tank is steered by a braking action on two large brake drums on each side of the engine. Water had got into the engine and brake drums and I could not steer at all. I could reach out through the visor and touch the bottle mines just in front of me. The other tanks started to pass me and thread their way through the obstacles up the beach. Mustn't brush those mines — the least that would happen would be a track blown off and then you were stuck.

We *were* stuck and a sitting target. The first tank that passed us had reached a point about 30 yards ahead. It stopped. Flames were licking out of the turret and along the edges. I remembered that all our tanks were stacked with 808 high explosive.

As I pulled the lever that moved the two inch armoured plate across my visor our tank shuddered with the force of the explosion. When I opened the visor two seconds later the burning tank had gone — blown to smithereens.

The next tank up the beach suffered the same fate. We later found the turret, which weighed about five tons, over 100 yards away — blown completely off the tank.

And then the next one started to burn. Two of the crew managed to get out. They jumped down onto the beach, clothing on fire, — burning torches rolling over and over on the beach in an endeavour to extinguish those agonising flames. Part of the defences on that stretch of beach consisted of two 105mm fixed gun emplacements, one at each end of the beach with a fixed traverse so that one or the other could cover the area. The gun on our right had fortunately been knocked out, either by the RAF or by the RN gunfire. The gun slightly to our left was very much in action. Later on that day we found out why we were not hit when we were stuck. The gun had a limited traverse and we were just out of range. About 30 yards ahead of us the tanks came into range and were being picked off.

If the gun on our right had been in action we would have been knocked out long ago. If we had landed 50 yards to our right we would have also had it from this same gun that was now doing all the damage. There were tracer bullets flying all over the place, there were fires and smoke and noise. Some flail tanks had landed. These are the tanks with the revolving chains which beat the ground in front of them and explode the mines. The commander of one of them should have got a medal. He spotted the 105mm that was doing all the damage — wheeled round to the left — came in at the rear of the gun and blew it up. I was putting pressure on the steering arm in the hope that the drums would dry out so that I could get on up the beach. I dared not move until I could steer sufficiently to negotiate around those spikes and mines.

Suddenly I felt the steering respond. I

backed off a little and went forward in and out of the obstacles towards the beach. We succeeded in releasing the small round plate in the well of the tank and as we reached dry land the water inside drained out. It was only about 7.30 a.m. and there were all sorts of people on the beach: flails and assault tanks, infantry and commandos, characters sticking flags in the sand keeping their heads down and ducking under the cross-fire.

I felt much better. The dry land was moving about just like the LCT and I did not stop swaying about until about three days later. 'Eddie Advance' — I was still outside the tank and looked up at the turret to see the tank commander grinning down. I scrambled in and we trundled up the beach over the top and out on the road.

'Fire at anything that moves,' said the briefing officer. 'The Germans have cleared all civilians out of the area some five miles beyond the beach line. Anything that moves in that area is the enemy.'

We had moved 50 yards inland when out of the German defences and billets came the girls. Bottles of wine held high, 'Tommee'! 'Tommee'! they cried.

The crack of small arms fire was just ahead. An infantry sergeant bent down low ran up to enlist our help. They were pinned down, he said. A German strong point, built in the corner house 100 yards up the road round the corner. Yes we would help. 'Advance Eddie,' round the corner up the road, there they are, the tracers are coming from here 'Halt! traverse front, stop, load,' the poor old front gunner had to push the Flying Dustbin [bomb thrower] vertical, above his head, up into the gun. Quickly, I thought, or your forearms will be sprayed with machine gun fire. 'Gun loaded, flap back, traverse left, aim, fire.' The Flying Dustbin could be seen arcing through the air towards its target as the velocity was quite low. 'Bang!' The strong point and the corner house disappeared and all that was left was rubble and dust. 'Thanks mate,' said the sergeant and we passed on. The Germans lying about and the prisoners being herded up were a mangy looking lot. Some seemed slant-eyed and looked Mongolian, not like Germans at all; some were in their pants and pyjamas and others only half dressed. They must have been surprised when we landed. Throughout the day we milled around. We could hear our shells coming over from the direction of the beaches and the German shells going the opposite way. We were somewhere in the middle.

During the evening we rendezvoused in an orchard, deployed our tanks around the perimeter, dug holes in the ground and settled down to eat. The German Air Force dropped flares, bombed and machine-gunned. Tanks cannot hit back against aircraft, so we dozed and D-Day was over.

About a week after D-Day Edwards's tank was blown up on a mine. He was wounded and returned to England on a hospital ship but within four weeks had rejoined his unit in France. He was in Luneberg Heath when Germany surrendered. After the war Edwards was able to return to his old job and married in 1946. His company was bought out by Ranks Hovis in the Fifties and he retired in 1981 as general manager. He now lives in Fareham, Hampshire.

JULY 1944

German army officers attempt to assassinate Hitler but fail.

AN SAS MISSION IN FRANCE
Bob Walker Brown

Walker Brown's account of his escape from a POW camp in September 1943 was narrated on page 299. The then official view was that escaped prisoners were probably psychiatric cases at best, so it was necessary to appear before a medical board, some of the members looking like psychiatric cases themselves! Posted to an infantry training centre at Aberdeen and temporarily medically downgraded, Walker Brown soon became bored and frustrated. He saw an exotic looking officer wearing parachute wings and a pistol who proved to be a SAS officer. Within a week Walker Brown had joined the 2nd Special Air Service Regiment at Prestwick. Having made a successful escape he was excused the rigorous SAS selection course *and was at once sent on a parachute-jumping course. On his first balloon jump he landed on the roof of a double-decker London bus which was full of Wrens! Hard training followed in preparation for the invasion of France when parties of the SAS Brigade were dropped behind the German forward areas, or infiltrated by armed jeep in July and August 1944. Walker Brown's account follows:*

All SAS operations were mounted against the background of Hitler's personal order that all special troops captured outside the immediate battlefield were summarily to be shot; and, that any German commander failing to implement the order was himself to be shot. This was no idle threat. Several members of the regiment were thus murdered. My fellow Troop Commander in Italy, Ross Littlejohn (Black Watch) and his signaller, Corporal Crowley were captured by German ski troops near the Brenner Pass, brutally interrogated and then shot. In France a party of five was betrayed by the French, captured, interrogated, suspended by the ankle from trees, doused with petrol and ignited. This certainly concentrated the mind.

Since D-Day SAS reception and reconnaissance parties had been dropped or infiltrated into Central France. By late July operations had become fluid. The American and Free French divisions withdrawn from Italy had landed in the South of France and were advancing up the Rhone valley to link up with the US 3rd and 7th Armies north of Dijon. The 1st and 2nd SAS and the French and Belgian SAS squadrons had established operational bases in the thick forests of Central France from which attacks were mounted on enemy supply routes, especially those leading from Normandy to Belfort. No 1 Squadron, 2nd SAS had established a base in the Forest of Chattilon and now there was a need for an additional troop. I dropped as a 'stick commander' with a troop of armed jeeps at night on a DZ (Drop Zone) in the Forest of Chattilon. The troop commander was Count Mike Pinci (a Roman Count). We were dropped by five Halifax bombers, modified for para dropping. Each carried an armed jeep, equipment containers and up to a 'stick' of ten parachutists. In continuation para training there had been fatal casualties due to the failure of static lines, stored under a row of batteries in the Halifax fuselage. Acid leaking onto the webbing strap weakened it and it parted under tension. On the flight over France there was heavy flak and my aircraft sustained damage. Running in over the DZ, just glimpsing a T in torches the first half stick jumped. The last man's static line parted and flapped about in the slip stream. He went straight in and made a deep impression — in the ground. As the pilot positioned the aircraft for the next run-in I was next to jump. I had a few moments to contemplate the future as my static line had been stored next to the one that failed. When my canopy opened I was pleased — if I may put it that way. Clearing the DZ with a dead man was sobering. Moving into forest cover with the SAS reception party and some FFI (Forces Francaise de l'Interieur) we were briefed about the immediately forthcoming attack on the German garrison of Chaumont where it occupied the chateau.

After several 'stand tos' with wild boar making Teutonic noises we drove to link up with the rest of the squadron and some FFI and took part in a stand-off attack on the chateau and adjacent area. With some 30 or so twin and single Vickers K MGs, five Browning HMGs, numerous Bren LMGs and three inch mortars we made a formidable noise, with tracer, ball and AP flying all over the place and return German fire with green tracer. German reinforcements soon appeared so we pulled out leaving brewed up vehicles, smouldering fires and according to the French some 110 casualties. We lost one killed and two wounded.

In view of certain enemy retaliation Major Roy Farran (who was squadron leader, No 1 Squadron, 2nd SAS Regiment) decided to take two troops east across the present RN75 and resume operations there while leaving the troop I was in to attack from the west. The troop established a temporary base with FFI and learned from them that an escorted column of fuel bowsers was due to leave Langres early the next day for Dijon. We decided to ambush it. Unwisely accepting a French-advised fire position we motored into position the next morning. The position gave a long field of fire towards Langres; it was sited at a minor road junction where a small country road crossed the main road. It was blind to the rear towards Dijon and there was no covered line of approach or withdrawal. As bells tolled and churchgoers appeared on the road in front, the sound of approaching vehicles was heard. Yelling at the French, 'Courez vous comme un lievre,' they dived off the road as the leading escort vehicle appeared, the bowsers some five or six trucks further back.

We had been told by the French that all enemy columns headed for Dijon and the approaching Free French. The lead vehicles were allowed through; as the fuel tankers came within close range we opened up with everything. As the tankers went up in flames and smoke the escort put in a very determined counter-attack. As we were disengaging, my right hand twin Vickers gun had a stoppage; the torque effect swung the mounting round and fired an unaimed burst almost behind me. At the same time my pistol lanyard fouled the cocking handle and almost choked me. But that burst was a stroke of luck. The leading escort had not headed for Dijon but had turned right behind our position; it fired in response to my unintended burst and revealed the danger. Grabbing our two casualties we were very lucky to have got away with it. We failed to observe the elementary principle of all round observation and field of fire and should never have accepted the position without reconnaissance ourselves but time was short. After withdrawing to forest cover, country roads and forest tracks parallel to the Langres-Dijon main road were used to mount a series of other road ambushes.

Mike Pinci very intelligently decided that we should use air strikes as a better way of slowing traffic on the main road. He called for a strike on the road just south of Langres at first light next day; commandeering a civilian car hidden under a hay stack he drove himself onto that very stretch of road at the same time as the strike request. He was immediately attacked by two cannon-flying Thunderbolts. We buried him that same day in a village churchyard after a service by a RC priest.

Taking over the troop, I decided to mount a stand-off attack on the southern approaches to Langres where German troops were digging in. Having lost some of our jeeps we enlisted a motley bunch of vans and civilian cars. In a Peugeot with its sliding roof open, we mounted a three inch mortar with the baseplate on a pile of sandbags and the muzzle just clearing the roof line. With a good view of the enemy positions we opened up with everything at a range of about 400 yards. The Peugeot-mortar made a stupendous noise as the wretched car bottomed every time a bomb was fired no one quite knew where. The poor chap hanging onto the bipod legs was understandably fussed in case the bomb hit the edge of the roof. As we pulled out, the advance guard of General Leclerc's Free French appeared — very impressive Spahi in kepis. The General had his Tac [Tactical] HQ well forward and after introducing myself, the troop joined the French in the capture of Langres. Many of the prisoners we took were mere boys and very frightened.

Being ordered to exfiltrate, Walker Brown returned to England sometime in September 1944. An account of SAS Operation Galia by Walker Brown can be found in December 1944 on page 401.

AUGUST 1944

Burma falls to the Allies and Paris is liberated. The Allies land in Southern France. The Soviet forces strike into Romania which surrenders.

LETTERS FROM
A SOLDIER IN ITALY
David Bertram

David Bertram was born in 1911 in Bengal where his father was assistant manager of the Paper Mills. Before the war he worked as a trainee assistant manager at a paper mill in Lancashire. He married in 1940 and had a son in 1941 before being called up in 1942. He joined the Royal Army Pay Corps and after serving for a while in the UK was stationed in Italy in 1944.

GS Coy, 35 AO, CMF

14th August

Towsie Darling
What wonderful news your letter gave me on
Saturday night. I feel so proud and happier
than I can ever tell you and greatly relieved
that it is all over. You have done better than I
thought possible in presenting me with a girl
— it is just what I had been hoping for and
it's happened. I have read and re-read your
letter and I am just fair delighted with myself.
Best of all darling is that you are so bright
after what you have been through. I am sorry
to hear that it was so bad in the last stages
but it's all past you now and you have all the
pleasures of our little daughter in front of
you. It was certainly a much bigger baby than
Bobbie and 8lbs seems to me pretty good. Do
let me know about my wee girl and describe
her to me if you can . . . I just can't get over it
— you know the sort of feeling you get when
you want something very much and then
suddenly you get it. By God I hope this
bloody war is over pretty quick as I have a
terrible urge to get home — more so than
ever. Won't it be wonderful when we get
settled down again and can concentrate on
our family. I might tell you I have got our

little girl's career mapped out but won't tell you what it is — you might be alarmed! Until I get home and can show you what you mean to me all I can say is thank you for what you have done. I love you all so much — you my darling more than any other thing in this life, then my son and daughter; and I have one desire and that is to see them growing up into two decent normal people. As there is nothing I can send as a gift meantime I want you to start Rosemary Anne off in life with £10 from her Daddy who would give his right arm to see her right now. Take the £10 from my account. Longing for details and praying that you are both as well as can be.

All my love D

19th August

Towsie Darling
Just wondering how you and little Rosemary are getting along and hope everything is going all right and that you are getting stronger every day. It's fine that the baby sleeps so much as that's all to the good and will save you a lot of trouble later on . . . We are going elsewhere now. It's been short and quite unexpected but, speaking for myself, I am delighted at the prospect as it's in the right direction this time. It's not near any fighting

so don't worry on that point. It may be some days before I will be able to write to you again but you will know and not worry . . . Well darling I am always impatient to get your letters but more than ever now to hear all about my wee girl . . .

All my love D

26th August

My Darling Towsie
Sorry for being so long with my letter but you will note the change in my address and realise what's happened. We are still on the same side but much further up — not near the fighting so don't get alarmed! We had a very pleasant journey and took it by easy stages by road. Our mail will once again be all upset but I am grateful that I got news of the baby before leaving Bari. How are you getting along now — back home again and taking things easy I hope. And what of my wee girl — is everything going all right and no trouble of any kind? I do hope she gets on well as I know how much you worry if any little thing goes wrong. Are you feeding her yourself or has she been put on the bottle?

Well, I don't know what's going to happen to us now — it looks as though we are transferring into 35 ADO and we are not very

377

happy about it as naturally we prefer our own unit but still the war is almost over I think so it doesn't matter much . . . We are in tents here but I rather like it as it is much cooler at nights — when the rain starts it will be another matter . . . Take care of yourself and let me have all details of the baby.

All my love D

On discharge in 1945 Bertram completed his training in the paper industry. In 1947 he and his wife established their home in Edinburgh and Bertram started his own business as a paper merchant. He died in 1981.

SEPTEMBER 1944

The V1 and V2 rockets are launched on Britain. Allied troops capture Dieppe and Arras reaching the Belgian frontier on the 1st September. On the 4th they cross into Holland. On the 17th September the Allies launch Operation Market Garden. The British 8th Army continues to advance up through Italy and take Rimini.

THE AMERICAN
Brian Guy

Brian Guy was born in 1925 and joined up in Newcastle in 1943. He trained in Clitheroe and became a sapper in 246 Field Company, Royal Engineers, 8th Brigade. In the autumn of 1944 he was in France.

Always on the move, the British and Americans had broken through into the French countryside and then their tank columns had turned north to enclose the enemy in what was to become known as the 'Falaise Pocket.' We were pushing at the back of the pocket, driving the enemy towards the ever tightening noose at the head of this great trap. The fire inside this pocket was devastating; Germans died in their thousands and left behind a mangled mess of the paraphernalia of war. The Germans in some places were running for their lives, in others they stayed and fought it out. In some skirmishes they fought like demons. The line between our forces and the enemy had become very fluid; one was never sure if we had passed the enemy, or, whether he was still in front. To pay tribute to the Germans, they put up a fierce and spirited resistance in some of the rearguard actions that took place, actions that were fought with the purpose of giving their comrades time to get away. During this time our company was battling down the Vire-Tinchebray Road in hot pursuit and had stopped for food and refuelling. We set about digging our fox holes. Spud Murphy, our DR, and myself always tried to share the task of digging! First back from the day's operation would start the hole for both of us. We decided that a door over our hole would improve our creature comforts and help keep the rain off so we set off for a farm a short distance away. When we got there, as there was no sign of the enemy, we started to look for our door and found the farm cattle in an enclosed yard, all suffering from wounds that had been sustained by setting off booby traps. This made us a great deal more cautious. We came to an outhouse, a typical Normandy one where great cider barrels were kept up on racks at the back of the cobble stone floor.

Spread-eagled on the floor was a dead German officer, resplendent in full uniform with sword and Nazi dagger, his medals including the Iron Cross, pinned on his chest. Knowing the Germans and their dirty tricks, we were only too aware that moving him would set off a booby trap. Now with even greater care we moved on to a hay loft, then saw a door that had very narrow steps leading up to the loft from the outside. We decided that we would get it off its hinges when we heard footsteps coming down the loft steps and a pair of German jackboots appeared.

Spud pointed his empty Sten gun at him and I drew my trusty Bowie knife and prepared to do this fellow some very serious harm, when a voice with an American accent called out, 'I want to give myself up.' In these unusual circumstances, we let him come on. Having seen what they were prepared to do with their own officer, we took no chances. I have never seen anyone so keen to give himself up. He told us that he was the son of an American mother and a German father. While they were on holiday in Germany the war had broken out and he was unable to get home, subsequently he was called up to serve in the German army and sent to Normandy. He told us that his mum had told him to stay behind and give himself up to the Americans. I was convinced that he was telling the truth; we gave him a cigarette and had quite a chat before turning him in.

Brian Guy's account, The Garden Roller Man appears in November 1944 on page 396.

OCTOBER 1944

Operation Market Garden was divided into two parts — Market was to be the seizure of bridges by airborne troops along the Rhine. Garden was to be the advance of troops and tanks across the bridges. British paratroops managed to capture the northern end of the bridge at Arnhem but the Germans held onto the town and the British Guards Armoured Division were unable to link up with the paras.

OPERATION MARKET GARDEN — MEERBEEK TO ELST
Reginald Romain

Reg Romain was born in 1918 and was employed as a dairyman before the war. He was conscripted as soon as war broke out in 1939 and joined the 5th Wiltshire Regiment. After training he was involved in coastal and training duties in Kent. He became a Sergeant and section commander in an *anti-tank platoon of the 5th Wilts. Romain took part in the Normandy landings and fought with his regiment as they advanced through Belgium and Holland to the Elbe in Germany.*

During the early hours of October 1st we were attacked by German Marine troops; they came in, seemingly oblivious to our intensive fire and it was clear that they would over-run our position in an orchard by sheer weight of numbers. I ordered my gun crew to stop firing, removed the firing mechanism and instructed them in no uncertain terms to make for the farm buildings to the rear of our position. These were of course almost in ruins but the barn joined to the buildings might offer some sort of protection and we could remount our firing position there. We all made it to the barn. Corporals Les Timbrell [known as Tim] and Sid Seymour were close behind and alongside me.

We came through the hedge on the farm track where some carriers were burning and turned to go into the barn. This had two big wooden doors, which we dashed through. I waited long enough for the last man to come through and then swung it closed. Just then, there were a number of explosions inside our refuge, which could have been German grenades or mortars or even our own retaliatory fire.

I noticed a long shallow trough running the length of the floor of the building and I shouted to the lads, 'In here!' we all dived into the trough to find it awash with wet cow dung. It smelled awful and permeated our clothes.

All four of us decided to find other refuge but as we did so there was a terrific ripping sound from the doorway and half of it tore away.

The next thing I can remember was hauling myself to my feet, while Sid and Tim stayed huddled on the ground. My position was directly between the two. I saw a heavily armoured vehicle backing up in the lane outside and it was apparent that it had fired its machine gun through the door, killing both of my companions while missing me.

This armoured vehicle appeared to be supporting the German attack through to B Company and was firing at random. I had no time to think on a personal level because we were being ordered to take up all round defence of the buildings. I took Corporal Mellors to what remained of an upstairs window and we took up a position with our Bren. It was while we were making our way to this position that I saw a group of Germans who had been hit; at a quick glance it seemed that two or three of them had been killed. I particularly noticed one man had all his clothing blown off and lay with his rump in the air.

From our position at the window, we saw a wounded Jerry crawling away towards a ditch, dragging his leg and we let him go as it seemed clear that his fighting days were over. We needed to conserve our ammunition as it was apparent that we had quite a fight on our hands.

After a while we heard a group of the enemy doubling back through our positions and they came back so tight to the buildings that we could not train our Bren on them and they escaped unharmed. There are probably three blokes alive in Germany today, who owe their lives to the steepness of that barn wall.

From then on, the German attack just fizzled out and our B Company counter attacked and retook our earlier positions. We were marched there by B Company Commander, Major Norris and rejoined our guns at the old D Company position.

During the early hours of the next day, we managed to get back to the barn although in the meantime, we had lost Stan Greenman. He was killed bringing round the early tea over the top of my slit trench. Once inside the barn we had a meal, the first for a couple of days, when we noticed poor Tim and Sid's bodies still lying where they had fallen. Out of respect we covered them with a layer of ash and debris.

I am almost sure that we were relieved that day by our 4th Battalion who were then counter attacked again by another wave of Germans.

By this time the push up to Arnhem had been halted, the remaining Airborne chaps brought out and we moved into a village, which I think was called Weert, for a rest. It did not last long, within a few days we were back in the line at Mook.

It was whilst we were relieved at Elst by the 4th Wilts and were resting at the side of a road near Nijmegen, when a party of Airborne troops, who had recently been evacuated from Arnhem, marched past.

One called out, 'It took you a bloody long time to get here!'

One of our lads replied, 'Yeah, quite a few bastards didn't get this far!'

Romain finished the war near Bremen not far from the Belsen concentration camp. After the war he returned to work as a dairyman. He married in 1955 and had two daughters. Romain later worked for an electricity company until retirement in 1979. His wife died in 1976 and Romain now lives in Southampton and has six grandchildren.

THE GENTLE AUSTRIAN
John Slatterley

John 'Jack' Slatterley was born in 1920 and lived in Manchester. He joined the army at the start of war and was in the Airborne Division.

Operation Market Garden was over, and Arnhem was a deserted town as we were driven through it on our way to prison camps and hospitals away from the crippled bridge that had been held so helplessly, the bridge to freedom now a twisted ruin, its broken fingers washed by the River Rhine.

I had taken no part in the cruel battle, but had flown over from Brize Norton airfield near Oxford with the first Airlanding Brigade, a boy going to war for the first time, eager and afraid at the same moment.

It was a glorious Sunday morning when we left. We, in our glider towed by an American-crewed Dakota, were in the first wave and were soon over the coast of Holland. Fighter planes had gone in before us and there were fires below, then suddenly the landing zone Oosterbeek, a small holocaust of fire and noise. Tracer bullets were crossing the sky and puffs of smoke erupted as shells exploded all around the silent descending gliders. There was no returning now. The planes had cast us off and we hissed our way to earth. Our glider was tree high when the tracers found us. The glider pilot was hit first in his right shoulder, the same burst picked its way along the length of the glider and shattered my femur in an explosion of blood as the glider nosedived into the trees.

I awoke on Monday morning in a farmhouse with my leg encased in cold wet plaster. I was lucky, our doctors had operated on me on the Sunday evening, and in a slight hangover of morphia I lay on my stretcher and wondered what was happening outside. Two stretcher bearers came in, full of banal chatter that I welcomed. (Home for you tonight lad, sending a plane specially they are) and carried me out to a utility truck, another shot of morphine (because the roads are a bloody mess and we want you to be comfy, don't we) and then oblivion.

I came round to find myself lying in the lounge of the Hotel Tafelberg, still on my stretcher and still in Oosterbeek just a couple of miles from Arnhem. I lay there with other casualties all through the bitter days, hungry and afraid, with the daylight blocked out by mattresses at the windows, night becoming day and each hour worse than the last, until suddenly there was silence. The battle was over, the only sounds now were the singing of the birds and the noises of the German trucks arriving to transport us to captivity.

Apeldoorn is about 12 miles from Arnhem and it was here that Queen Wilhelmina had her summer palace Het Leo, which was now being used by the Germans for a hospital. We were brought here where the wounded were sorted out: badly wounded — not fit for travel and walking wounded — able to be moved to Germany when transport was available.

My leg by now was a mass of maggots, corrupted flesh and bad blood and the stench was overpowering. I was given another operation to cut away the rotted flesh and generally clean me up and then along with 72 other badly wounded was taken to the Juliena Hospital, which the strange reasoning Germans had renamed the Hospital. After the discomforts of the barracks of Oosterbeek, the hospital was an oasis of comfort and the rapport between the British patients and Dutch staff was natural and affecting.

We were tended by all Dutch doctors,

sisters and maids, supervised by their German overseers and were in 12 bed wards in this modern hospital. The windows in the ward doors were blocked out in an effort to prevent civilian visitors from looking in, but each visiting day the doors would suddenly open and gifts of tobacco or cigarettes thrown on the nearest bed, the victory sign given by a stranger's hand or a muffled greeting shouted and the doors would close again. On Sundays, however, the Germans relaxed the non fraternisation rules and we were allowed a Dutch choir, accompanied by a portable organ, singing outside our doors. These good people could then enter the wards and pass a few pleasantries with us. Our two Church of England padres, who had surrendered with us, also visited on Sundays to administer communion and to give us the news of the week from St Joseph's Hospital, also in Apeldoorn, where they were incarcerated. They always arrived very grandly in neat battle dress and red berets, and although on parole, were accompanied by a German guard. We were allowed to have three cigarettes per day from the Germans, delivered by elderly guards, who apologised for the small ration; these jaded soldiers knew the war was going to end in defeat for them and were the absolute opposite of the arrogant young zealots of the Herman Goering Division who had guarded us in the barracks.

I had another operation two days after entering the hospital. The plaster was taken from my leg and a steel pin was inserted through the femur bone, slightly below the break. The pin was attached to a horseshoe, also of steel, through which a cord was threaded, this going over a pulley at the end of the bed. Weights were attached to the cord thus pulling the broken bones apart allowing new bone to grow. I, along with every other man in my ward, was immobile and so the Germans were unable to move us further inland as the good Dutch Dr Pilar, who performed the operation, told me, 'I intend to keep you all here until we are liberated.' We were visited almost daily by beautifully smelling German officers in all manner of mysterious uniforms and insignia who were apparently curious to see us whilst passing through Apeldoorn.

It was my second Tuesday in the hospital when the three sisters in our ward cleaned the supper away more quickly than usual. I asked the reason and was told, 'More Germans are coming to see you and don't bother us; we are busy.'

The latter remark was spoken quite

good-humouredly as in jest. My bed was the first on the left as one entered the ward and invariably any persons, German or Dutch, coming in to do a round would start from the right. Consequently I was always the last man to be approached. At 6.30 p.m. the ward doors opened and in stepped six of the most elegantly dressed German officers I had yet seen. Usually the visiting officers wore their caps and sometimes overcoats, but these men looked as though they had just stepped from a mess room and were entering the ward for an after dinner drink. Immaculate was the only word to describe them from head to foot they were perfect.

The first to enter gave us their usual all time greeting, 'Heil Hitler,' and then stepped back slightly to let his jack-booted superior enter, a tall man with a slight limp, wearing rimless spectacles, with his hair cropped short in a crew cut. As they started the round, scent pervaded over everything, the hospital smell vanished and there was the strange aroma, almost a combination of Eau de Cologne and cigar smoke. The sister assisted the officers, pulling back bed covers, which moments before had been meticulously straightened, to allow wounds and leg contraptions to be viewed.

I watched the entourage stop at each bed,

their chief asking questions in German which were translated to the man in bed and the answers re-translated back into German. He looked sympathetic nodding his head as though agreeing with the replies. Then they came to me, seeming relieved that the round was over and questions were few, but just as they turned to go the senior officer touched my wounded leg and glanced again at the wounds, with the pus flowing quite freely from them. 'Pain?' he asked in English and then they were gone. Shortly afterwards one of the sisters came into the ward with four bottles of Advocaat sent to us by the high ranking officer with his compliments, 'Who was he?' I asked. 'He seemed quite a gentleman.' 'That man,' she replied softly, 'is our German Governor of Holland.'

(This was Seyss Inquaart, who had become Governor of Austria at the time of the Anschluss and then with the occupation of the Netherlands, overseer over the Dutch people. Shortly after his visit to us, this eminent man was to have over 100 hostages shot on the Arnhem-Apeldoorn road, on the very spot where an ambush by the underground on the Dutch collaborator, Rueter failed. This gentle man was to be tried after the war

**at Nuremburg as one of the principal
Nazi criminals, tried, condemned and
executed for his crimes against humanity.)**

*After the war Slatterley went every year for
his annual holiday to Apeldoorn, Holland.
He never married and died in 1978.*

NOVEMBER 1944

The *Tirpitz* is finally sunk by RAF bombers. The Allies continue their advance across Europe and enter Strasbourg.

THE GARDEN ROLLER MAN
Brian Guy

Brian Guy's account of the plight of a German American featured in September 1944 on page 379.

We were now battering at the gates of the German homeland on the Dutch side of the border in the Limburg area, and had to set about breaking his hold on the vital Dutch/German border areas. What follows is a recollection of one of the hardest fought, bloodthirsty, and sometimes, for us, very peculiar episodes of the war in North West Europe.

The American 7th Armoured Division took a real pasting trying to take the towns of Overloon and Venraij, then retired to the south, never to be seen again. Afterwards, British 3rd Infantry Division had to go in and take these towns, where others had failed. The resulting battles were bloodthirsty in the extreme, tremendous shell and mortar fire, coupled with heavy small arms and machine gun fire on both sides, and, as usual 8th Brigade with my company up, had to lead off, (8th Brigade led off the attack by tradition, from D-Day onwards).

This battle took place in driving rain amongst the muddy tracks that wandered through the dense conifer woods and over the Molen Beek, this little stream that had been mined on the banks and even under the water, and at the same time was under heavy shell and mortar fire. Sometimes, sadly, whole groups of men were blown to pieces. During this ferocious fighting, our guns at Oploo made the ground tremble beneath our feet. But by now Overloon and Venraij lay safely in our hands, taken against fierce resistance. Meanwhile we had to deal with a new type of mine: we called them Rigler mines. Under heavy fire we cleared them by the thousands, and not knowing what to do with them, we stacked them up in ditches or on top of the ground criss-crossed in stacks. With an officer on a motor bike, I made my way down from our battle area to where they were clearing the thickest of these mines and on the way we had to run over a dead German who was lying in the deep-rutted sand tracks. We could not avoid him. The sand ruts were very deep; when we got there the officer told one of the men to take a mine off away from the rest and see if it was booby trapped. We had turned round and were on our way back to our own area of the fighting when, from behind us, came a gigantic explosion. We yanked the bike around and went back but the whole area was devastated, swept clean of all life. All those that had been present had disappeared. Sadly, as happens in these circumstances, we put wooden crosses there in the knowledge that later, when they were to be buried in a proper place, there would be nothing for the burial squad to find.

During this battle we had to deal with a quarter of a million mines, the worst of these was the Schu mine which was made of wood and could not be detected. These mines were causing a continuous stream of casualties with horrific injuries. The accepted way to find these mines was to crawl along on hands and knees prodding the ground in front with bayonets. Under heavy fire, an unpleasant task, coupled with the loss of those of us, who unfortunately, prodded them in the wrong place and paid with our lives. How to counter this carnage? Then someone came up with the idea of getting an ordinary garden roller which we did. We welded spikes around the roller barrel, then a soldier would push this roller in front of him, and when it went over a Schu mine, it would blow up and the garden roller would fly up in the air on its specially elongated handle, and then drop down again. To protect the soldier, he had a cut down gas mask over his eyes with long gauntlet gloves and a woven rope protector strapped round his groin. Just try to imagine a full scale, ferocious war going on, with heavy artillery and mortar fire and, in the middle of it all, a lonely soldier pushing a garden roller across the battle field and in not too much of a hurry, in case he went too quickly and missed detonating the mine. I was one of those lonely soldiers. And this was demonstrated in front of Field Marshal Montgomery's second in command, Air Vice Marshal Tedder. The outcome of all this was, a short entry in the company's war diaries, stating simply: 'The garden roller experiment was a washout.' In fact, it worked surprisingly well, but could not cope with uneven ground.

Brian Guy was severely wounded in Holland in December 1944 and flown back immediately to England. After the war he remained 100% war disabled but worked in engineering until retirement in 1979. He lives in Swanage, Dorset.

DECEMBER 1944

The Battle of the Bulge begins on 16th December. The US 3rd Army reach Bastogne.

2ND SAS OPERATION GALIA
Bob Walker Brown

Walker Brown whose accounts of escape and an SAS mission in France were told in September 1943 on page 299 and July 1944 on page 366 tells of another SAS operation. He had been ordered to exfiltrate and return to England in September 1944. In December No 3 Squadron to which Walker Brown had been posted as a Troop Commander was ordered to fly to Italy landing at Bari shortly before Christmas. Walker Brown takes up the story:

In late December 1944 a unit of the German division holding the right of the Gothic Line mounted a reconnaissance-in-strength against the division holding the left flank of the US

401

5th Army. The forward elements of this division fell back, leading to the possibility of deep enemy exploitation, without immediate Allied resources to mount an effective counter attack. It was at once decided to mount a deception operation in order to make the enemy think that the 2nd Parachute Brigade, which had just left Italy for Greece, had returned. My troop was ordered to parachute behind the advancing enemy division and to attack enemy main supply routes behind the Gothic Line with or without Partisan support. It was hoped that the enemy would be persuaded for a short time, that a substantial airborne operation was being mounted in their rear.

A SOE [Special Operations Executive] Mission consisting of an officer and signaller were located at the mountain village of Rossano, north of La Spezia. They were in contact with local Partisan forces. The officer was Major Gordon Lett, whom I knew, having been a POW with him in the same camp. Instead of making for the Allied Lines like myself, he stayed with the Partisans and was taken on by SOE.

My briefing was: we were to operate in front of the US 5th Army; enemy forces consisted of one German Panzer Grenadier Regiment (brigade), one composite German/

Italian division, Fascist Militia and unidentified elements. (It was an underestimate: a German Mountain Corps was in the area). Friendly Forces consisted of Partisan bands of varying effectiveness and reliability and a SOE Mission at Rossano. Because of an unusual radio transmission pattern from Gordon Lett's signaller, it was thought that the SOE mission had been captured, transmitting under duress. (In fact the signaller was suffering from frost-bite to his fingers).

Nevertheless, on the 26th December, it was decided to drop my troop, of 31, as a matter of urgency, in dreadful flying conditions. We took off from Bari in four C49s with fighter escort. The DZ was very difficult to identify, the mountains being under deep snow. A guinea-pig officer, Captain Chris Leng, SOE was detailed to drop first. Green signal light: drop. No green signal: choose random DZ from the air and drop. The green signal was observed and the troop jumped. The DZ was the side of a terraced vineyard grossly unsuitable and we had several minor injuries. My leg bag broke free at about 400 feet, smashing my carbine.

Gordon Lett, with an excellent knowledge of the terrain and the situation gave a first rate brief:

The enemy was in the deep valleys four

hours' march away.

The mountain passes were covered in thick snow and ice.

There were no motorable roads (in contrast to today).

Some Partisan bands were well disposed; others — the Communist Red Brigades were unreliable.

News of our arrival would reach the enemy rapidly via informers, suitably greatly exaggerated, as we hoped.

With such an excellent brief there was no need to waste a moment. Tasks were therefore given to the three sticks (patrols) of ten as follows: By descending into the valleys, to attack enemy transport; to attack by fire isolated posts; to use limited explosives as opportunity allowed; above all, to maintain a high level of activity; sticks were to split into two patrols of five as required; Troop HQ with three inch mortar acted as a patrol.

Within 24 hours all patrols had successful shoots, except one half stick which made the classic mistake of moving into an empty building while waiting to ford the River Taro at night. It was spotted by Fascisti and surrounded. The Partisan guide was summarily shot. Five SAS were put in the bag, not handed over to the Germans who would have shot them.

During the following 18 days we kept up continuous attacks against transport on main supply routes and on small enemy posts. Because of the bitter weather it was impossible to use the ice-covered mule and goat tracks by night. The descent of the steep mountains, with much slipping and noise, had to be by day against a background of fresh snow. The approaches to the valleys were few and under enemy observation. One had a limited time to carry out a shoot before a pair of field guns went into action, firing over open sights at ranges of about 1500 — 2000 yards. Scrambling up the steep, icy tracks under fire was bad for the adrenalin. However, we had several effective, three inch mortar shoots, including direct hits on a horse-drawn field battery (stationary).

Ammunition expenditure was high and there was difficulty getting bombs and mules near the mortar base-plate. With severe weather and poor flying conditions air re-supply was a constant problem. Following one airdrop in atrocious visibility the lead aircraft made a final farewell pass over the DZ and flew straight into a mountainside. The recovery and burial of the brave American crew was difficult. DZs were sometimes refused or changed at the last minute, often entailing forced marches

405

through the snow and much wastage of time and security. Red Brigade parties sometimes put out false ground signals in order to steal SAS supplies. A long burst from a Browning HMG put a stop to that, but did not improve relations.

With four experienced gunners in the troop a 75mm pack Howitzer was requested and dropped. Firing in the general direction of La Spezia caused few casualties, but greatly impressed the Partisans. It also caused the enemy to react, as intended.

With the troop concentrated, there was a report, via Gordon Lett, that Mussolini was at the town of Pontremoli, with a strong escort of Germans, en route to visit the Monte Rosa Division. This was a composite German/Italian Alpini formation in the Gothic Line.

Leaving four sick with Gordon Lett and Chris Leng at Rossano the troop marched with maximum speed to a deserted village overlooking Pontremoli. From the church tower it was possible to select a fire position south of the town on the road leading towards the Gothic Line. The position selected was on a bend in the road with a fast-flowing river between the road and the ambush position. There was a drop of some feet to the river, with a steep bank opposite

— a good position and there was a long field of fire. The approach was down a steep, ice-covered mule track. Soon after taking position at first light the next day, the head of a long column of vehicles approached from Pontremoli. At the same time a battery of horse-drawn field artillery appeared moving towards the town. Waiting for both columns to meet we opened up with two Vickers MMGs and LMGs at a range of about 300 yards. With vehicles on fire, horses bolting and men trying to escape into the river, we inflicted substantial casualties.

At the height of the action I fortunately noticed movement on our side of the river. Through binoculars it proved to be a column of German mountain troops in dirty snow smocks, carrying skis. Had the smocks been clean I would not have seen them until too late. The column was approaching us. This was an extreme emergency. We pulled out rapidly and, as the enemy was less than 1000 yards away, we had to use the track we had approached by in the interests of speed, extremely dangerous though it was.

On reaching the track, leading into the mountains, I was horrified to find ourselves some 200 yards behind the rear of a German column. Simultaneously a message came from the rear of the troop that we were followed by a second column of enemy. To avoid immediate identification we left the track and plunged into waist-deep snow, heading for the deserted village, on a high ridge, where we had left mules, spare ammunition and radio.

On reaching the village, after an exhausting climb through deep snow, there was nothing for it but to split into groups of four and head for a previously briefed RV. Before doing so, in order to travel as light as possible in the thick snow we smashed the radio, buried and destroyed the codes in deep snow, abandoned the mules, ammunition, MMGs and LMGs, first throwing weapon essential parts away. As we moved off we were observed and came under heavy small arms and mortar fire.

Leaving the RV we headed for Rossano, avoiding tracks, but we bumped into a German patrol and took two prisoners. One, a feldwebel, said that two German Mountain Regiments, Fascist units, Ukrainians and Mongols were engaged in a search and destroy operation for 400 British parachutists. We were suitably flattered. The situation, however, was very dangerous. The sound of automatic fire could be heard and columns of smoke from burning villages could be seen. Any village suspected of harbouring SAS or Partisans was destroyed; suspected Partisans were shot out of hand.

I later saw 20 young men and girls who had been machine-gunned to death against a cemetery wall.

In order to gain some height advantage we headed for the summit of Monte Gottero, about 7,000 feet and reached there after a continuous forced march through deep snow of just over 59 hours since leaving the RV. It was necessary to change the leading man every five minutes, the snow being waist-deep for much of the way. With no communications and short of rations it was ten days before the enemy operation appeared to slacken. Without radio it was now essential to establish contact with Gordon Lett, his signaller, radio and the four SAS sick, hoping that they had survived, but there was a strong possibility that they had been captured. Making a cautious recce at night I approached a mountain village, down an icy track. There was a full moonlight. Approaching the first house there was shouted challenge and a long burst from the distinctive German MG42. The burst missed me by inches. The next day most of the enemy left the area.

Arriving at Rossano we found that Gordon Lett and party had also evaded capture. Using the SOE radio I signalled for a complete re-supply, weapons, ammunition, radio, clothing etc in order to resume offensive operations as rapidly as possible. Following re-supply and the dropping of a MO [Medical Officer], the previous pattern of attacks on transport was resumed. However, we had lost surprise and following the savage reaction of the enemy, local Italian support diminished. I therefore signalled a request to exfiltrate with a view to re-deployment. This was agreed and I was given a point in the Gothic Line, between two German battalions, for the passage through the strongly held enemy positions. The location of the forward Allied unit was also given.

The approach to the rear of the Gothic Line took several nights of cautious movement in the valleys. As a recently escaped POW I had had useful experience. Particularly hazardous moments were the night fording of deep, fast-flowing rivers, with linked arms to avoid being swept away, without knowing if enemy were on the far bank. On one crossing a German Hauptmann [Captain] was found in over-friendly contact with an Italian girl. He came with us. Before fording that river my troop signaller, hoping to keep more or less dry, sat on what he thought was a low wall and removed his trousers. He was actually sitting on the side of a well and dropped his pants into it. He wanted the German officer's trousers. But I firmly said NO. The German with my pistol at his back, was to say the right things if we bumped an enemy patrol. He would not have looked the part without trousers. My signaller may have been the first man to cross the enemy lines without any trousers. It took him a long time to live it down.

The transit of the Gothic Line had to be made in one night, using old shepherds' tracks. Twice enemy patrols were met, but we parted by mutual consent with the Hauptmann in the lead. Just before first light I thought that we were close to the Allied forward position. Suddenly the German activated a trip flare. Instead of artillery defensive fire, nothing happened. Another 100 yards and the same thing happened, with no reaction.

Some minutes later the outline of a village could be seen. Carefully approaching it there seemed no sign of occupation. Thinking it might be the wrong place we covered a house and threw stones at a window. Seconds later a complete Allied platoon came out with their hands up, thinking we were Germans. Their gunners must have been asleep as well. Moving to the rear on an ammunition track

411

we were in a happy mood, having exfiltrated without casualties except for five prisoners, until we attracted the attention of La Spezia coast battery of 14 inch guns, which could fire inland. Two very near salvos brought us back to the real life of soldiering.

Operation Galia was considered to be successful. According to HQ 5th US Army some 6,000 enemy troops had been deployed to carry out search and destroy operations lasting two weeks, the only SAS operation to have provoked a major enemy reaction. Additionally, we had accounted for about 60 vehicles and a substantial number of casualties. It is unlikely that the deception plan worked. It took 18 days of intensive action to provoke the enemy reaction, although the strong enemy reconnaissance was halted soon after we dropped. Had a complete squadron been deployed the enemy response would probably have been much quicker. The principal lesson to be learnt is that if you irritate the enemy, SAS mobility is vital. Mobility is a relative factor. Although the distances covered on this operation were small, there were exceptionally difficult conditions of terrain and weather. In spite of a forced march of 59 hours without halt, except for one enemy contact, things could have been much worse had the German ski troops used their skis, which they carried, but did not use. At that time radio communications were primitive. Troop HQ had one set in contact with the joint SOE/SAS HQ at Florence. Each stick had a one-way receive-only set which could pick up coded signals. There was no means of knowing if a signal had been received.

After the war the Special Air Service Brigade was disbanded and Walker Brown joined the Parachute Regiment. He was in Palestine taking part in anti-terrorist operations until 1948. He then rejoined the Highland Light Infantry and spent a period of time in Malaya teaching jungle warfare to Malay officers and NCOs. Returning home in 1952 he was immediately posted to the 1st Battalion Highland Light Infantry in Malta — from there he took the Regimental Coronation party home to take part in the Coronation procession in 1953. He subsequently undertook postings to Egypt and Cyprus but was back with an SAS regiment engaged in deep jungle operations in Malaya before taking early retirement as a Colonel in 1968. He joined the Defence Intelligence Staff and finally retired in 1980. He now lives in Wiltshire with his wife, Helen.

THE BATTLE OF THE BULGE AND CAPTURE
Johnnie R Beaver

Johnnie Beaver was born in America in 1921. He served in the US Army and joined a heavy weapon's platoon. He arrived in England in October 1944 but did not see action until December 1944.

On the morning of 16th December 1944, all hell broke loose. Most of us were young and had never fired a gun at another human, much less fought in a war. The only fighting any of us had been involved in were a few night patrols. We had gone from the States straight into the hell known as the Battle of the Bulge.

St Vith had seen battle before this day but the battle it saw from the 16th December through to the 19th was like nothing it had seen before. German Field Marshal von Rundstedt began the shelling, laying down a thunderous artillery barrage which was totally deafening to our ears. The Germans would lift the barrage and then send in troops and tanks against us. Time and time again we held them off so other units could regroup and strike back.

Food and ammunition were running low

and we couldn't parachute any supplies in because of the fog. We had radio contact for the first couple of days but then we lost it. We spent all of our time trying to fight off the German forces that were overpowering us.

The Germans had finally driven a wedge between the 423rd and the 422nd Regiments and we were surrounded. On the 18th orders were given to attack in the direction of Schonberg to the West, in an attempt to break out of the German encirclement. Our 81 mm mortar was on a hill above Schonberg, dug in. Some time during the first few days of the battle, ammo bearers had brought us a few rounds of white phosphorus. Since we could not take the town we could do a little damage to it. We laid those rounds down on the town and started some fires. We fought without armour, virtually no artillery and ammunition fast running out. We had had no food or water for four days and nights; we were forced by the sheer weight of number and artillery to try to make it on our own back to the American lines, every man for himself.

The four of us: our platoon leader Lieutenant Philipson, Corporal Dopp, Jack and I headed out in our jeep with our 81 mm mortar on the trailer. We went down through the woods but as we rounded a curve we found the road was blocked by a jeep knocked out by a German machine gun nest. The Germans started firing at us: Corporal Dopp jumped out and managed to crawl down a ravine to safety; Philipson and I went out on the right hand side of the jeep onto the road. We had no more than hit the ground before the Germans shot a grenade into the jeep which exploded. I was knocked unconscious and when I came to Philipson was lying on the ground. As I crawled to him, I realised I had been hit in the side with shrapnel and pulled it out. Philipson had shrapnel that had gone in right under his shoulder blade and came out in the front of his chest. I managed to bandage his wound before I heard a German on the other side of the jeep. As I looked up he motioned with his gun for me to stand up. He took our weapons and I picked up Philipson. My relief at not being shot was short lived, for now I was a German POW.

We were marched back into the German lines to a farmhouse being used as a headquarters. Philipson was put upstairs with other wounded soldiers. They put me in the cellar with a few of our guys who had been captured along the dirt road. It was a long, terrifying night. Early the next morning on 20th December began the Death March. Having marched for a few hours, we came to a railroad siding where there were some railway carriages which the Germans filled with prisoners. I helped Philipson into one. I went to crawl in after him but a German guard shoved me back and shut the door. I felt like this was the last time I would see him alive. I learned years later that the Allied forces strafed the train and Philipson was shot quite a few times but he recovered and made it home.

We started marching again, heading back into Germany and were joined by other small groups of prisoners. We still hadn't had any food. We were eating what we could find in the fields along the way, such as sugar beet. Some old people would try to give us pieces of bread. The guards didn't like that at all and would push them away.

On the March our worst times were given to us by the Hitler Youth Corps. They were kids that should have been in the Boy Scouts but instead they were supposed to be the new Nazi Germany. Dressed in uniforms they would stone, spit on or hit us with sticks while the guards did nothing to stop them. At night they would bed us down in the fields or bombed out buildings. We were told if one of us tried to escape, others would be shot. The German guards told us that until we were registered with the American Red Cross, no one knew whether we were alive or dead. They could do anything they wanted to us. We knew that the ones that dropped out on the March were being shot.

As we went further into Germany, we began hearing about Jews being gassed from other prisoners who joined us. One day we came to what looked like an old factory. We were told to strip off our clothes, pile them up and to remember where they were. Then we were told to go through the door at one end of a long narrow building, to take a shower and come out through the door at the other end. From the high ceiling hung what looked like shower heads with pull chains which we were afraid to pull for fear of gassing. We went to the other door and beat on it. The guard opened it and we put our clothes back on. We were deloused and off we marched again.

My feet were giving me problems. The snow and water kept my feet wet and cold. At night I would pull off my boots, wring out my socks and lie on them to dry them. But the wet socks and boots kept rubbing my feet. I knew I was suffering from frostbite. At night, even as tired and as weak as we were, we could not sleep because of cold, hunger, pain and fear.

We started each morning at daylight.

Usually there were new guards and we marched until dark. We were all weak from not eating. Most of us had wounds of one kind or another and were suffering from frostbite, fear and homesickness. Some of us just couldn't go on any longer and fell out. We didn't have any choice but to leave them and knew when we got further down the road the Germans would shoot them.

Late on Christmas Eve, we marched to some barracks in a small village which we thought were built for the Hitler Youth Corps. This was the first time we had been inside. The barracks were empty except for a piano which none of us knew how to play. We lay down on the floor and tried to get some sleep. Christmas morning we waited for our guards to show up to continue the March but they didn't. We assumed the guards were in one of the other buildings. Mid-day came and along with it some men with buckets of meaty soup, our first meal in days. We figured it was horse meat and were thankful to get it. The Germans wouldn't let us observe Christmas in any way. After everything was cleared away we heard bombing. We got down around the walls and covered our heads; we heard one hit close and then another one. After a few minutes it was over. So we got together and decided to take some poles that we found in the barracks and go outside and spell out POW in the snow. The guards caught us and lined us up to start marching again. We saw that one bomb had hit the road and one the building next to us. This had been the British coming back from a bombing run and unloading their bombs.

A few days after Christmas, we came to a village and were put in a small wire enclosure with three barracks. There were some prisoners in another compound across the way. We found out they were Polish and they worked in a sugar beet factory. In the evening as they came by from work they would slip us small packages of brown sugar. The whole compound including the factory was enclosed with fencing. One night we got the door to our barracks open. We headed for the sugar beet factory to get brown sugar and any other food we could find. We got into the factory but the German guards heard us and marching us back to the barracks, locked us up. Fortunately the Germans didn't retaliate. We were so hungry and all we could think about was food. To try and occupy our minds, we wrote menus of the meals we wanted when we got back home. The guards at this compound would bring us a watery soup with kale and grass in it. There was a small stove in the barracks and we would try to fry some of the kale and grass. After a day or so, this mixture started going straight through us. Diarrhoea and stomach pain were constant companions to us all. This would make us weaker. After a few days there, we were marched to the main camp, Stalag IVB.

Beaver remained in captivity until the end of the war. He worked in the printing business for many years and now lives in St Marys, Georgia, USA.

JANUARY 1945

The Allies force the Germans back and the Americans regain land in the Ardennes. Hungary signs an armistice with the Allies.

MORE ON BROTHELS
Alastair Gordon
(The Marquess of Aberdeen)

A previous visit to a brothel is described by Alastair Gordon in May 1942 on page 213.

In 1945 when the militant feminists of Paris demanded, and got, the closure of all the bordellos, just one remained open (I dare say half the French Cabinet were clients). This was the Vicomtesse de Brissac's house in the fashionable XVI arrondissement. She herself — no doubt long disowned by that great family — was stout and heavily made up, but the girls were soignée and elegant.

My favourite, a chestnut-haired beauty, was fluent in several languages. She once lost her professional cool and called out in her extremity, 'Ach, mein Gott!' Tactfully I didn't remind her that the Germans had left, defeated. But, with her gift for languages (and my lack of them), she was excellent company to take out to dinner, followed by further romps in my hotel bedroom. Once again, no names please. Rosa Lewis of the Cavendish Hotel used to say, 'No names, no lawyers, and kiss my baby's bottom.'

One particular night in Paris a friend of mine and I had a two bedroom suite in the Georges Cinq Hotel: it was a very hot night, so at half time we all got into a cold bath off one of the bedrooms with glasses of brandy; it was a very big bath, but we all managed to get in amid shrieks of laughter. Having cooled off we returned to our respective bedrooms to resume exertions. My linguist girlfriend said, 'You British are happily different to French men who are played out by their mid twenties.'

Gordon was demobbed as a Captain in 1946 and resumed his art studies at the Camberwell School of Art. He married Anne Barry in 1950 and worked in life assurance but also pursued his career as a botanical artist. He succeeded to the Aberdeen peerages in 1984 on the death of his elder brother and became the 6th Marquess of Aberdeen and Temair. Lord and Lady Aberdeen had two daughters and a son. The Marquess of Aberdeen died in August 2002. In Who's Who he lists his recreations as 'Wine, women and song.'

ESCAPING EXECUTION
BY THE RUSSIANS
Henry John West

An incident in the desert by West was recounted in March 1941 on page 132. Having been captured in North Africa he has spent the majority of the war in prison camps.

After some time, I was sent to another work camp in Czechoslovakia. Teshen was the name of the place where I was one of a gang making a road into a power station. I was driving a diesel roller up and down the crushed rock one day, when they rushed us back to camp and told us to take any small things that we could carry and at about 3 p.m. they marched us out of the camp. They said that we were going to march right into Germany as the Russians were getting close. At midnight we were still marching and my foot started to play up and I was getting some pain. I had had enough so I said to the fellow next to me, 'Are you game to make a break for it?' He answered, 'Yes I've had enough too.' We waited until we saw a deep ditch at the side of the road with bushes. I looked out for the guard behind and he kept his eye on the one in front, and when we saw that they weren't taking too much notice we made a dive into the ditch which was full of slushy snow.

We stayed there for some time until we almost froze to death. When all was quiet, we slowly got out of the ditch and started to walk back towards, we hoped, the Russians. We were so cold that we decided to find shelter and we eventually found an unoccupied school which had a cellar. We stayed here for about five days, sleeping under some old potato sacks, which kept us warm but hungry, as we could find virtually no food, only some old rotten swedes or turnips which no doubt saved our lives.

One day I happened to look out of a little spy hole that we had made when I saw a massive tank parked at the end of the road, about 600 yards away. The turret was swinging around in all directions and kept pointing to our building. We were afraid to move in case those inside saw the movement and fired. Looking at the markings on the tank we realised it was Russian, and as they were Allies we decided to show ourselves. They had guns trained on us as we walked towards them and then they pushed us up against the tracks of the tank and started shouting at us which of course we couldn't understand. I had learnt a bit of German from the coal mine so I tried to speak in broken German that I thought I had mastered so well and that only made it worse. They knocked us around and I do believe they were going to shoot us. They had already tied my hands behind my back. Then a young Russian officer arrived from somewhere and as luck would have it he could understand English. He took some photos from my pocket, one of which was of my wife and little daughter taken in Cairo and it also had some addresses of POW mates whom I was going to contact after the war. They released us telling us which way to go and giving us a note that would pass us through and we went quickly in case they changed their minds. We walked up through Poland but we had to go slowly as we weren't fit, having been prisoners for so long. I had been three years in Italy and Germany. We must have walked almost 200 miles, picking up bits of food and drink on the way from abandoned houses. Eventually we were allowed to get on a train and landed up in Odessa on the Black Sea.

West stayed in a large house with other ex POWs for about a month and arrived back in England during March 1945 — all the POWs were divided up and returned to England on a convoy of ships. West now lives in Melbourne, Australia.

FEBRUARY 1945

Churchill, Roosevelt and Stalin meet at Yalta to redraw the map of post-war Europe as the Soviet Forces advance into Germany. The British and Americans bomb Dresden, killing tens of thousands of German civilians.

CAPTIVITY
James Romine

James Monroe Romine was born in 1913. When war broke out he enlisted in the USAF and, joining the 544th Bomber Squadron, became a tail gunner, flying as part of the crew on a B-26. There were 150 tail gunners in the squadron and only eight came home. He was known as an ace gunner (ace gunners were those who had shot down five or more enemy planes). He had married Anne before the war and told her he was part of the ground crew so as not to worry her.

I flew my last mission on 10th February as a tail gunner in the lead ship of a squadron of 36 planes, with Euskirchen, Germany, as our target. We had received our first hit before reaching the target, while flying at an altitude of 12,600 feet. Then right after 'bombs away,' we received a direct hit in the right engine. We began losing altitude immediately and Colonel Bentley warned the crew that we would be forced to bail out. We were just east of the Ruhr River. Shortly after my parachute opened, I was hit four times by machine gun fire from ground forces, breaking my leg in two places; this made for a bad landing, the impact of which dislocated my hip.

I got my chute off and felt tempted to try swimming back across the Ruhr River, but it seemed too risky to expose my position so openly in the daytime, when all about me were trees and hedges for protection. The field was heavily mined and I had to be very careful crawling through the snow, though there seemed some hope of escape if I could just get back to the river bank at nightfall and try somehow to get across. But the Germans were thicker than hell and were keeping a sharp watch, and wherever I crawled I left behind a bloody trail. After about three hours, between sundown and dark, a concussion grenade landed in my hiding place.

I was taken prisoner by SS troopers who forced me at fixed bayonet to walk on my injured leg to a village about two and a half miles away. Had I at any point come across with the information they sought I'm sure they wouldn't have gone to the trouble of taking me prisoner. Before we got to the village I sat down and refused to walk further, so they held a confab and sent for transportation to carry me the rest of the way. There was a German first aid station in the village, but they merely took a look at my wounds and replaced the bandages I myself had put on. Three SS officers proceeded to question me for several hours, then stripped me of all my clothing, wrapped me in a blanket and took me about 16 kilometres by horse and wagon to a point somewhere west of the Rhine. We arrived at a German evacuation hospital, where there were about 300 wounded Germans and where they left me for a day and a night with no medical attention. Then we started on another trip further into Germany, to the finest hospital one could ask for anywhere — large, modern and shining. Here at last, I thought, was a chance to have my wounds dressed. Instead, they tossed me into a small room in the attic of the three-storey hospital along with nine other American infantry boys, two of whom were to die during my three days there. There were four legs left among those nine men in that room, their stumps were raw and uncared for. We lay on filthy straw mats, lice-covered and nauseous from the indescribable stench that hung over the room. The daily diet consisted of coffee and a piece of black bread in the morning and at night a small cereal bowl of potato soup. SS men came in periodically to question me further; how they could endure entering the room is beyond me. The cruel deaths which those fellows were left to face, amid supposedly civilised surroundings where all medical facilities were at hand, is a testimonial to German brutality that will never be forgotten by those of us who lived to relate the facts.

After three days of futile questioning the Germans put me in an ambulance and drove me across the Rhine to a waiting train, the carriages of which were painted white with red crosses and which, I found out later, were loaded with ammunition for the Russian front. I was laid in a carriage, with a foot-deep layer of horse manure and straw as a mattress. Inside with me they put a Polish pilot who spoke very little English and for six days we lay there with no water to drink and just two or three sandwiches during the whole trip. The train was stopped several times by American planes but they were fooled by the red crosses and it wasn't strafed.

MARCH 1945

Allied troops are now crossing the Rhine in large numbers. The Americans are dropping incendiary bombs on Japanese cities.

RESCUE BY THE US 3RD ARMY
Romine's story continues:

It was about the beginning of March when we arrived at Badenoheim and the Polish pilot and I parted company. I was taken to another fine, modern SS hospital, which might have been a luxurious hotel in peace-time. Here again I was given no medical care, except twice they made 16-inch cuts to allow drainage from my leg, which had now swollen to twice its normal size. I was kept alone in a litter room, sleeping on straw and, of course, with no sanitation facilities. Ridiculously enough, an armed guard stood over me all day long. I was never allowed water to drink and during my entire imprisonment I was given just two cigarettes. The living conditions and starvation diet continued here until that unforgettable day when the US 3rd Army walked in and took over. By this time I was so weak, my pain had seemed to become fainter too, and my recollections of the details are hazy. But I do remember that a sergeant and a captain suddenly appeared before me one day, and they had a hard time deciding whether or not I was American. I must have mumbled something, for I know it wasn't long before the Captain had sent a jeep to collect four army medics and a supply of blood for transfusions, delousing powder and dressings. Since I was in no condition to be moved, the medics stayed right there with me for two days. After I had gained strength they carried me several blocks by stretcher to an abandoned German house they had converted into an aid station. It was there I learned that 24 other American flyers had been imprisoned in various parts of the town other than at the hospital and some of them looked as if they had had as rough a time as me. Eventually they moved us all by ambulance to an American field hospital somewhere East of the Rhine. They kept me there for four days and then taking me across the Rhine to an airstrip loaded me onto a C-47 bound for Paris. After several weeks I arrived at Rhodes General Hospital in Utica, New York.

After the war Romine had a series of operations on his left leg and gained partial use of it. He loved horses and went to work as a cowboy on a ranch in the Hunboldt mountains in Nevada. However, his leg never healed and was finally amputated in 1951. Afterwards he said that getting rid of his leg was the best thing that had ever happened. Later he joined his brother working as a tile setter on a large government housing project. Romine never liked to talk much about the war but did tell his nephew this story: 'I was on a mission over Northern Germany and due to fatigue fell asleep at my gun. I suddenly awoke to find an ME-109 coming out of a cloud about 50 feet away straight at me. I was very lucky because my twin 50 caliber guns were pointed right at him and I just jerked both triggers and riddled the plane. When the German pilot was hit he passed right by the tail end of the bomber (about 15 feet away). I'll never forget the look on that guy's face . . . he had crystal blue eyes and looked just like a kid I grew up with in Missouri.' James Romine died after a riding accident in 1978.

APRIL 1945

The Allies begin their attack on the Gothic Line. The British are deeply shocked by what they find at Belsen Concentration Camp. On the 12th April Roosevelt dies. On 30th April Hitler marries Eva Braun and commits suicide.

ANOTHER LETTER HOME
Terence C Irvine, MC

Terence Irvine's letters to his mother also appear in April 1943 on page 275.

We are on the move and so you probably will not hear from me for a bit. I am writing this on my knee in a very nice garden of a little provincial Dutch town up near the German border. Last week I was up in Germany doing a reconnaissance and got as far as Osnabruck of which little is left. I am delighted to say that I saw a lot of very depressed looking Germans wherever I went. Those that have not had their houses knocked down by the

RAF get kicked out by us to put our troops in. We also eat their vast food stores looted from all over Europe and give them ours instead, so that eggs, ham, pork and fresh milk are now on the menu. We are of course waiting to go into our final destination — the big 'city' of which I am to be the Chief Constable. Lovely sunshine this afternoon and I am sunbathing in shirt sleeves only. One of the girls of the house has been to Birmingham on a visit and speaks good English. They cannot do enough for us as they have just been liberated. No electricity, gas or fuel, very little food, we are helping in whatever way we can. Had a long letter from Roger Cattell who is still in Aleppo. He wants to get home to France to see after his business, I want him to do so too! I have been asked several times if I wish to stay on in Germany as a policeman and I always say 'yes' if it is made attractive enough! Am not allowed to tell you much news. Have got a new motor car, which is an improvement on the old one. I don't know when our mail will catch up with us.

On 22 May 1945 Irvine was appointed Lieutenant Colonel DPM Hamburg. As the Army Group moved through Germany Irvine followed. He was appointed Local Colonel

DPM Berlin. On 17 December 1945 Colonel Irvine, the Head of the Police in the British sector of Berlin, was arrested by Brigadier Kingsley-Foster and held under close arrest for 79 days. On 4 March 1946 at the Courts Martial Centre, Hanover, Major Irvine, having been stripped of his rank of Lieutenant Colonel was tried by court martial.

At Hamburg it was alleged while enforcing the army's non-fraternisation policy Major Irvine befriended a German woman, Frau Rosemarie Von Zimmerman whom he said he intended to marry as soon as conditions allowed. Aged 50, it was alleged that Irvine had employed Frau Zimmerman, formerly the wife of a German officer, first as an informant and then gave her a car and requisitioned a private house which was later used for parties at which she was present. Irvine then set Frau Zimmerman up in an apartment near his own in Berlin. As a result of the court martial, Irvine was dismissed from the service. He arranged for Frau Zimmerman to be smuggled into Britain and married her in September 1946. He subsequently divorced her in 1960. Irvine worked in the bloodstock business and later hotel management, becoming the manager of the Hong Kong Hilton. He died in 1966.

THE LIBERATION OF DACHAU
Thomas McQuillan

Dachau was the first concentration camp used by the Germans, having been established in 1933, and was located about 12 miles north of Munich. It was also the first and most important camp at which medical experiments were carried out.

Thomas McQuillan was born in 1919 in Pennsylvania and worked as a coal miner before the war. To introduce his account he writes: In 1941 I arrived at Fort Smith, Arkansas to begin my military training. We were trained by the academy at Fort Knox by General Pritchard and then by General Smith when General Pritchard was replaced. I was then transferred to Camp Campbell, Kentucky. I departed from Camp Shanks in New York and landed at Marseilles in France. We met up with the Moroccans (very big men) and went straight to the Front Line and then into Germany.

When I entered the concentration camp, the first thing I remember seeing were the railway wagons filled with people, mostly dead but a few still alive. My battalion was divided into

439

different companies and sent into the different POW huts. We disarmed the prison guards, which was no real problem as they were ready to give up, and threw their guns into a pile. We then made the prison guards the prisoners. The now ex-prisoners were helped into the main compound. Those prisoners who could help, would then help their fellow prisoners, who could not walk by themselves, into the compound. We gave what 'K-Rations' we had to the newly liberated prisoners. The sight of so many human beings looking like walking skeletons was very upsetting. How anyone could do what was done to these people is incomprehensible. Their clothes hung on them as if on a hanger. The haunted look of the people as they sat and watched what was going on around them is still etched in my mind. I could count their ribs and see the bones in their backs. Men and women about the same age as I was (26) looked as if they were in their 60s. There was crying and wringing of hands wherever you looked in the camp. Our following orders were to have the SS troopers remove the bodies of the victims that were mass buried in a huge ditch. This 'ditch' was approximately half a mile long, and the dead had been dumped in and covered up with dirt. The troopers were now ordered to bury each victim in an individual grave. The townspeople were marched past the open ditches to see exactly what had been done in the camp in their town.

Some of the people would pretend to cry; having an onion placed in a handkerchief, so it would look as if they were truly sorry. Maybe the onion helped them against smelling the stench of decaying flesh. When it was discovered that someone had an onion, it was taken away. The SS troopers were also forced to clear out the crematoriums and bury the ashes and bones of those prisoners murdered there. The Allied Governments then ordered that the guards be loaded into a truck and took them away to face charges. I spent four or five days at Dachau. The mistreatment and torture of civilians was the most sickening scene that I had seen during my entire tour of duty. I do not know how the prisoners survived such treatment. Adults who weighed maybe 60 pounds were walking! Some of the prisoners were taken out of their huts on pallets obviously unable to walk. Some cheered, some cried, some were incapable of emotion. These were innocent people, raped body and soul.

After the war Thomas McQuillan became a factory worker in Cleveland, Ohio. He now lives in a suburb of Cleveland, Ohio, USA.

LIBERATION AT
STALAG 4B MUHLBERG
Tom Barker

Tom Barker's account: Captured on Crete was told in June 1941 on page 149. By now Barker has spent almost four years in captivity.

You could not by any stretch of the imagination say that my last day as a Prisoner of War was uneventful. I woke up to cries of, 'There is no bloody guard on the wire,' and, 'Look up at the tower, the guard has gone.' I leapt out of my bunk and sure enough as I looked up at the tower there was no one there.

I noticed it had suddenly gone very quiet and I saw everyone was watching something happening over in the Russian POW compound so I went outside and joined the crowd to see what was so interesting and I wished I hadn't. It was grisly and haunting.

There was a German guard called Blondie, who was in charge of the Russian work parties. In my mind he was also the meanest bastard in any army. He would hit a POW for no reason; he usually carried a pick handle and would lay into anyone who got in his way. He was about six foot tall and heavily built with blonde hair, blue eyes and a permanent scowl and looked what he was, in his grey uniform with all the relevant badges to show he had been in the Hitler Youth, a typical SS bully boy. And we knew for certain that he had killed eight blokes in this camp, blokes who could not fight back.

One day a cart with rubbish and potato peelings had been on its way to the rubbish pit to be burned when some hungry Russian POWs grabbed some of the peelings. Blondie saw them, put his pistol to the back of one bloke's head and shot him. He then beat the other senseless with his pick handle and broke his arm and lashed out at others who came too close to him. He made the other prisoners pick up the dead man and put him on the rubbish cart while hitting anyone within range of his pick shaft and the dead man was taken to the pit and burnt along with the rubbish.

Some Russian POWs, now free, were applauding a woman on a horse and she was basking in this adoration. They had been busy raiding the small allotment garden in the camp to get anything that was edible and that was where they found Blondie, the German guard, hiding in one of the tool sheds. He had been found asleep in a drunken stupor and was now struggling to keep his feet while a group of very determined Russian POWs steered him to a lamppost in the camp.

A large group had gathered and two or three Russians had hold of Blondie by the arms. Blondie was struggling and shouting and screaming but to no avail. The woman on the horse just sat there and watched as a skinny Russian POW threw a rope over the lamppost nearby and fastened it round Blondie's ankles. Three or four thin Russian POWs got hold of the rope and pulled while two more held on to Blondie's arms and pulled him off his feet. The Russians on the rope pulled Blondie's legs off the ground and the two holding the arms let go so now Blondie is grabbing at tufts of grass to stop himself being hoisted upside down. The Russians kept hoisting until Blondie was about two or three feet clear of the ground.

For a short while Blondie was swaying back and forth and trying to reach up to untie the rope round his ankles. When it looked like he might succeed, one Russian grabbed his arm and cut and hacked until the hand fell off to the ground, while Blondie's other fist is flailing at the bloke's back until another Russian POW grabbed the arm and hung on to it. The bloke with the knife did the same to the other hand.

Meanwhile Blondie is screaming and

writhing upside down and blood is being spattered on the watching Russians who move back to avoid getting wet. After a while the screaming stops and the body twitches as the blood is just a drip now and then. Another Russian moved forward and it looked as though he was giving the German a hug. But when he stepped back he suddenly held up the severed head for all to see. Then looking at it, he spat on it, and as though in disgust, he threw it to the side of the road, and urinated on it, and one or two of the others walked over to it and did the same.

This was the ultimate savagery of war. Blondie was also responsible for the death of a bloke I knew, so I shed no tears but to see a bloke die like this was like being in a nightmare. To the Russian POWs it was justice but to everyone else it was war. How thin too is that veneer we hide under that we call it civilisation. I would like to point out here to those sceptics who say the Holocaust and some of the war stories by different authors are not true. How come they were seen by not only me, but thousands of POWs in that camp: British, French, Russian, Greek, Americans and Dutch.

Tom Barker married in 1947. He worked in various fields, making bricks and tiles for a time and then ran his own electrical goods service and repair shop. He and his wife had five children, emigrating to Australia in the Sixties. They now have six grandchildren and one great grand-daughter.

MAY 1945

On the 2nd May the Soviet Forces complete their capture of Berlin and German forces surrender in Italy. On the 7th May all German forces surrender unconditionally. VE Day falls on the 8th May.

CLEANING UP AT BELSEN
contributed by George Bower

At Belsen, near Celle, an estimated 37,000 prisoners had died from starvation, disease and overwork. It is the first camp to be liberated by the Allies on 15th April 1945.

George Bower was born in 1910 near Rotherham. He was a coal miner before war broke out and was called up in 1940. Having temporarily worked in a hospital he joined the newly formed Light Field Ambulance and took part in the Normandy landings. Bower writes:

'I really cherish this letter, my unit was one of the first into the horrible place, a truce was called to allow us in, owing to typhus raging in the camp.'

SPECIAL ORDER OF THE DAY
By LIEUT COLONEL M W GONIN, RAMC

I wish to thank all ranks of the 11 (Br) Light Field Ambulance and every member of 567 Coy American Field Service Unit who have worked with us so closely for what you have done since coming to BELSEN Concentration Camp on 17 April 1945.

The Unit will always be remembered for what some of you did on D-Day with 27 Armd Bde, for those uncomfortable weeks at Hermanville before Caen fell, for the restless months from Caumont to the Maas when you made for yourselves a reputation with the Guards which any unit might envy. With the Guards you helped to clear the Sittard Triangle and with them took part in the muddy, bloody battles of Cleve and Goch. Since 27 Feb and the formation of the Bank Group you have had not more than two days' consecutive rest and at the Rhine you evacuated 1,700 casualties in 56 hours — a role which has never been undertaken by any unit in the history of warfare. Finally and again with 6th Guards Armoured Brigade you shared with the Americans in the capture of Munster. For all this you have received well deserved acknowledgement from Higher Command.

You then undertook what, for this unit, was the thankless and unspectacular task of clearing Belsen Concentration Camp. Our American friends and yourselves, with the BRCS have moved well over 11,000 sick from Belsen. To do this, 63 of you have worked for a month amid the most unhygienic conditions inside huts where the majority of internees were suffering from the most virulent disease known to man. You have had to deal with mass hysteria and political complication requiring the tact of diplomats and firmness of senior officers. During the first ten days in the Concentration Camp and before any organised attempt had been made to feed the sick in those huts you distributed 4,000 meals twice daily from what RSM Marno could scrounge by initiative and subtlety.

By collecting medical equipment from all over Germany you produced a dispensary which has supplied drugs for 13,000 patients a day and has met the demands of excitable medical officers of all races requiring the most exotic drugs in half a dozen different languages. You have, without hesitation, acted as undertakers, collecting over 2,000 corpses from the wards of the hospital area and removing them to the mortuary — a task which the RAMC can never before have been asked to fulfil.

The cost has not been light: twenty of you contracted typhus — a disease causing great personal suffering. Thank God all the patients are doing well.

One of us will never leave Belsen — the dawn attack by the German Air Force on our lines was the price paid to come here.

Life can never be quite the same again for those who have worked in the Concentration Camp but you will go with the knowledge that the 11 (Br) Lt Fd Amb has once again done a good job.

Brig HL Glyn Hughes, CBE DSO MC and

Lt Col JAD Johnston, MC SMO Belsen Camp join me in thanking you all for the part you have played in achieving the impossible.
Lieut Colonel M W Gonin RAMC
Commanding No 11(Br)
Light Field Ambulance

After the war Bower worked for BT and now lives in Oxford.

THE END OF WAR IN ITALY
Michael Bereznicki

Bereznicki whose accounts have appeared in September 1939 on page 1, February 1940 on page 41, September 1942 on page 237 and December 1943 on page 324 celebrated the end of the war outside Verona.

After we captured Bologna I noticed that our advances were happening faster and faster. Our opponent was getting weaker and weaker because he was not putting up much of a fight anymore. He just kept retreating. As we moved northward, our regiment captured lots of abandoned enemy equipment — motorcycles, troop carriers, machine guns, and even a four-ton truck. The Germans were running out of gasoline and they had no choice but to ditch their equipment. I remember one of the more entrepreneurial guys in our unit, who took a captured four-ton truck and sold it to a group of Italian farmers for several million lira. He took the money and bought wine, cheese, a stereo and some records. He threw a big party, which was thoroughly enjoyed by everyone. Afterwards, we knew which tent was his — the one with the loud, blaring Italian music.

We chased the enemy up into the northernmost parts of Italy. Outside Verona, our regiment passed a group of American soldiers sitting on a hillside, drinking wine, and waving. They all said, 'The war is over. The war is over.' None of us could understand English, being Polish so we kept on going. When our column finally reached the town, I saw a long, long line of German POWs shuffling dejectedly past us. Most avoided eye contact, preferring instead to look at the ground below. Every building in Verona, had white flags and bed sheets hanging from balconies, rooftops, windows, and flag posts. A sea of white stretched out as far as the eye could see. The civilians were delirious with joy. They ran around singing and shouting and dancing down the streets. My truck was pelted with flowers and champagne. The war was definitely over.

After the war Bereznicki stayed in Italy as part of the Occupation Forces to help maintain law and order. He was discharged from the Army in 1946 and worked in a Scottish coal mine from 1947 to 1948. Bereznicki then emigrated to Canada, married in 1960 and worked for the Alberta Government Telephones until retirement in 1972. He has one son and lives in Edmonton in Alberta.

VE DAY
Joan R Gilmour

Joan Gilmour was born in Birmingham in 1921.

Joy at the news of the end of the war went to our heads. The church bells rang (the first time for the duration) and we threw open our windows the better to hear them. We were given a day off work and went wild with joy going out on to the town where the whole of Bath seemed to be milling around. There were many Forces personnel. Flags came out everywhere. The Bandstand in Parade Gardens was full of soldiers, airmen, civvies, yanks, sailors on leave, children and old people, all singing different songs. It was like a joyous madhouse. Lights returned and the feeling of immense relief was overwhelming, after all the years of the blackout. We were madly inflated with happiness but also sad at the deaths of loved ones, friends and comrades who had given their lives in the cause of peace, including my beloved Canadian Seaforth Highlander killed in Sicily. Later I met the brother of my friend with whom I worked. I shall never forget seeing the change in him — aged 28 he was grey and haggard looking like an old man. He had been a prisoner and made numerous escapes being moved from one camp to another hopefully more secure. His suffering was highly visible.

There was sheer relief and almost disbelief that peace was actually there. However, we were aware of the continuing war in the Far East, especially for me personally as some of my friends' relatives were serving out there. We had already experienced the dismay and horror of Singapore falling and the ensuing conflict in that theatre of war.

Joan Gilmour is a poet and lives in Bath.

PERMISSIONS ACKNOWLEDGEMENTS

For permission to reproduce material, acknowledgement and thanks are due to the following:

Ron Bereznicki for On a Farm in Poland as War Breaks Out; Deportation; You're in the Army Now; Welcome to the Front; The End of War in Italy; — all extracts from unpublished memoirs by Michael J Bereznicki. Mary Edwards for 18 Years Old and Too Young for France; The Battle of Keren; Tobruk; Monte Cassino; all extracts from unpublished memoirs by Captain Alec J Barthorpe. Brenda Glass for Life on *HMS Hood* as War is declared; Life continues on *HMS Hood*; Tragedy at Oran; all extracts from memoirs by Leonard C Williams. Colonel Vic S Senior for Raw Recruit. Brigadier Peter A L Vaux for Balance of Payments. Barbara Willis for Getting used to the French by Robert C Clemishaw. Jennifer Schofield for *HMS Exeter* at the River Plate by Norman Schofield. James C Slater for The Phoney War and Home Life; Bombs and Life in the Country; Life in Lincoln — all extracts from unpublished memoirs by May W Cannan. Arthur Heartfield for The Phoney War in France. Basil Rabbits for Brief Action and Speedy Retreat to Dunkirk. James W Fyfe for Dunkirk. Heath Quittenton for The Lancastria Goes Down by Edwin R G Quittenton. Silvester Macdonald for Cleaning up after Dunkirk; The Torpedoing of *HMS Phoebe*. Bob Harris for Evacuation Memories. Dennis L A Farr for The Night the Bombs Fell. Jessica A Frank for Waiting for the Return of the Bomber Squadron; also for A Bombing Mission by Alan D Frank and Evacuation by Mrs Evans. Tony West for An Incident in the Desert; Escaping Execution by the Russians by Henry J West. Kenneth Welch for the Torpedoing of *HMS Capetown* by Albert Welch. Walter Fudge for On Board *HMS Dorsetshire*; The Sinking of *HMS Dorsetshire*. Tom Barker for Captured on Crete; Liberation at Stalag 4B Muhlberg. Charles Hanaway for Training. Jack Durey for Prisoner of War. Marie Robson for The Sinkings by Ralph Robson. Charles Mallett for On the Run in the Desert and Tobruk and Recapture by Bob Mallett. David Melville-Hays for Evacuation by Sea from Singapore; Becoming a Japanese POW; Dysentery,

Disease and Death all extracts from Memoirs by Charles C Weston. The Oldie Magazine (March 2001) for extracts from The Good Whore Guide by The Marquess of Aberdeen: Brothels I Knew as a Bachelor and More on Brothels. Alan Shard for The Loss of Putney Hill. Ernie W H Huntley for The Battle of Alam Halfa and Events Leading up to the Battle of El Alamein. Kay Berryman for Letters from the Desert by Sidney A Wigglesworth. Doreen Sweetman for Christmas as a POW by George Sweetman. The Tank Journal (February 1994) for After El Alamein, an extract from Alamein and After; A Reminiscence by Major Harold Limer. Andrew Sewell for Full of Insolence. Peter Hawkings for Letters to Mother and Another Letter Home by Terence C Irvine. Valentine J Wrigley for Talking with the Enemy and Working in Intelligence at Monte Cassino. Colin Johnson for A Letter to Mother by Louis Johnson. Ted Gumley for The Invasion of Sicily. Alexander H Smith for The Italian Armistice. Colonel Bob Walker Brown for Escape; An SAS Mission in France; 2nd SAS Operation Galia. Lord Henniker for Tito, Partisans and Working with Fitzroy MacLean. Fulvia L S Gent for Life in Albania and Back to Italy. William Renwick for Escaping While Wounded. Allan P Seggie for An Episode in

Italy. James Pearce for Training Mules in Burma. Gail Farrell for D-Day Landing by Melvin Farrell. Les Edwards for D-Day. Rosemary Jones for Letters from a Soldier by David Bertram. Brian Guy for The American and The Garden Roller Man. Reginald Romain for Operation Market Garden. Betty Greenhalsh for The Gentle Austrian by John Slatterley. Johnnie R Beaver for The Battle of the Bulge and Capture. Jerry D Romine for Captivity and Rescue by the US 3rd Army by James M Romine. Thomas McQuillan for Liberation of Dachau. George Bower for Cleaning up at Belsen. Joan R Gilmour for VE Day.

We do hope that you have enjoyed reading this large print book.

Did you know that all of our titles are available for purchase?

We publish a wide range of high quality large print books including:
Romances, Mysteries, Classics
General Fiction
Non Fiction and Westerns

Special interest titles available in large print are:
The Little Oxford Dictionary
Music Book
Song Book
Hymn Book
Service Book

Also available from us courtesy of Oxford University Press:
Young Readers' Dictionary
(large print edition)
Young Readers' Thesaurus
(large print edition)

For further information or a free brochure, please contact us at:
Ulverscroft Large Print Books Ltd.,
The Green, Bradgate Road, Anstey,
Leicester, LE7 7FU, England.
Tel: (00 44) 0116 236 4325
Fax: (00 44) 0116 234 0205

A GOOD MAN'S LOVE

Elizabeth Harris

Hal Dillon and Ben MacAllister had been deeply affected by the appalling death of their university friend Laurie. Hal journeyed to Mexico to continue his anthropological studies, and there found distraction in his passionate affair with Magdalena. But was he inviting even more heartache? Ben became a wanderer. While working in Cyprus he had met English girl Jo Daniel, and, after a nomadic summer together, they travelled to England to embark on what promised to be a lifetime of marital bliss. But Jo discovers that promises don't always come true.